BEYOND
THE NUMBERS

BEYOND
THE NUMBERS

Understanding the Institutions for Monitoring Poverty Reduction Strategies

AUTHORS

Tara Bedi, Aline Coudouel, Marcus Cox, Markus Goldstein, and Nigel Thornton

THE WORLD BANK

ISBN-10: 0-8213-6484-7
ISBN-13: 978-0-8213-6484-0
eISBN: 0-8213-6485-5
DOI: 10.1596/978-0-8213-6484-0

Cover design and image by W. Drew Fasick.

Library of Congress Cataloging-in-Publication Data

Beyond the numbers : understanding the institutions for monitoring poverty reduction
    strategies / Tara Bedi ... [et al.].
        p. cm.
    Includes bibliographical references and index.
    ISBN-13: 978-0-8213-6484-0
    ISBN-10: 0-8213-6484-7
    1. Poverty—Government policy—Developing countries—Evaluation. I. Bedi, Tara,
1978-

HC59.72P6.B476 2006
363.5'561091724—dc22

                                                                2006045190

Contents

Part Two

Diagnostic and Guidance Tools for the Practitioner

Part Three

Country Studies—Institutional Arrangements
for PRS Monitoring Systems

Foreword

Five years ago, the international development community adopted a major shift in how it relates to low-income countries by putting developing countries in the driver's seat and promising to align its support behind national poverty reduction strategies. This shift in how aid is delivered relies heavily upon the ability of governments to design, execute, and monitor national strategies with prioritized goals and policy interventions that are well integrated into national processes and budget frameworks.

This book concentrates on one of the cornerstones underpinning this new relationship: a monitoring system that guides the elaboration of the poverty reduction strategy, the design of policies, and the evaluation of the impacts. It focuses specifically on what has proven to be one of the most difficult aspects in the design and implementation of monitoring systems: the institutional arrangements, that is, the formal and informal processes, procedures, rules, and mechanisms that bring monitoring activities into a coherent framework.

By drawing out the lessons and good practice from an analysis of 12 countries and proposing a diagnostic tool to assess country systems, this book equips policy makers and practitioners who struggle to design and run such systems and makes an important contribution to strengthening the effectiveness of development assistance and the quality of poverty reduction strategies.

Luca Barbone
Director
Poverty Reduction Group
World Bank

Sharon White
Director
Policy Division
U.K. Department
    for International Development

Acknowledgments

This volume draws on a work program developed and led by Aline Coudouel (World Bank) and undertaken by a team consisting of Rachael Beavan and Sarah Hennel (both with the U.K. Department for International Development), and Francesca Bastagli, Tara Bedi, Markus Goldstein, Giovanna Prennushi, and Cécile Wodon (all with the World Bank).

The volume builds strongly on experiences in 12 low-income countries. Marcus Cox and Nigel Thornton (both with Agulhas Applied Knowledge) developed the analytical framework and prepared the synthesis of the country experiences. The background country reports, which Natalie Schur masterfully edited, were prepared by Ivy Papps and Shkelzen Marku (Albania), Elizabeth Jimenez (Bolivia), Aline Coudouel and Ferdinando Regalia (Guyana and Nicaragua), Margarita Diaz (Honduras), Elvira Ilibeozova (Kyrgyz Republic), Ephraim Chirwa (Malawi), Francesca Bastagli (Mali and Niger), Christian Bonifas (Mauritania), David Booth (Tanzania), and David Booth and Xavier Nsabagasani (Uganda).

We wish to thank Graham Eele for extensive comments and guidance and Naoko Watanabe for comments on the diagnostic tool. We are also grateful to Pedro Arizti, Nicola Baroncini, Marcelo Bisogno, Kevin Carey, Ghislaine Delaine, Neil Fantom, Andrew Follmer, Louise Fox, Poonam Gupta, Richard Harris, Makiko Harrison, Kerstin Hinds, Michael Howells, Jody Kusek, Ulrich Lachler, Haeduck Lee, Richard Martini, Keith McKay, Soraya Mellali, Carlos Mollinedo, Alia Moubayed, Antonio Nucifora, Chris Pain, Stefano Paternostro, Sonia Plaza, Nicola Pontara, Jaime Saavedra, Antoine Simonpietri, Susan Stout, Ekaterine Vashakmadze, Hawa Wague-Cisse, Vera Wilhelm, Elizabeth White, and Quentin Wodon for comments and suggestions at various stages of the work program. Contributions to specific country studies are acknowledged in the relevant section.

In addition to funding from the World Bank and the U.K. Department for International Development, the work program has been financed through grants from the Trust Fund for Environmentally and Socially Sustainable Development supported by Finland and Norway and the World Bank–Netherlands Partnership Program funded by the Netherlands, which are gratefully acknowledged.

For any questions, comments, or suggestions on this volume, please contact Aline Coudouel at the World Bank (acoudouel@worldbank.org). For further information on poverty reduction strategies and the related monitoring systems, please visit, respectively, http://www.worldbank.org/prsp and http://www.worldbank.org/povertymonitoring.

About the Authors

Tara Bedi has been working on monitoring and evaluation as a junior professional associate with the Poverty Reduction Group at the World Bank since 2004. She received a Masters Degree in Public Administration in International Development from the John F. Kennedy School of Government, Harvard University. She previously worked on issues in the sustainability of nongovernmental organizations, refugee resettlement, and health policy. Tara grew up in India involved with the nongovernmental organization her parents founded to solicit the participation of the rural poor in addressing social and economic development issues.

Aline Coudouel is a senior economist with the Poverty Reduction Group at the World Bank, where, for the past two years, she has been leading the team working on poverty analysis, monitoring, and impact evaluation. Her work has focused on poverty measurement, poverty monitoring, the poverty and social impact analysis of reforms, development impact evaluation, labor markets, social protection, and poverty reduction strategies. Her work at the World Bank has mainly focused on Africa, Europe and Central Asia, and Latin America. Previously, she investigated the welfare situation among children and women in Europe and Central Asia for the United Nations Children's Fund.

Marcus Cox is a consultant advising a range of bilateral and international development agencies. He is senior editor at the European Stability Initiative, an interdisciplinary research group specializing in the political economy of Southeastern Europe and the European Union enlargement process. He has worked for the past decade as a practitioner and analyst in post-conflict reconstruction and nation building in the Balkans. He holds a PhD from Cambridge University, where his work focused on the Bosnian peace process. He has supported the World Bank and the U.K. Department for International Development through research on institutional development and aid effectiveness, including a recent study on poverty reduction strategies in low-income countries under stress. He also provides design and evaluation services for programs on civil society development, access to justice, and human rights.

Markus Goldstein is an economist in the Poverty Reduction Group at the World Bank, where he works on poverty analysis, monitoring, and impact evaluation. His research interests include poverty measurement and development economics. His recent research involves work on HIV/AIDS, land tenure, poverty over time, risk, and intrahousehold allocation. Prior to joining the Bank, he taught at the London School of Economics and the University of Ghana, Legon.

Nigel Thornton is a director of Agulhas Applied Knowledge (http://www.agulhas.co.uk). Over the last 10 years, he has designed, managed, and evaluated development projects and programs in Africa, Asia, and Eastern Europe. He has wide experience with aid instruments and in work with multilateral and bilateral partnerships. Originally a health services manager in the United Kingdom, he has both operational and policy level experience in the United Kingdom and South Africa. He was an adviser to the minister of public service and administration in the first South African government after the end of apartheid. Prior to joining Agulhas Applied Knowledge, he was a governance and institutional development adviser for the U.K. Department for International Development in the Balkans and Bangladesh.

Executive Summary

As part of the poverty reduction strategy (PRS) initiative, countries have been developing monitoring systems to track PRS implementation and its impact on poverty. PRS monitoring systems are central to the effective design and implementation of a PRS. They support decision making, foster accountability, and promote dialogue.

In this study, PRS monitoring is defined broadly to include the tracking of overall progress in poverty reduction, monitoring and evaluating the implementation of PRS policies and programs, and the monitoring of budgets and expenditures. The system therefore focuses on the entire results chain that links the various elements.

While most countries involved in implementing a PRS already have in place a range of individual monitoring mechanisms, drawing them together into a common system is a relatively new undertaking that poses substantial practical challenges. In many countries, the systems suffer from fragmentation, lack of coordination, lack of demand, unclear mandates and responsibilities, lack of relevance and timeliness of data, and limited accessibility. This underlines the importance of institutional arrangements that bring all activities together in a coherent framework: roles and responsibilities, rules, procedures, reporting mechanisms, and so on.

A PRS monitoring system therefore also incorporates a range of institutional functions, which include mechanisms to coordinate among data producers, develop common technical standards and platforms, build monitoring capacity, organize information flows, compile and analyze data from various sectors, analyze monitoring data and evaluate PRS programs, generate annual progress reports and other outputs, disseminate outputs across government and to the public, provide advice and support to policy makers, and organize the participation of civil society.

While there is much literature on the technical side of PRS monitoring, less guidance is available on the institutional challenges. Part I therefore reviews the experience in 12 countries according to different themes covering both the organization of monitoring activities and the use of monitoring information in the policy process. Part II provides a diagnostic tool and offers guidance for policy makers. Part III concludes the study with summaries of the 12 country studies. The volume closes with a bibliography.

Progress to Date

The case studies demonstrate that progress in establishing effective PRS monitoring systems has been limited. Few systems have created functioning links between monitoring and decision making. Organizing a coordinated monitoring system and ensuring that monitoring data are used in the policy process are both proving major practical challenges. The difficulties described in the case studies include the following:

- practical issues with data collection, especially routine administrative data
- difficulties in the coordination of activities; territoriality among public sector agencies, combined with a lack of incentives to participate, has led to resistance to rationalization and coordination and hampers the translation of formal plans into practice
- a lack of operational detail, costing, and prioritization in many PRSs, making it difficult to select meaningful indicators for monitoring PRS implementation
- weaknesses in public expenditure management systems, making it difficult to track PRS expenditures
- a deficit in analysis and evaluation
- low demand among policy makers for monitoring information

Most of the PRS monitoring systems are still too young to permit proper assessments. Nonetheless, there are signs that the process of establishing PRS monitoring systems and selecting monitoring indicators is prompting a review of sectoral policies and institutional arrangements to ensure consistency with PRS objectives. In many countries, civil society is actively engaged as members of monitoring committees and through independent monitoring activities, thereby helping to sustain the participation initiated during PRS formulation. There are also signs of increasing transparency around the policy and budget processes, with potentially important transformative effects.

Organizing Monitoring Activities

Before establishing a PRS monitoring system, most countries already possess a range of monitoring mechanisms, usually as a result of diverse donor programs. The lack of a consistent monitoring framework causes problems, including duplication and redundancies in information systems, excessive administrative burdens, lack of data compatibility, and poor information flows. Adding new monitoring obligations without simplifying existing arrangements is unlikely to help. The main challenges in establishing a PRS monitoring system therefore revolve around rationalizing existing monitoring mechanisms and coordinating numerous separate actors.

Typically, countries have devised formal plans for their PRS monitoring systems, but these are not fully implemented. This may result partly from the process of designing the systems themselves. Often, this process is narrow and based on limited stocktaking and few consultations with stakeholders, and actual designs are frequently elaborated by external consultants. Many of the plans are also particularly weak in terms of operational details such as roles, responsibilities, standards, modalities for cooperation, and so on. This results in limited buy-in by the actors and limited accountability and compliance.

A process of designing and implementing a PRS monitoring system that generates a buy-in by stakeholders may therefore be as important as the selected design. Ideally, the institutional design should emerge out of a shared commitment to solving the practical problems of PRS implementation. Systems are consensual in nature and tend to function only if participants find them useful and legitimate and agree on a common purpose.

Most existing PRS monitoring systems contain the following broad elements:

- a high-level steering committee to provide political support, oversight, and a link to the center of government
- a coordination unit or secretariat responsible for coordinating among agencies, compiling data, and drafting reports

- interagency committees or working groups for facilitating coordination and dialogue, often with civil society and donor representation
- a national statistics institute that sets data standards and provides technical support for producers of administrative data
- line ministries and other agencies that are required to appoint PRS monitoring system liaisons who are responsible for collating sectoral data

Experience suggests that the following variables in institutional design are important.

1. *Strong political leadership.* Placing the institutional lead close to the center of government or the budget process is likely to give the system greater authority, while facilitating the creation of links to the policy and budget process. Countries have typically located the core of their PRS monitoring systems in the ministry of finance, the ministry of planning, or the office of the (vice-)president. Experience suggests that leadership is more effective if it resides with a single agency rather than an interagency committee. Similarly, a champion is important in helping a system take root, but could be dangerous if the system becomes tied to a personality. Experience shows that flexibility is important in the broader components of the PRS monitoring system, as the locus of leadership may eventually need to be changed.

2. *Coordination of actors.* The coordinating structure should be designed to encourage active participation by key stakeholders, without imposing too great a burden on participants. Elaborate coordination structures have shown a tendency to weaken over time. Incentives often work to the disadvantage of coordination because each agency tries to protect its own program. The experience in the 12 countries offers lessons. An effective system avoids burdensome structures and focuses on building functional relationships among actors, with clear roles and responsibilities and well-defined activities. A capable secretariat facilitates information flows, organizes dialogues, assists monitoring system members, and mediates among actors. The identification of roles and responsibilities, advocacy for the system, and broad political leadership are critical. Donor funding for separate monitoring mechanisms at the project level provides disincentives for coordination. Donors should be involved in the design process so as to ensure that their monitoring requirements are served through the national PRS monitoring system.

3. *Links with line ministries.* Most PRS monitoring systems are second-tier systems that rely on a supply of routine data from line ministries. The link works best when the nominated liaison points are substantively involved in monitoring and evaluation for sectoral policy making and management purposes and have the authority, time, and incentives to play this role effectively. Where sectoral monitoring itself is weak, the PRS monitoring system may need to include an active strategy for promoting sound monitoring practices, such as rules requiring that monitoring and evaluation functions be incorporated into departmental budgets, work plans, and job descriptions. Ensuring that the needs of the PRS monitoring systems and of donors are aligned with sectoral information systems is likely to increase compliance and performance.

4. *Involvement of national statistics agencies.* National statistics agencies are often the most institutionally advanced elements in PRS monitoring systems. However, the system arrangements must ensure complementarity with existing statistical systems and statistical planning so as to avoid duplication, limit potential rivalry between the statistical systems and the PRS monitoring system, and strengthen links between central agencies and line ministries. In addition, PRS monitoring systems should ensure that statistics agencies have sufficient resources and mandates to play their role in setting standards, providing technical assistance, and building the capacity of other system members. This may help increase the compatibility and complementarity of the data supplied by numerous agencies.

5. *Involvement of local governments.* PRS monitoring in a decentralized system poses particular challenges that have not been satisfactorily resolved in any of the 12 countries examined in the case studies. Capacity constraints at the local level are usually critical, especially in the poorest areas. During the process of decentralizing service delivery, some countries have encouraged local authorities to develop their own monitoring arrangements, while others have preferred to strengthen the monitoring of local governments by the center. Strategies for improving local monitoring include carefully selecting indicators to minimize the administrative burden, linking quality control mechanisms to targeted capacity-building initiatives, using secondary monitoring methods to cross-check local reporting, providing feedback to local governments on monitoring results, and strengthening information flows between local governments and the communities they serve.

Making Use of PRS Monitoring

From the case studies, it appears that more attention has been paid to organizing the supply of monitoring information than to ensuring the effective use of this information to improve PRS policies and programs. Low levels of demand for monitoring information also tend to impact on the supply of adequate information. If the results of monitoring are not sought out and used by policy makers and public sector managers, then monitoring comes to be seen merely as a bureaucratic burden, and compliance with monitoring procedures deteriorates. The most promising strategy for strengthening demand is to tailor PRS monitoring system outputs to key points in the policy-making process where information on the performance of policies and programs is likely to be influential, such as around the budget, the medium-term expenditure framework, planning cycles, updates of the PRS, parliamentary sessions, public dialogue, and donor strategy elaboration. Most of these processes are outside the PRS monitoring system, but should guide system activities.

Important elements in encouraging the greater use of PRS monitoring information include the following.

1. *Analysis and evaluation.* If PRS monitoring is to influence policy making, the practice of analysis and evaluation needs to be institutionalized in the PRS monitoring system. This is a striking deficit in most systems to date. Some countries have created central analytical units in the office of the president, the ministry of finance, or the national statistics institute. These units have worked best when they have remained small, been close to government, and focused purely on analysis. Another useful technique has been joint analytical exercises between donors and government, including during public expenditure reviews. Finally, since governments typically face constraints in terms of the capacity for analysis, the PRS monitoring system should ensure that the analytical capacity of nongovernmental actors such as universities, research institutions, nongovernmental organizations, and donors is harnessed.

2. *Outputs and dissemination.* If they are to have an impact, the information and analysis resulting from monitoring activities must be compiled into outputs and disseminated across government and to the public. This is another area of major weakness in existing systems, many of which have focused on donor requirements. This means that information should be circulated back among central agencies, local and

regional governments, and service providers. A PRS monitoring system should also meet the needs of parliaments, the media, the general public, and donors. A dissemination strategy should be a central part of PRS monitoring systems. To this effect, the PRS monitoring system must develop outputs that are tailored to the needs of the various decision makers and users and are timed to feed into policy cycles. Making information accessible to various audiences requires presenting monitoring data in both technical and nontechnical ways, which is often a new skill for governments.

3. *Links with budget and planning.* Perhaps the most promising strategy for building demand is to link PRS monitoring to the budget process. Wherever public sector agencies are bidding for public funds (for example, through the annual budget, public investment plans, or a medium-term expenditure framework), this presents an opportunity to require them to justify their bids according to PRS objectives and evidence on program performance. This has been done in two of the countries under study, Tanzania and Uganda, with a notable (if uneven) boost in results-oriented policy making. For this to be more effective, it is helpful to have an agency in the ministry of finance or close to the center of government with the capacity and authority to engage with the sectors on their policy choices and play the challenge function around budget preparation. When linking a PRS monitoring system to the budget, care needs to be taken to avoid creating perverse incentives that may distort the monitoring process. Results take time and are influenced by many factors. In addition, there is a danger in linking budgets to the ability to monitor rather than to the ability to deliver and to punish the low performers who might be most in need of support. Overall, the link between PRS monitoring and the budget process is difficult to implement and depends on the maturity of the medium-term expenditure framework and the public expenditure management system.

4. *Links with parliament.* Finally, the lack of involvement of parliaments in existing PRS monitoring systems represents a missed opportunity to help ensure parliaments are able to carry out their role of oversight and control of the executive and their role of representation for their constituencies. Possible strategies to strengthen the capacity of parliaments include engaging with existing parliamentary groups, building the economic literacy of representatives, presenting data in a nontechnical and timely fashion, identifying existing venues to present the information, and developing alliances between parliaments and civil society groups.

Organizing Participation

Nongovernmental organizations, private interdisciplinary research entities, universities, unions, lobby groups, and other members of civil society can play a role in PRS monitoring on both the supply side and the demand side. Among the countries in the case studies, the level and type of civil society involvement varies considerably; it includes performing monitoring activities (whether as part of the PRS monitoring system or independently), participating in monitoring committees and working groups, providing analysis and policy advice, and interpreting and disseminating monitoring outputs to the general public.

Typically, apart from most of the countries in Latin America, the participation of civil society has not been formalized. Selecting civil society representatives can raise questions of legitimacy if civil society does not already have well-developed representative structures, and it may not always be appropriate to try to reflect a single civil society voice in the PRS monitoring system. Civil society organizations do not always wish to be part of a formal PRS monitoring system for fear of compromising their independence, and funding modalities should respect this choice.

Conclusion

The experience of the 12 countries under study teaches us that, in elaborating and implementing a PRS monitoring system, one should build on existing elements; recognize that changes will be gradual; aim at starting a process of change rather than at designing a "perfect" system; focus on building flexible arrangements that can be adapted to change; clearly define relations, incentives, and activities; identify entry points in decision-making processes and, in particular, the budget process; and adapt the various outputs to the intended users.

Acronyms

The acronyms below are used throughout this volume. Individual chapters also sometimes contain lists of acronyms that are particular to those chapters.

CSO	civil society organization
HIPC	Heavily Indebted Poor Countries (Initiative)
M&E	monitoring and evaluation
MDG	Millennium Development Goal
MTEF	medium-term expenditure framework
NGO	nongovernmental organization
PRS	poverty reduction strategy
PRSP	Poverty Reduction Strategy Paper

All dollar amounts ($) are U.S. dollars unless otherwise indicated.

Introduction

One of the key components of a successful poverty reduction strategy (PRS) is a system for monitoring the implementation of the strategy and for tracking progress in poverty reduction. The system is critical for the entire PRS cycle, feeding information into the elaboration of the strategy, influencing the design of the related policies, monitoring policy implementation, and evaluating the impact. The system is a cornerstone in the success of the PRS, ensuring that the strategy is solidly based on evidence, focuses on results, and evolves over time.

In this book, PRS monitoring is defined broadly to embrace both the monitoring of PRS implementation (through input, output, and outcome indicators) and the monitoring of impact indicators that capture the many dimensions of poverty. Poverty is understood as a multidimensional concept, covering all dimensions of well-being. The PRS monitoring system is also understood to encompass both intermediary and final indicators, including input, output, outcome, and impact indicators. The data produced and used by the PRS monitoring system therefore incorporate administrative data and administrative data collection systems, as well as surveys, censuses, and quantitative and qualitative data.

The PRS monitoring system encompasses a broad spectrum of activities, including data and information collection, analysis, dissemination, reporting, feedback into the policy process, and the overall management and coordination of the activities. PRS monitoring systems also involve a broad range of actors. The producers of the data typically consist of the national statistics agency, the monitoring and statistical departments in line ministries, other government data producers in line agencies and at lower levels of government, and nongovernmental data producers, including donors, universities, nongovernmental organizations, and research centers. Analysts usually belong to various governmental agencies, universities, consulting firms, private interdisciplinary research entities, and donor agencies. Users range from government decision makers to parliamentarians, civil society groups, the donor community, and researchers. Different actors are also involved in the coordination and overview of the PRS monitoring system. These may include the government agency in charge of the PRS, advisory committees, and parliamentary oversight committees.

In addition to these activities and actors, an effective PRS monitoring system requires institutional arrangements—coordination, roles and responsibilities, rules, processes and procedures, reporting mechanisms, and so on—that bring all activities together in a coherent framework by allowing communication and information flows between the various actors. Unless this interface is established, a vicious circle spins, wherein adequate information is not available for decision making, and decision-making processes do not demand adequate information.

This volume uses the word "system" to describe these institutional arrangements. The concept is not applied in a strict sense, which would suggest a coherent set of organizations working within a single agenda and trying to achieve common objectives. In reality, in most countries, agencies operate under differing sets of rules and with multiple and sometimes conflicting objectives, and institutional issues are sometimes very complex. The word "system" could also suggest a focus on the design of a set of static arrangements. On the contrary, one of the main lessons learned from this work is the need for a greater focus on a process of elaboration that acknowledges the complexity of existing agencies and arrangements and the evolution of institutional arrangements over time. In addition, the broad sets of objectives of a PRS monitoring system may come into conflict, and there is no single, optimal design. Hence, the word "system" is used here rather loosely to mean the set of rules and regulations that govern the interactions between different actors.

When they embark on the development of a PRS, most countries already have a range of discrete monitoring arrangements in place. There are usually sectoral systems and monitoring mechanisms attached to specific programs and projects, and many developing countries have received extensive donor support over recent decades to establish their own statistical systems. However, the PRS initiative in most cases has highlighted the need for improved monitoring mechanisms. The elaboration of a PRS therefore often represents the first attempt to integrate different monitoring activities into a single, national system able to meet the diverse information needs of a comprehensive strategy.

The record in establishing PRS monitoring systems has been modest. Many countries have produced detailed plans for monitoring strategies and created working groups and committees, but few have made much progress in rationalizing existing monitoring arrangements into unified systems. There is little evidence that the information collected through PRS monitoring is being used by policy makers to improve the effectiveness and efficiency of PRS programming. However, most of the existing monitoring systems are still at an early stage of development.

In particular, in most PRS countries, fragmentation is a key constraint. Lack of coordination, lack of demand for information from decision makers, unclear mandates and responsibilities, lack of relevant and timely data, and limited accessibility are often identified as key impediments to the promotion of results-based decision making.

Capacity-building efforts and financial support have mostly focused on the activities or actors mentioned above and, in particular, on technical aspects. Much less support has been provided for improving the actual functioning of systems. Similarly, while there is a substantial body of literature covering the technical aspects of PRS monitoring and issues such as indicator selection and data requirements, the institutional dimension has received much less attention. The literature does not offer a clear overview of the different institutional elements needed for an effective PRS monitoring system. Nor does it furnish much guidance to policy makers on how to go about designing and implementing a monitoring system despite the substantial challenges they are likely to encounter.

The objective of this book is to shed light on institutional arrangements, draw lessons, and provide guidance on good practice in the design and functioning of the institutional arrangements of PRS monitoring systems. The lessons from early experience will equip practitioners involved in running or advising on such systems, such as government officials, World Bank staff, other development agency staff, and researchers.

This book concentrates on the institutional arrangements linking the various actors and activities. It does not aim at addressing issues related to how each of these actors or activities function. For instance, it does not cover questions related to the organization of data collection activities, to technical information management systems, to decision-making processes, or to public expenditure management systems. This study is also cursory in its treatment of questions about the legal environment, funding mechanisms, and the role of donors and civil society organizations in the systems. This is not meant to suggest that these elements are secondary, but rather reflects the needs of the focus of the volume.

The analysis is based on the experience of 12 PRS countries in three regions: Bolivia, Guyana, Honduras, and Nicaragua in Latin America and the Caribbean; Albania and the Kyrgyz Republic in Europe and Central Asia; and Malawi, Mali, Mauritania, Niger, Tanzania, and Uganda in Africa. The country studies were undertaken in the spring and summer of 2004 and, hence, may not reflect changes that have occurred since then. Even where this is the case, however, the lessons acquired from the experiences are still a very useful basis for learning.

The authors of the case studies were asked to provide both a static mapping of the PRS monitoring system—the formal allocation of responsibilities among various actors—and a dynamic mapping of how monitoring and information flows actually function. The case studies therefore range beyond the terrain of monitoring in a strict sense to include the challenges of organizing information flows within and outside government and the way that monitoring information is used within national policy cycles.

The country studies have been examined to provide a framework to draw lessons and for the analysis of institutional arrangements for PRS monitoring. This framework has been used to edit and synthesize the country studies that are presented in this book. The analysis has not been undertaken to produce particular blueprints for the elaboration of PRS monitoring systems. Rather, the lessons have provided a series of principles and options that the practitioner can adapt to a local reality. The findings and analytical framework have been used to derive a diagnostic tool that practitioners may find meaningful in assessing, designing, or implementing PRS monitoring systems.

The book is organized as follows. Part I, chapter 1 assesses achievements in the development of PRS monitoring systems and summarizes the substantial practical challenges that have been encountered, thereby providing a context for the subsequent discussion. Chapter 2 considers the organization of monitoring activities, including the process of establishing a shared system, structures for oversight and coordination, the relationship with line ministries and the statistical system, and the challenges of decentralization. Chapter 3 reviews options for encouraging the use of poverty monitoring information, including analysis and evaluation, outputs, dissemination, links to the budget process, and the role of parliaments. Chapter 4 assesses the experiences of civil society as participant in poverty monitoring both as producer and user of monitoring information. Chapter 5 offers conclusions on PRS monitoring systems.

Part II, chapter 1 provides a diagnostic tool that supplies pointers for designing or reviewing a PRS monitoring system. Chapter 2 offers guidance for policy makers and their advisers who are engaged in the design and implementation of a PRS monitoring system.

Part III presents the country studies in the form of edited summaries. The country studies cover Albania, Bolivia, Guyana, Honduras, the Kyrgyz Republic, Malawi, Mali, Mauritania, Nicaragua, Niger, Tanzania, and Uganda.

The volume closes with a bibliography.

PART *One*

Lessons from the Experiences of 12 Countries

Part I summarizes the findings and lessons that have emerged from the analysis of poverty reduction strategy monitoring systems in 12 countries (Albania, Bolivia, Guyana, Honduras, the Kyrgyz Republic, Malawi, Mali, Mauritania, Nicaragua, Niger, Tanzania, and Uganda). Chapter 1 assesses achievements in the development of poverty reduction strategy monitoring systems and summarizes the substantial practical challenges that have been encountered, thereby providing a context for the subsequent discussion. Chapter 2 considers the organization of monitoring activities, including the process of establishing a shared system, structures for oversight and coordination, the relationship with line ministries and the statistical system, and the challenges of decentralization. Chapter 3 reviews options for encouraging the use of poverty monitoring information, including analysis and evaluation, outputs, dissemination, links to the budget process, and the role of parliaments. Chapter 4 assesses the experiences of civil society as participant in poverty monitoring both as producer and user of monitoring information. Chapter 5 offers conclusions.

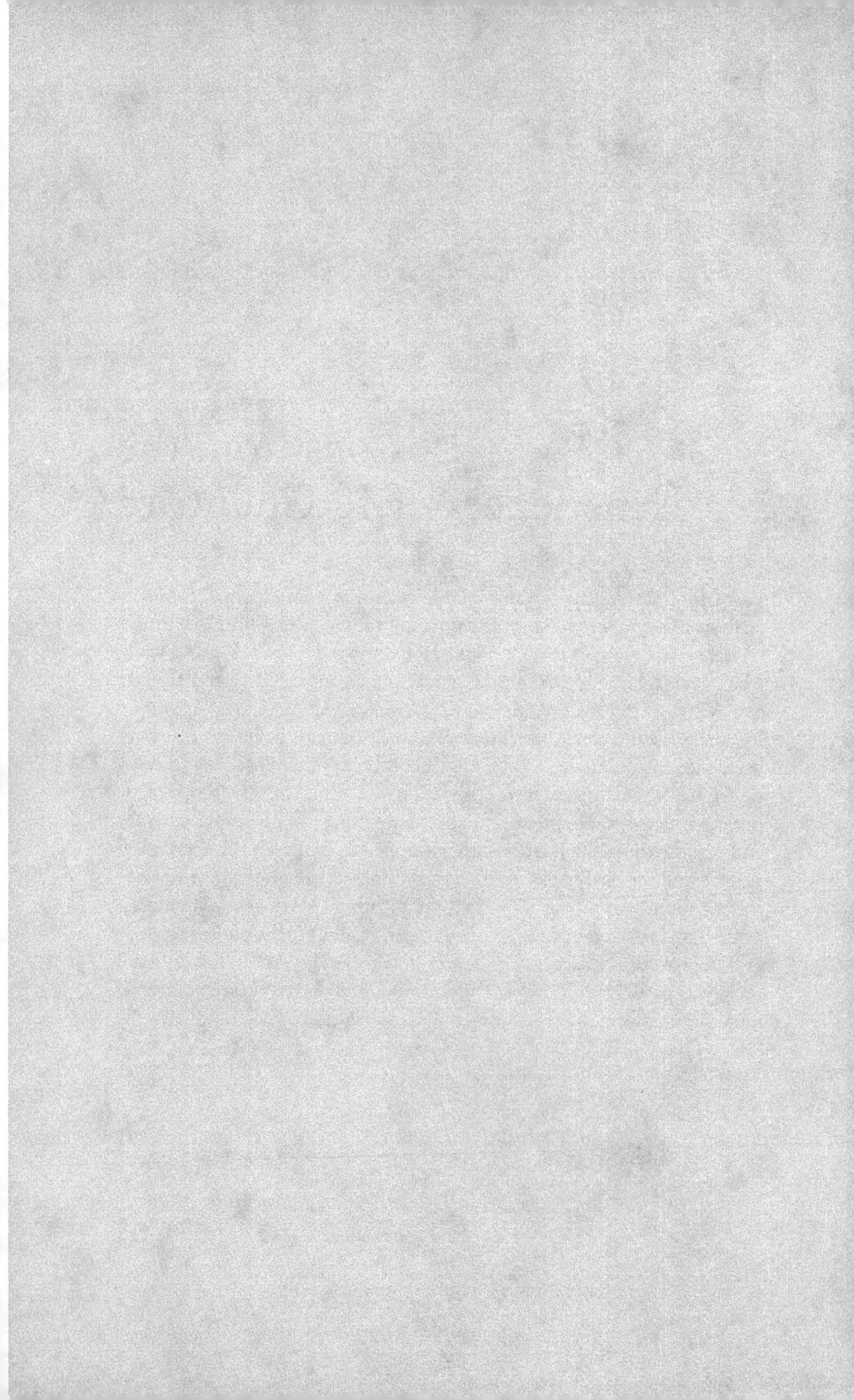

1

Expectations and Realities

The development of a monitoring system is a critical component of a successful poverty reduction strategy (PRS). Such a system is intended both as a way of ensuring continuous improvement of the PRS and as an instrument for influencing the nature of the development policy process by making it more evidence based and results oriented. A recent review of the PRS approach (IMF and World Bank 2005) underlines the centrality of a monitoring system as a pillar upon which a PRS can be elaborated; it helps open the policy space for dialogue, establish priorities, design programs and policies, set realistic targets, and assess implementation with a view to refine the strategy.

However, the country studies upon which this analysis is grounded indicate that the achievements against these rather ambitious goals have been limited. In most countries, both the supply side (organizing the monitoring and reporting of indicators across fragmented administrations) and the demand side (ensuring that monitoring information is actually used in national decision-making processes) are posing major practical challenges.

This chapter therefore begin by reviewing the goals and functions of a PRS monitoring system and comparing these against the experiences described in the country studies in order to provide a realistic perspective on the challenges ahead.

What Are the Objectives of a PRS Monitoring System?

Ideally, a PRS monitoring system serves a number of larger objectives:

- It supports government decision making on poverty reduction policies, budgetary priorities, and the continuous updating and improvement of the PRS.
- It supports the accountability of government before the public for its policy choices and their impact on poverty.
- It promotes evidence-based dialogue between government, civil society, and donors on development policies and priorities.
- It supports the reporting requirements of donors for their own account-ability and for program management purposes.

This is a broad set of goals, and not all are served equally by the same institutional arrangements. When designing a PRS monitoring system, policy makers need to bear in mind the possibility of trade-offs among these different goals.

To achieve these goals, a PRS monitoring system typically incorporates three functions, each with somewhat different institutional leads, as follows.

1. *Poverty monitoring.* The system should track overall progress in poverty reduction against national targets and international measures of development success, such as the Millennium Development Goals, through the periodic measurement of selected poverty indicators. This focuses on monitoring impact indicators and is accomplished through the use of censuses, surveys, and other investigative tools and is usually led by a national statistics institute. In most of the countries studied, poverty monitoring is the most developed area conceptually, technically, and institutionally. Poverty monitoring is relatively easy for donors to support even in weak institutional environments because the capacity needs are fairly concentrated and technically difficult elements can be readily outsourced.

2. *Implementation of the monitoring of the PRS.* The system should allow for the monitoring and evaluation (M&E) of the progress in the implementation of PRS policies and programs. This involves the measurement of inputs, activities, outputs, and outcomes across the various sectoral programs and thematic areas. Implementation monitoring relies on administrative data from a wide range of actors, from line ministries down to

local service-delivery units, and is therefore the most difficult to manage and coordinate. The capacity constraints are often severe and difficult to address because of the number of actors involved. Implementation monitoring depends upon a careful selection of indicators based upon explicit result chains (that is, causal links between interventions and their desired impacts) in order to support effective assessments of programs and policies.

3. *Expenditure tracking*. Although conceptually a part of implementation monitoring, the measurement of expenditure is a somewhat discrete area, usually under the leadership of the ministry of finance. While expenditure tracking is not always explicitly articulated as a part of PRS monitoring, reliable and timely data on expenditure are indispensable to a well-functioning PRS monitoring system in practice. Indeed, information on poverty outcomes and implementation can only be used to improve strategies and interventions when these outcomes are associated with cost and resource requirements. Expenditure tracking depends upon parallel progress in budget and public expenditure management reforms. These are under way in all PRS countries, but at very different stages. A new system may take many years to become effective.

The balance among these functions varies in different countries. Among the countries studied, the African systems are oriented more toward poverty monitoring (measurement of indicators of impact), which has been the focus of donor support in recent years. By contrast, the Latin American systems are influenced by strong civil society mobilization around debt relief and the use of funds from the Heavily Indebted Poor Countries (HIPC) Initiative and tend to focus on accountability in public expenditure.

In a weak institutional environment, poverty monitoring is the easiest of these three functions to accomplish. This part of the PRS monitoring system is critical to ensuring that the focus is on results and that poverty impacts are not seen as "somebody else's business" (Hauge 2003). In line with the PRS philosophy, one of the functions of a PRS monitoring system is to keep poverty impacts in constant view.

Restricting monitoring only to impact indicators, however, is of limited value for program management and policy development. Impact variables normally respond to policy interventions too slowly to support annual decision making. In addition, monitoring the changes in impact indicators on poverty without simultaneous monitoring of programs and policies (inputs and outputs) and changes in intermediary variables (outcomes) does not directly provide policy-relevant lessons. Finally, monitoring needs to be supplemented with evaluations of the impact of policies and programs on poverty in order to attribute changes in the welfare dimension that is of interest in particular interventions.

Results orientation does not mean prioritizing the monitoring of results or impacts over the monitoring of implementation processes. Rather, it means focusing on the entire results chain, that is, the causal links between interventions and their intended outcomes posited through explicit hypotheses that describe *how* the interventions will take effect at different stages and that may eventually be tested against the evidence.

A PRS monitoring system needs to perform this integrating role by bringing existing monitoring arrangements together to permit this focus on the results chain. As such, a PRS monitoring system does not take over all other monitoring activities, but merely coordinates and organizes them.

Some authors describe most PRS monitoring systems as second-tier systems that operate by extracting data from existing sectoral and central monitoring arrangements so as to analyze and guide PRS elaboration and implementation. "It is of central importance that a [PRS] monitoring system not attempt to collect all the data itself," one study concludes. "Rather, it should rely on other, existing monitoring systems" (GTZ 2004a, 39).

However, a PRS monitoring system should coordinate among existing systems if it is to generate relevant, timely, and compatible data. It may also be the case that sectoral foundations are missing or too weak to support the PRS monitoring process. In this situation, the PRS monitoring system needs to become involved in promoting the take-up of more effective monitoring techniques across agencies.

A monitoring system therefore incorporates a range of additional functions that are specifically institutional in nature. These include coordinating among different actors, filling gaps and eliminating redundancy in primary data collection, building up monitoring capacity where it is deficient, organizing information flows among actors within and outside of government, compiling data from various sources, organizing analysis and evaluation, producing annual progress reports (a HIPC requirement) and other monitoring outputs, disseminating outputs across government and to the public, providing advice and support to policy makers, and organizing the participation of civil society.

All these elements are conceptually part of a PRS monitoring system and are therefore important for planners to consider. However, at the outset, most of the actors involved in monitoring will not see their activities as part of a national system. Whether they will choose to participate in building a common monitoring system depends largely on their interests and incentives. These incentives may be influenced to a degree, for example, through the rules governing budget processes or through donor practices. The rules—both formal and informal—that shape public service incentives to generate and use monitoring information are therefore a key dimension of a PRS monitoring system; they shape the structure and functioning of the system.

The Record

Measured against these rather ambitious goals, the achievements of PRS monitoring systems have been fairly modest. In all the country studies, the PRS monitoring systems are recent innovations, and, in many cases, implementation is not yet sufficiently advanced for an assessment. Only a few (for example, Honduras, Tanzania, and Uganda) have made real progress in linking existing monitoring activities into a single system. Few have been able to establish functioning links between PRS monitoring and government policy making, and none has yet triggered any sustained shift toward greater effectiveness or efficiency in development programs (Williamson 2003). Overall, the 2005 PRS review notes that:

> While the challenges are large, there is some evidence that the PRS process has contributed to improvements over time. For instance, in countries that have been implementing their PRS for at least two years, three-quarters had systems that were largely developed or were taking actions. . . . For countries that have been implementing their PRS for less than two years, only about a quarter were in the process of taking actions. (IMF and World Bank 2005, 24)

The following common obstacles to an effective PRS monitoring system were identified in the country studies.

1. *Shortcomings in PRSs*. PRSs often lack operational detail, costing, and prioritization. Indicator sets are poorly selected, and many goals are not associated with indicators. Few countries have reasoned out satisfactory result chains, developed logframes, or provided explicit ex ante expectations for interventions. These are objectively difficult tasks for administrations unused to comprehensive development planning, and

it is not surprising to find them lacking in first-round PRSs. Nonetheless, without well-articulated PRSs, it is difficult to carry out effective monitoring. The 2005 review of the PRS (IMF and World Bank 2005, 14) noted that "specifying clear targets, for which data are available, and identifying intermediate indicators remains [*sic*] particularly challenging for countries" and "many PRSs would benefit from a more explicit link between goals and targets and the policies needed to achieve them." The Tanzania country study notes that:

> It is hard to monitor plans that do not themselves reflect strategic policy thinking, that is, which do not say how the specified outcomes are going to be achieved with the specified inputs, and how the obvious obstacles are to be overcome. (Booth 2004, 33)

A review by the German Agency for Technical Cooperation has commented that:

> The attempt to superimpose a monitoring system onto this kind of a strategy paper is correspondingly complicated. Basically, the goals must be operationalized, before goal achievement can be measured. So far, none of the countries visited has managed to do this in a satisfying way. (GTZ 2004a, 63)

2. *Difficulties in coordination* among data producers and users are exacerbating the capacity constraints on data producers. Duplication and redundancy are widespread, which increases administrative burdens and complicates analysis. Agencies are often protective of their separate monitoring responsibilities, which come with staffing and resource entitlements, and are resistant to initiatives to rationalize the workload or introduce common standards. As a result, committees and working groups created to facilitate consultation have often been unsuccessful in promoting practical cooperation. In some cases, donors are contributing to the coordination problems by continuing to impose discrete, project-level monitoring requirements. Given these problems, one study concluded that, "in terms of the current state of things and the needs to be met, the chances of assembling in short order, or even in the medium term, the conditions for effective monitoring seem very slim" (EEC Canada 2002, 10).

The 2005 review of the PRS notes that:

> progress in building monitoring systems that coordinate the collection of data, [their] analysis and [their] use for policy making has been limited in many countries. This is the area that the joint staff advisory notes most frequently mentioned as a significant constraint to PRS implementation. (IMF and World Bank 2005, 23)

3. *Practical problems with data collection* are proving very difficult to overcome. In particular, all the country studies report that capacity constraints in administrative data systems are serious, especially at the local and regional levels. As a result, indicator data are often incomplete and of inconsistent quality. (The Kyrgyz Republic is able to report on only 25 percent of its indicators.) According to Booth and Lucas (2002, 17), routine administrative sources are "at best highly unreliable and at worst unusable" and therefore ill suited to capturing small, annual movements in indicators. Overall, there has been some progress in statistical capacity in PRS countries since the inception of the PRSs, especially in terms of availability and quality. But the constraints remain severe, especially in African countries (IMF and World Bank 2005).

4. There is a marked *deficit in the evaluation and analysis* undertaken on the basis of poverty-monitoring data. Annual progress reports are often loose compilations of indicator data without substantial analytical content and, during a first PRS cycle, are often produced in an ad hoc manner. This is symptomatic of monitoring carried out to meet donor reporting requirements, rather than to support domestic policy making.

5. The success of PRS monitoring systems is closely tied to the development of *budget planning and public expenditure management systems*, which, according to many of the country studies, are still at an early stage. Most of the countries do not have functioning medium-term expenditure frameworks (MTEFs). Some are unable to report accurately on expenditure or to attribute expenditure to policies or programs. Budget releases are often irregular, undermining accountability for program and policy implementation. Without reliable data on expenditure, it is difficult to assess interventions, especially in light of large, extrabudgetary donor programs.

6. The *link between PRS monitoring and government policy processes* are proving very difficult to institutionalize, and, in most of the country studies, there is little or no evidence that monitoring outputs are being used either

for policy making or advocacy. Demand for monitoring information remains weak, and national policy making is based on evidence only at the margin. Weaknesses in demand and supply are mutually reinforcing: if monitoring outputs are not used effectively, monitoring comes to be seen as a mere bureaucratic requirement, and compliance deteriorates. There is evidence that the PRS process has encouraged greater access to information, but more effort is still needed (IMF and World Bank 2005).

7. *The alignment of donor monitoring and reporting requirements around national PRS monitoring systems* remains at an early stage of development. Most donors do not seem to find annual progress reports sufficient for their own accountability and management purposes both because of quality concerns and because the focus on poverty outcomes rather than on inputs and outputs makes the reports poorly suited for assessing national development efforts in the short term. Therefore, donors tend to incorporate a separate M&E system in each of their individual projects. This leads to duplication of efforts and spreads M&E resources thinly. Furthermore, donors often make funding available to ministries for M&E activities in order to ensure that the required information is available. This practice may create resistance in government agencies to efforts by donors to align their M&E requirements, as this could reduce the resources channeled for monitoring. In countries that receive budget support (for instance, Tanzania and Uganda), development partners have often begun to align their support around common conditionalities, which can reduce donor reporting requirements. These conditionalities, however, are typically only a very small subset of the overall PRS (rather than a single conditionality of "successful PRS implementation"), and this may represent an incentive for governments to focus exclusively on the monitoring of this selected subset of indicators rather than on the overall PRS monitoring system.

Clearly, the obstacles preventing PRS monitoring systems from achieving their stated objectives are therefore widespread and entrenched. Many of the authors of the country studies are pessimistic about the prospects of surmounting these obstacles in the short to medium term. The Albanian country study concludes:

> Although all the machinery necessary for the effective functioning of the policy cycle is in place, the actual operation of the system does not correspond with these intentions and, the outputs from

the PRS monitoring system have not yet had an impact on policy choices. (Papps and Marku 2004, 5)

This is in keeping with the findings of the World Bank's overall PRS evaluation:

> governments in most countries are monitoring results as a require-ment, and results are not being used to adjust strategies or to enhance accountability for performance. (World Bank 2004b, 17)

On the other hand, positive messages are also emerging from the country studies. In some of the more advanced cases, the initiative to develop PRS monitoring systems has helped to make the PRS process focus more on results. The process of selecting a good set of monitoring indicators, where it is taken seriously, requires line ministries to review both their sectoral strategies (in particular, to identify *how* proposed programs and policies are likely to impact on poverty) and their institutional arrangements (to review data collection processes). In Honduras, for example, this has helped to encourage greater strategic focus in sectoral planning.

According to many of the country studies, civil society is becoming more involved in the monitoring of PRSs, particularly in relation to HIPC expenditures. In some instances, the participation of civil society is institu-tionalized in the design of the PRS monitoring system both as a producer and as a user of monitoring information. In other cases, civil society organ-izations prefer to remain outside the formal system and contribute through independent monitoring techniques such as citizen scorecards, public service satisfaction surveys, and public expenditure tracking surveys. PRS monitoring systems are helping to create a political space where dialogue and debate on PRS implementation may take place and build on the progress achieved during PRS formulation.

The country studies also support the view that increasing the trans-parency of government policy making can have important transformative effects over time. The Mauritania country study comments that, in the past, reviews of economic policy were treated as "almost confidential." Now, government policies and their consequences for poverty are the subject of public debate. Through the PRS process, a more pluralistic model of poverty knowledge is emerging, broadening the opportunities for stake-holders to engage with the decisions that affect them. PRS monitoring systems are beginning to make a contribution to this process.

Tactical Choices and Tailored Solutions

The challenge of developing an effective PRS monitoring system is obviously very different in each country and depends on the initial conditions. In some countries, sectoral monitoring is already well established, and the challenge is to overcome territoriality in order to create a unified system. In other countries, sectoral monitoring arrangements are weak or nonexistent, and a PRS monitoring system must begin by promoting the adoption of monitoring practices and building monitoring capacity broadly across administrations and jurisdictions.

In some countries, public scrutiny of government performance is already an established part of the political process, and governments depend upon monitoring to promote their achievements and build their legitimacy. In other countries, the interest and capacity of civil society in monitoring the development process is at a low level, and government is unaccustomed to external scrutiny of its performance.

In some countries, budgetary systems are technically advanced, and the budget process is the key policy tool for ensuring that resources go to projects with proven impact on poverty reduction. In other countries, the official budget bears little resemblance to the real distribution of resources.

In addition, the organization of government itself varies greatly across countries. A single organization, such as a finance ministry or a statistics agency, will have different responsibilities and exercise authority over different areas in different countries. Hence, the variables affecting the design of a PRS monitoring system are too numerous and complex to allow for any simple catalogue of best practices or ideal institutional choices.

Creating a PRS monitoring system usually involves tactical choices and solutions adapted to specific problems rather than the application of a set model. The design of the system should conform to current political and institutional realities rather than to an idealized model of how policy processes should function. In addition, it takes a long time to change practices, and the new sets of roles and responsibilities will need to be introduced gradually according to country conditions. Finally, environments change constantly, with new rules of the game, growing capacity, changing political landscapes, and so on, and this calls for a constant evolution of the systems. The experiences described in the country studies presented hereafter should help to inform these tactical choices even though they are not proposed as a model or even a series of models.

2

Organizing the Supply Side of PRS Monitoring

This chapter addresses the challenges involved in putting in place a coherent system for monitoring both the implementation of a poverty reduction strategy (PRS) and the impact of the strategy on poverty. Broadly speaking, this is the supply side of the monitoring equation. The chapter covers the process of designing and implementing a system and some of the more important organizational choices. Chapter 3 examines the other side of the equation: the use of the information and data gathered by the system. Chapter 4 addresses the question of the participation of civil society in these two sides of monitoring.

Why Create a Unified PRS Monitoring System?

When they embark on a Poverty Reduction Strategy Paper (PRSP), most countries already have a range of monitoring mechanisms in place, including survey and census programs led by national statistics institutes, administrative data systems at the sectoral level, and project-level systems. This last type of mechanism has typically emerged as a result of discrete donor initiatives on different occasions. Overall, these systems tend to operate in isolation even when they involve the same public bodies.

For example, Niger's PRSP contains a diagnosis of existing monitoring arrangements. The diagnosis found that there were 10 distinct databases and government information systems, resulting in "duplication, dispersed effort and absence of harmonization among data collection methodologies, making it difficult to compare information coming from different data sources" (Bastagli 2004a, 3).

The disadvantages of fragmented monitoring arrangements in terms of the production of data and analyses noted in the country studies on PRS monitoring include the following:

1. *Duplication and redundancies in data collection.* Local and regional governments face excessive reporting requirements, often producing the same data in different formats for different sectoral information systems. For instance, in Uganda, the annual cost of monitoring inspections runs to 1,400 staff years in the health sector alone (Hauge 2003). A lack of strategic focus often leads to redundant monitoring obligations. The greater the administrative burden caused by redundant systems, the lower the level of compliance, especially if the activity is not considered useful by the data producers.
2. *Gaps or imbalances in monitoring.* Certain sectors, particularly health and education, have received a large amount of donor attention in recent years and are often more advanced in terms of monitoring. By contrast, sectors such as agriculture have far less developed systems and practices despite their importance in the PRSP. There are also gaps within sectors.
3. *Lack of data compatibility.* To the extent that monitoring mechanisms use different collection methodologies, monitoring periods, and levels of disaggregation, this hampers joint data analysis.
4. *Poor information flows.* The information produced through monitoring is poorly disseminated across government agencies, and feedback is rarely provided to the producers of the data. This inhibits the design of effective policies and programs and makes the pursuit of cross-sectoral and thematic policies and programs more difficult.

In light of these problems, the countries under study have pursued two main supply-side objectives through the creation of a common monitoring system: rationalization and coordination.

Creating a unified PRS monitoring system usually involves rationalizing existing monitoring activities rather than introducing new ones. Such rationalization may include the termination of activities that are not central to the implementation of the PRS, the consolidation of activities duplicated by various agencies, the adoption of common definitions for all actors in the system, a reduction in the number of data platforms used in the country, and so on. Indeed, unless the administrative burden of monitoring is lightened, simply adding new monitoring requirements, even if they are technically superior to the existing ones, may do more harm than good. One study on Uganda (Hauge 2003, 7) concluded that, "new systems, even if logically sound, are unlikely to constitute any improvement unless they are also accompanied by simultaneous reductions in monitoring and evaluation elsewhere." A PRS monitoring system aims to achieve greater strategic focus by shifting resources across monitoring activities in order to reflect PRSP priorities.

Creating a system also usually involves defining relationships among the various actors in the monitoring field. Setting up a system does not mean consolidating all activities within a central agency or under a single superstructure. Rather, a monitoring system should provide a clear allocation of responsibilities, including a calendar of activities, thereby increasing transparency and enabling the various agencies to be held to account for their performance. It should also help foster stronger working relationships between the actors both inside and outside government. It should map and organize information flows to ensure that data are available to the appropriate people at the proper time. It should develop modalities for consultation and cooperation and mechanisms for agreement on common needs and standards. A monitoring system is therefore not the sum of monitoring activities; more accurately, it is a network among a wide range of actors, and it ensures that the activities of these actors complement and inform each other and respond to policy-making needs.

Designing and Implementing a PRS Monitoring System

Both rationalization and coordination pose substantial challenges. Among the countries under study here, all but four have taken steps to create a common PRS monitoring system, although, in some cases, this has so far been limited only to a proposal; and only three countries (Honduras, Tanzania, and Uganda) have begun to operate systems with a fair degree of correspondence between formal design and actual practice. Even in these cases, however, the authors report continuing problems in coordination. In other countries, efforts to systematize PRS monitoring remain at an early stage.

In the country studies, the authors report strong disincentives to rationalization and genuine coordination. As the Tanzania country study notes, agencies tend to defend their separate monitoring activities because these justify more staff and attract per diems and allotments to cover field expenses, which are an important source of civil service earnings. This leads to what has been described in Uganda as "bureaucratic segmentation and fierce territoriality" (Hauge 2003). Ironically, it is the more advanced subsystems in education and health, where donor assistance has been concentrated, that are likely to be the most resistant to central coordination.

In the face of these disincentives, the obvious danger is that PRS monitoring systems will remain purely notional and will not change bureaucratic realities. Though it may be too early to judge, this appears to have been the result in a number of the countries under study. Many coordination efforts are abandoned or simply run out of steam within a short time, leaving monitoring to continue in an ad hoc fashion. Some of the countries have already gone through several different design processes, without much implementation.

In such cases, the problem is probably not in the institutional design itself, but in the process of design and development that has failed to secure the necessary buy-in by stakeholders. Most of the design processes appear to have been fairly narrow exercises. In a few cases, they have begun with surveys of existing monitoring arrangements and capacities and the identification of the need for rationalization and coordination in general terms. There has usually been some consultation with stakeholders across government (and, less often, in civil society), but formal stakeholder analysis and participatory design processes have generally not been used. In most instances, external consultants have been engaged to produce a monitoring strategy or master plan setting out the main features of the system. Usually, this has been done two or three years after the first PRSP.

In most cases, the original design of the system consists of a conceptual representation of information flows, the nomination of a central body to collect and compile monitoring data, and the formation of one or more interagency committees or working groups where stakeholders meet to agree on indicators and monitoring priorities. The details of the system—definitions of roles and responsibilities, standards, modalities for cooperation, calendars of activities, and so on—are left to be resolved within the working groups. However, if the working groups are not effective or the political will dwindles, the initiative may stall at this point without achieving much real coordination.

A number of the country study authors call for greater clarity and detail in the definition of mandates and responsibilities in order to reinforce accountability and promote greater compliance. They point to the importance of formal obligations in overcoming bureaucratic inertia. Most of the monitoring systems are not supported by a regulatory framework, although regulations are anticipated in some situations. In a few instances

(Albania, Bolivia, and the Kyrgyz Republic), monitoring strategies have been formalized through a government or presidential decree. In Latin America, there are plans to elaborate responsibilities in the form of inter-institutional agreements, but these have yet to be developed. In Africa, the monitoring strategies (like the PRSPs themselves) appear to have no formal status.

While the argument could be made that a legal framework is needed to support a monitoring system, there are also clear limits to the cooperation that can be achieved through top-down authority if the design process has not established buy-in by stakeholders. In the Kyrgyz Republic, the central coordinator of the PRS monitoring system (the Comprehensive Development Framework Secretariat), located in the presidential administration, is an extremely powerful organization on paper, with the authority to compel line agencies to produce information on pain of sanctions. It is also the principal advisor to the president on economic policy. However, with severe capacity constraints across the administration, low interest in monitoring among line agencies, and a lack of expertise within the secretariat, this centralization of authority has not brought about any apparent benefit, and the system functions poorly.

Overall, experience suggests that PRS monitoring systems are basically consensual in nature and function properly only if participants consider them useful and legitimate. Once there is a level of agreement on the need for and the main characteristics of a system, regulation appropriate to national administrative traditions can be introduced to reinforce predictability and mutual accountability. Without an initial common purpose, however, imposing legal or administrative obligations is likely to produce only token compliance. It is also important to ensure that the system remains flexible. Indeed, priorities, capacity, and institutions are not static in nature, and the system needs to be able to adapt to this changing environment to harness the capacity of the various actors for the shared objective of PRS implementation.

The sponsors of a PRS monitoring system therefore need to be effective advocates of the need for a common monitoring system. An approach that seems to be successful in Honduras is the use of a participatory process for selecting indicators in order to demonstrate the benefits of cooperation. If the process is taken seriously, selecting quality indicators requires participants to revisit their strategies and the hypotheses and assumptions that underlie them and to examine their administrative structures and the data these structures generate. This creates a snapshot of policies and institutional realities among the agencies active in each sector, thereby help-ing to encourage a coherent focus on PRS priorities.

One example offered by a participant in the Honduran process concerned illegal logging, a cross-cutting priority area in the PRSP. In order to select appropriate indicators, more than a dozen public agencies that were engaged in some aspect of the issue (law enforcement, forestry, conser-vation) were brought together for the first time to analyze the problem, define their roles, and compare strategies; reportedly, they came to recog-nize the need for a joint monitoring framework. Where the monitoring arrangements emerge out of a shared commitment to solving practical problems, they have a much greater chance of success.

Choices in Institutional Design

Among the countries under study here that have developed PRS monitor-ing master plans, the institutional designs look broadly similar on paper. Each PRS monitoring system contains the following basic elements:

1. A high-level *steering committee* to provide political support and oversight and usually chaired by the prime minister, minister of finance, or, in presidential systems, a senior adviser to the president. This body is often also responsible for PRSP implementation as a whole. In terms of monitoring, it typically sets monitoring priorities, approves annual progress reports, and feeds monitoring outputs to the government.
2. A *coordination unit* or *secretariat*, responsible for coordinating monitor-ing activities, convening interagency meetings, compiling data, and drafting reports. It may be located within the office of the president or prime minister, or in a ministry of finance or planning, and it usually contains a small number of dedicated staff.
3. Several *interagency committees* and *working groups*, sometimes with a sec-toral or thematic mandate, that promote interagency cooperation and dialogue. They may be responsible for defining sets of indicators and information needs, preparing sectoral reports, and advising policy makers. They often include representatives of civil society and donors.
4. The *national statistics institute* is always a key component of the system as one of the most important primary data producers. It may also be responsible for compiling administrative data from the line ministries, setting overall data standards, developing information technology plat-forms, and providing technical assistance to other data producers.

5. *Line ministries* are usually required to nominate a point of liaison with the PRS monitoring system; this may be an individual official (such as a director of planning) or a dedicated monitoring and evaluation or statistical unit that has responsibility for compiling sectoral data.

While the institutional structures look broadly similar in outline, their performance is strongly influenced by power relations among the various actors, the administrative and political culture, and the relative capacity of agencies. The key institutional issues therefore relate to the relationships and modalities for cooperation among all these actors. The following sections set out key considerations in developing and strengthening these relationships.

Leadership

The country studies suggest that the initial choice for the institutional lead in the process of developing and implementing a PRS monitoring system is critical. The authors of the studies point to the need for strong leadership, located close to the center of government or to the budget process. The appropriate location will depend on country circumstances.

In the country studies, the range of institutional leads includes (1) ministry of finance (Albania, Mali, Niger, Uganda), (2) ministry of planning (Malawi, Mauritania), (3) office of the president (Bolivia, Guyana, Honduras, the Kyrgyz Republic, Nicaragua), and (4) office of the vice-president (Tanzania). Lucas, Evans, and Pasteur (2004) comment that it is more likely to be a ministry of finance in Africa and a ministry of planning in Asia. In Latin America, the trend appears to be toward the office of the president.

Given the rivalries that often exist between ministries of planning and finance, the choice of institutional home is likely to affect the orientation and authority of the system. Leadership by the ministry of finance helps to link monitoring to the budget process, which is often seen as a condition for an effective PRS monitoring system. Ministries of planning may be better equipped to analyze monitoring data, but may lack the authority to champion the system effectively. In Malawi, the Ministry of Economic Planning and Development is a relatively weak player in the political system, and the country study notes that other ministries are not even aware of its formal leadership role in the monitoring process. The Ugandan PRS monitoring system has benefited in recent years from the support of a combined planning and finance superministry, but there are signs that the authority of this institution is beginning to wane. In Tanzania, the national poverty eradication division is located in the Office of the Vice-President, which gives it political authority, but the country study notes that its institutional separation from the budget process does not support the goal of results-oriented budgeting.

Leadership appears to be more effective when it is invested in a single agency, rather than in an interagency committee. Leadership needs to be exercised actively, with commitments from senior politicians and supported by champions able to make the case for a common monitoring system across the administration.

The choice of the institutional lead should reflect current political and institutional realities and the way that development policies and resource-allocation decisions are actually made. It may also depend on where individual champions are located, although there are risks associated with tying institutional choices too closely to personalities. The country studies suggest that the leadership role may need to change over time in response to political and administrative developments.

Coordination

Organizing effective coordination among the institutional actors emerges in the country studies as one of the most difficult challenges. Most of the countries have created a series of interagency committees and working groups to gather the various agencies and discuss coordination needs. These often include representatives of civil society organizations and donors. Effective coordination means rationalizing existing monitoring activities and agreeing on common procedures and standards. Agencies are often protective of their autonomy and their separate monitoring roles, which attract resources. Against this background, several of the country-study authors are skeptical that simply bringing representatives around a table is enough to produce genuine coordination. Where incentives act against coordination, interagency committees tend to produce superficially plausible solutions, such as ambitious new training programs or information technology investments, without addressing underlying issues.

In light of these problems, the committee structures described in some of the country studies appear too elaborate for the amount of coordination they actually achieve. Mali, for example, has 13 thematic working groups and plans to add nine regional committees. According to several country studies, the working groups meet only once a year to prepare annual progress reports (for example, in Albania), and make little contribution to coordination.

Including representatives of civil society and donors broadens participation, but care should be taken to avoid losing group coherence. In Bolivia, the membership of the four working groups was very diverse, with few common interests among the members and few incentives to dedicate the time that was required. The working groups met irregularly and were eventually dissolved. The Mauritania study points out that data producers and users often meet in committees to discuss priorities, but that few concrete recommendations ever result. It is therefore better to avoid elaborate or burdensome coordination structures and, instead, focus on building productive working relationships between agencies.

Effective secretariat support is important. A secretariat is needed to prepare meetings, ensure that they are focused and substantive, follow up on agreed activities, and perform central tasks for the system, such as the compilation of reports, report dissemination, and so on. It should also play a mediation role among the actors. For example, national statistics institutes often complain that, when users of statistical information are asked to define their needs, they make complicated, unrealistic demands without identifying their priorities. This problem is unlikely to be resolved through occasional meetings. It requires the presence of a third party able to organize a structured dialogue between users and the statistics institute, to work through the issues, and to encourage the parties to identify their real needs and constraints. This requires certain skills within the coordination unit, plus dedicated resources. In some of the countries under study, this function has been undermined by high turnover among staff in the coordination units.

Donors can play an important role in fostering coordination by not undermining the national PRS monitoring system with parallel mechanisms, by using the system for their own reporting needs, and by supporting the system, as follows:

- Donor funding for separate project-level monitoring structures that are not related to the PRS monitoring system may create a strong disincentive to rationalization and coordination since agencies might be keen to secure such funding. Limiting such parallel structures may help promote PRS monitoring systems.
- While donor information needs are not necessarily the same as those of the government, donors should strive to support the PRS monitoring system and use it for their own purposes. To ensure that donor information

needs are met by the national system and to avoid the push for parallel systems, these needs should be considered during the design phase. In addition, donors should work toward aligning their reporting requirements and procedures with the PRS monitoring system to ensure they can effectively use the system for their own monitoring and reporting needs. This will then provide incentives for the government to improve the PRS monitoring system.

- Donors can also actively support the PRS monitoring system. Ideally, such support is best provided by championing the entire system. Indeed, as is often the case with statistics, donors tend to favor funding for particular activities, such as specific surveys, while the core administrative functions of the agencies are underresourced. This results in low capacity to organize, plan, retain staff, coordinate, and so on. In contrast, supporting the institutions and agencies more broadly is required for the strengthening of systems. To reduce the strain on capacity, donors should ideally also pool their support of the system through mechanisms such as common funding baskets.

Ultimately, however, a precondition for effective coordination is a shared commitment across the various agencies to the creation of a successful PRS monitoring system. This has as much to do with an effective design process, advocacy, and political leadership as with the system design.

Liaison with line ministries

All the PRS monitoring systems described in the country studies are second-tier systems in that they rely on routine administrative information from line ministries for an important part of their indicator data. As discussed elsewhere above, the PRS monitoring system should not seek to consolidate all monitoring activities under one agency, but, rather, should coordinate activities undertaken by a wide range of agencies for their own internal management, as well as for monitoring broader policies and interventions. The PRS monitoring system must ensure that information on basic sets of indicators is collected from line ministries in a timely fashion. This will allow the assessment of progress in implementing the PRS as a whole and strengthen the accountability of ministries with respect to the center of government.

Ministries and other public agencies, including social funds, are usually required to nominate liaisons to a PRS monitoring system. These liaisons may be dedicated monitoring units or officers such as directors of planning.

The liaison points are responsible for ensuring the timely delivery of indi-cator data and may represent their agencies on committees and working groups. Such links have not been functioning adequately in many of the countries under study, often because the liaisons nominated have lacked the authority, time, or incentive to carry out the role effectively.

In practice, this means that PRS monitoring systems are heavily dependent on the quality of sectoral monitoring arrangements. Weaknesses in administrative information systems represent critical constraints accord-ing to all the country studies. In Albania, for example, monitoring and eval-uation units in 16 line ministries have extensive responsibilities under the PRS monitoring systems, including for developing sectoral indicators and targets, establishing and maintaining databases, reporting, and policy advice. In practice, these units are more virtual than real. No specific budgets or dedicated offices are provided, and the staffs all have primary responsibilities in other sections of their ministries. Monitoring and liai-son functions are not included in job descriptions. As a result, the units are largely ineffective for both sectoral and PRS-level monitoring.

In Honduras, management, planning, and evaluation units have been created within line ministries to replace the former secretariat of planning, but are considered a poor substitute. They are run by low-paid, long-tenured staff with poor training and little information technology support. They are unable to provide quality control on the data collected by local offices. Reporting obligations under the PRS monitoring system are not aligned with sectoral information systems, and separate project-level monitoring and reporting requirements linked to donors often take prece-dence. According to one commentator, "An emerging lesson . . . is that performance information is primarily a management tool at the sector and organizational level" (Holmes 2003, 10).

PRS monitoring systems are more likely to be effective if line ministries are actively engaged in monitoring to fulfill their own management pur-poses and if the liaison role is performed by individuals who are substan-tively involved in sectoral monitoring and policy making. If there is no substantial practice of monitoring at the sectoral level, the PRS monitor-ing system will need to include a more active strategy to promote mon-itoring across government. One option is to require line ministries to dedicate funds and full-time personnel to the monitoring function and to include monitoring obligations in departmental work plans and job descrip-tions. There may also be a need for capacity-building programs at the min-isterial level, although a number of the country studies warn that poor monitoring practices are more likely the result of weak incentives rather than capacity constraints.

The role of the national statistical system

In many of the countries under study, national statistical systems have benefited from extensive donor assistance since the early 1990s and are the most institutionally advanced elements of the PRS monitoring system. This volume does not cover the organization of statistical systems directly, but a few issues concerning the relationship of these systems to PRS monitoring are noted in the country studies.

First, in a number of countries there have been initiatives to develop a statistical master plan, often accompanied by the establishment of inter-institutional committees designed to link national statistics institutes to data users. In some cases, these master plans and structures predate the PRS monitoring systems and have not been revised subsequently, leading to overlapping coordination structures and redundant committees. In a few cases (Bolivia, Honduras, Nicaragua, Uganda), the authors of the country study have noted the potential for institutional rivalry between the two systems. Care should be taken in designing a PRS monitoring system to ensure complementarity with the development of the statistical system. The recent effort by many countries to establish national statistical development strategies driven by the needs of the national PRS goes some way in this direction.

Second, national statistics institutes are often allocated a standard-setting, technical-assistance, and capacity-building role in relation to administrative information systems. In most cases, they have been slow in taking up this role. The problem may be partly a result of the existing funding modalities for statistical systems. National statistics institutes tend to prioritize large survey and statistical operations, for which donor funding is readily available, leaving little time for other functions. For instance, in Malawi in 2004, only one-fifth of donor funding for the statistical system was assigned to regular statistical activities; the bulk went for irregular or development activities (Paris21 2006). To remedy this, donors may need to consider more flexible ways of supporting the institutional development of national statistics institutes, such as through basket funding.

A third issue relates to the use of survey data within the PRS monitoring system. After large surveys have been conducted, national statistics institutes sometimes offer training to other agencies in the use of the data, but, in most cases, the wealth of data available from the surveys is not being used effectively to support PRS monitoring. In Albania, for example, despite substantial donor investment in a Living Standards Measurement Survey, the country study reports that senior management in line ministries distrust the survey data, preferring to rely on outdated and inaccurate administrative sources. None of the line ministries has even sought to access the data set. There may need to be more effort to train policy makers in the use of survey data.

A final point relates to the scope of statistical systems. Statistical systems are meant to encompass both central statistics agencies and other producers of statistics, including sectoral ministries and local-level government agencies. In many of the countries studied, there is a disconnect between the central agencies and the wider system, which often results in gaps and redundancies. The peripheral agencies also typically perform less well than the central ones, resulting in the weaknesses in administrative data mentioned elsewhere above. An analysis of the availability of statistics for monitoring the Millennium Development Goals identifies the peripheral agencies as the weakest part of the system (Paris21 2006).

Involving local governments and local agencies

A number of country studies note the particular challenges posed by decentralized service delivery, particularly during the actual process of decentralization. However, few of the countries studied provide for the representation of regional or local governments in the PRS monitoring system structure. Guyana has established, on a pilot basis, PRS regional committees that are responsible for regional monitoring, dissemination, and capacity building. Mauritania is unique since its regional governments each have their own monitoring arrangements and gather regularly to compare progress and the lessons learned.

Whatever the structure of government, the challenges of collecting accurate and timely monitoring information from the local level are substantial. A number of country studies comment that even line ministries have difficulty communicating with their own regional outlets, and the channels of communication for the broader PRS monitoring system may be even harder to establish. Local capacity is often acutely constrained. Agencies already find compliance with basic accounting rules for development programs difficult, which suggests that they are unlikely to be able to comply with more sophisticated performance-monitoring requirements. Finally, multiple reporting requirements impose a heavy burden on local-level agencies.

There are many types of decentralized systems, and the critical characteristic for monitoring is the direction of accountability of the local agency. In the case of deconcentration and delegation, funding comes from the central government, and the local governments or agencies remain largely accountable to the central government. This provides incentives to comply with the needs of the central government, but can limit the incentives for agencies to use information to manage their own activities. In the case of devolution, local governments have some degree of political and fiscal autonomy, which shifts their accountability downward toward their local constituencies. This increases the opportunity for local governments to use data to inform their own policy making and their reporting to local constituencies, but reduces the authority of the central government.

The process of decentralization poses particular challenges to the establishment of a viable PRS monitoring system, and these challenges have not been resolved satisfactorily in any of the countries under study. There appears to be two competing approaches available.

The centralized approach. Here, the central government retains control of the process by centrally monitoring local governments. Countries have recognized that the process of decentralization carries the risk of exacerbating regional inequalities and the local capture of services or funds and have tried to strengthen the monitoring of local authorities by the central government. In Peru, for instance, the transfer of functions to particular local authorities takes place if and when the central government certifies that these local authorities have the necessary management and financial systems in place.

The decentralized approach. A few countries have tried to encourage local governments to develop their own monitoring arrangements so as to define and meet their own monitoring needs, as well as to supply administrative and financial data to the center. This supports the basic objective of decentralization, that is, to bring policy decisions closer to the communities they affect, but it might be constrained by limited capacity. This appears to be the preferred approach in a number of the African cases, although there has been little progress in implementation.

A PRS monitoring system can be promoted in a decentralized context by establishing three channels of accountability, as follows:

1. The *accountability of local governments and agencies to the central government* involves reporting reliable data to meet the needs of the center. This requires incentives, especially in the context of devolution, such

as, for instance, linking fund allocations to compliance. In Uganda, for example, local governments receive the bulk of their funding in the form of conditional grants from the center. They are required to monitor service delivery and development expenditure as a condition of the grants, creating a financial incentive for local monitoring. This, however, could penalize poorer areas or weaker agencies, which tend to have lower capacity. Overall, the incentives needed for the system to function might have to vary for different local agencies and governments that have different constituencies.

2. The *accountability of the center to local governments and agencies* requires the center to feed back data and analysis disaggregated at a level of disaggregation that is meaningful and useful for local governments and agencies. Among the countries under study, only Bolivia approaches the accountability of the center toward local governments in a systematic way. The Vice-Ministry of Strategic Planning and Popular Participation coordinates monitoring and evaluation activities at the regional and municipal levels. It is charged with disseminating information back to municipalities and providing feedback on the monitoring information they provide.

3. The *accountability of local governments and agencies to their constituencies* may be enhanced through the introduction of requirements to communicate results locally, for example, by posting information at schools, health clinics, and community centers. This strengthens local demand and can be effective since local governments may be more responsive to community demands than to the central government. Thus, the local vigilance committees in Bolivia, which comprise representatives of community-based organizations and enjoy a high degree of local legitimacy, are legally empowered to scrutinize local spending and service delivery under a law on popular participation, and are entitled to funding from municipal budgets.

More generally, a number of strategies suggested in the country studies may help promote the production of high-quality, reliable data. These include the following:

1. The *careful selection of indicators* for monitoring at the local level. These should be readily measurable indicators so as to minimize the administrative burden. Evidence suggests that the best way to increase compliance in the short run is to make it easier to comply.

2. *Definitions of requirements that are adapted to local capacity.* Capacity constraints are difficult to address because of the number of actors involved and the small size of many local institutions (which may not have sufficient staff dedicated to monitoring). The central system also typically needs to build its capacity to process and analyze a growing volume of information. In Peru, for example, plans to extend the computerized financial management information system to local governments will triple the number of system users, creating daunting technical challenges.

3. The *adoption of a shared list of definitions and classifications* to be used systematically across reporting units and geographical areas. Such an effort helps prevent significant miscalculations in aggregating data and misinterpretations of the resulting information.

4. The *harmonization of reporting requirements* among various agencies (sectoral ministries, local government administrations, donor-supported projects, ministries of planning, ministries of finance, and so on) to reduce the burden on local agencies.

5. The *development of quality-control mechanisms at the central level* where the data are collected and aggregated, and the system should be able to deploy targeted technical support and capacity-building programs to address quality issues revealed through these mechanisms.

6. The *use of secondary monitoring methods* (such as public service satisfaction surveys) to triangulate local administrative data in order to identify biases in reporting.

7. An *understanding of the process of data aggregation and disaggregation*, which can be difficult because agencies and interventions may use different definitions and vary in coverage (for example, local health posts versus regional hospitals; district borders that do not correspond to the jurisdictions of the subnational agencies of central ministries). Understanding how data are aggregated and the level at which they are collected helps identify what is feasible at the local level and what is sufficient for the PRS monitoring system.

3

Making Use of PRS Monitoring

Both the country studies and the broader literature concur that an effective system for monitoring a poverty reduction strategy (PRS) must build demand for monitoring, while organizing the supply side. Unless decision makers actively seek evidence to support policy making and program management, monitoring practices are unlikely to take hold across government administration.

The most promising strategy for building demand is to establish a link between the monitoring system and key points in the decision-making process where monitoring information may influence the development of policy. As stated in the Tanzania country study:

> The demand will only arise out of the progressive growth among planners and their political bosses of incentives to improve policies by reference to evidence and analysis. The focus in improving monitoring therefore needs to be on the interface between monitoring and decision making, particularly those parts . . . where the incentives to results-based thinking are [being strengthened]. (Booth 2004, 25)

Some of these points of interface are within the formal policy process; the budget is the most obvious example. Others are outside government, such as informed media reporting, interest-group advocacy, or the electoral cycle. The broader goal is to create a virtuous circle whereby government uses sound analysis and information to formulate its policies, is open to informed discussion on its policy choices, and, in turn, seeks to build legitimacy and electoral support through evidence of its achievements. A PRS monitoring system can help support these dynamics by creating an information-rich environment.

It may be useful for the designers of a PRS monitoring system to think through the different entry points into the policy cycle where monitoring information might help to increase the results-orientation of government policy. These entry points will differ from country to country, but might include decisions on budget priorities, annual reviews of medium-term expenditure frameworks (MTEFs) or public investment plans, periodic reviews and updating of the PRS; scrutiny of government policy by parliament and parliamentary committees, setting priorities for targeted programs or investment plans, the development of budget-support agreements and policy matrices with donors, and the development of multilateral and bilateral assistance strategies. While these processes are outside the scope of PRS monitoring, the PRS monitoring system needs to be organized so as to ensure that information and analysis are available in the proper form at the appropriate time.

This chapter begins by looking at the organization of analysis and evaluation and strategies for dissemination. It then examines the key issue of linking PRS monitoring to the budgetary process. Finally, it discusses the role of parliament.

Analysis and Evaluation

Monitoring alone does not produce institutional learning. It is only by analyzing the results and using them to evaluate policies and programs that one may realize the benefits of monitoring systems. It appears from the country studies that analysis and evaluation are a deficit in PRS monitoring systems. Considerable attention has been focused on the development of indicators and data collection systems, but little has been done to institutionalize the practice of analysis and evaluation. A study produced by the German Agency for Technical Cooperation comments that, in many cases, the most that is done with monitoring data is to edit them into the annual progress report format (GTZ 2004a). The problem is caused by both a general lack of analytical capacity, particularly within line ministries, and weak incentives. Where accountability is weak, agencies have little interest in using information and analysis to define their activities and in subjecting their own programs to critical scrutiny. As the Albanian country study points out, this can trap a PRS monitoring system in a vicious circle. Without quality analysis of the data, there is no firm basis for setting targets, which then become divorced from reality. As a result, reporting on progress toward these targets is seen as a meaningless exercise and is not taken seriously.

In the countries under study, a few of the PRS monitoring systems incorporate strategies for promoting the analysis of data and the evaluation of programs. The most common approach is to create a central body mandated to lead analysis on behalf of the government. For example:

- In Bolivia, the unit for the analysis of economic and social policies, which is located in the Ministry of Economic Development, led in drafting the PRS and designed the monitoring system. As well as compiling monitoring data from line agencies, it is charged with reviewing proposed sectoral policies and programs for consistency with PRS goals.
- In Nicaragua, a poverty analysis unit located in the Office of the President and staffed by four sectoral specialists, is responsible for the analytical content of annual progress reports and other reporting.
- In Tanzania, the technical working group for research and analysis is mandated to set priorities in research and analysis and propose funding mechanisms. A nongovernmental organization (NGO) acts as secretariat, and the group includes representatives of the central bank, governmental agencies, the national statistics institute, civil society, and donors. It maintains close links with nongovernmental research institutes.
- In Uganda, the poverty monitoring and analysis unit in the Ministry of Finance, Planning and Economic Development was established in 1998 with support from the U.K. Department for International Development. It has three professional staff and one Overseas Development Institute fellow. It is not part of the regular civil service, but seems to be well integrated in ministry processes. It is responsible for generating analysis and for commissioning studies from outside sources.
- A number of Francophone countries in West Africa have established poverty observatories either inside the national statistics institute or as independent agencies. These units carry out analysis of poverty trends and are also responsible for reporting on the progress toward achieving the Millennium Development Goals.

Dedicated analytical units have been most effective where they have remained small and close to government and have focused purely on analytical tasks. If they attempt to expand their role into policy making or data collection, they become competitive with other agencies and are likely to fail. If they are funded directly by donors, the challenge is to ensure that they are responsive to the needs of government and other national stake-holders. Experience suggests that these units, if they are too far removed from the center of decisions, do not have the intended impact because their analysis is then typically less relevant and operational, and the findings they produce are not owned by decision makers. Some of these central analytical units have also lacked the sectoral focus useful to line ministries and have not concentrated on practical program evaluations. Also, in cases of relatively autonomous agencies in which the wages are significantly higher than those in the civil service, the units may deplete central government agencies of qualified staff.

Another useful technique has been joint analytical exercises which involve government and donors and which thereby help build both capacity and interest in analysis. Such exercises include public expenditure reviews, which are useful tools if routine financial management information is deficient. In a number of countries, including Mauritania and Tanzania, they are now conducted on an annual basis to provide a periodic picture of spending patterns. In Honduras, donors have supported the analysis of the poverty and social impacts of a number of reforms, such as the privatization of electric utilities and tax reform. If ministries are encouraged to use the analysis to justify their proposed policy measures, this helps them view analysis as a means of achieving their own objectives. Similar positive dynamics can be seen in sectorwide approaches, whereby ministries need to justify their policy choices by indicating the impact on poverty in order to make the case to donors for greater alignment. Overall, donors should be taking every opportunity to encourage governments to defend their policy choices by bringing forward evidence and analysis.

Analysis should not be the exclusive preserve of government. The interpretation of monitoring information is best performed through exchanges and debate among a plurality of well-informed actors. In addition, nongovernmental entities, such as universities, research centers, consultants, NGOs, or donors, can supplement limited government analytical capacity (see chapter 4). The difficulty then resides in ensuring that the analysis is effectively used by decision makers. This requires scientific, neutral analysis; the dissemination and explanation of the tools and methods deployed; and the transmission of results in formats adapted to the needs of decision makers. This may sometimes be challenging for donors and nongovernmental advocacy groups since their agendas and ambitions could interfere with the analysis and limit broader acceptance.

Outputs and Dissemination

If they are to have an impact on the policy process, monitoring information, analysis, and evaluation must be compiled into outputs and distributed to actors inside and outside government. A good monitoring system will produce a range of outputs appropriate for different audiences and purposes, plus a dissemination strategy that provides those outputs across government and to the public at appropriate moments in the policy cycle.

The production of specific outputs and their dissemination is a major weakness in the PRS monitoring systems examined in the country studies. Most of the monitoring systems are focused mainly on the production of an annual progress report. Under the rules of the Heavily Indebted Poor Countries Initiative and the Poverty Reduction Strategy Paper (PRSP), the annual progress report is an opportunity to review and update the PRS on a regular basis. In practice, these reports are typically not being used this way. They tend to have weak analytical content and, in the first PRS cycle, are often produced in an ad hoc manner, sometimes by external consultants who do not draw on the monitoring system. They are usually inappropriate for domestic audiences, being long, technical, and full of donor language. Though they are sometimes circulated to civil society in draft form for comment, they are poorly publicized once adopted. On the whole, they are seen as an external reporting mechanism, rather than as a tool of national policy making. (A notable exception is Uganda, where existing government publications are used as the basis for the annual progress report. Poverty status reports are biannual. In alternate years, the annual progress report is based on the background to the budget.) The PRSP evaluation of the Operations Evaluation Department, World Bank, concluded that:

> the annual progress report requirement does not help to validate or strengthen existing institutionalized domestic monitoring processes. This lack of alignment implies duplication of effort and decreases the relevance of the annual progress report as an operational tool. The costs of reporting requirements are high for PRSP countries; many need to report to donors while continuing institutionalized or legally mandated reporting requirements in-country. As currently constituted, the annual progress reports are an additional strain on limited country capacity. (World Bank 2004b, 25)

It is important to ensure that the outputs of the PRS monitoring system are appropriate to the needs of the national policy process. This may require a range of publications in different formats and designed for different users, such as ministries of finance, sectoral ministries, other agencies, and parliamentary committees. Users that are often neglected are local-level decision-making agencies, as well as sectoral agencies. These users need outputs particularly tailored to their functions, that is, appropriately disaggregated and focused on policy recommendations in their respective areas.

In addition to format, the timing of outputs is also important. The outputs should be linked to key moments in the policy cycle, such as budget submissions, annual reviews of MTEFs, or parliamentary debates. Unless these outputs are aligned with the key entry points in the decision-making process, their full potential is unlikely to materialize (see more elsewhere below).

Making monitoring information accessible to the general public is also an important objective. The monitoring system should promote informed dialogue and debate around PRS implementation. It can enable governments to explain the choices they have made in selecting priorities and to demonstrate the impacts of these choices in terms of poverty reduction. Similarly, by increasing transparency, it should enable citizens to engage more productively in the decisions that affect them and empower citizens and civil society to hold governments accountable for their policy choices and interventions. Wide dissemination to the public, however, can be difficult if the results of monitoring are somewhat disappointing. In such cases, it takes a strong political commitment to transparency and dialogue for governments to disseminate potentially damaging information voluntarily.

Given the importance of these objectives, it is disappointing to note that little information from poverty monitoring systems is currently entering the public arena. The German Agency for Technical Cooperation has concluded that the dissemination of monitoring information in a form appropriate to a national audience is "largely neglected":

> It is quite astonishing to ascertain how little information makes its way to the public in a form that would permit an assessment of how seriously the government is carrying out its poverty program, and with what degree of success. . . . Those governments that take seriously the participation of and accountability to their citizens have the duty to provide their populace and the national authorities with relevant information. This obligation is not being

adequately met. Publicity work related to the implementation of poverty reduction can be significantly improved almost everywhere, to state it positively. (GTZ 2004a, 80)

In the country studies, examples of outputs intended for the general public include the following:

- Bolivia: booklets on population and poverty statistics at the regional level and thematic booklets on poverty issues
- Honduras: a number of Web sites, although the content is still under development
- Mauritania: a CD-ROM containing survey data and including 108 poverty-related studies and reports produced over the past 20 years
- Guyana: local information centers to disseminate information on poverty programs

Producing material in a form meaningful to the public might be a new skill for governments, and more use could be made of civil society partners in interpreting monitoring data and producing materials. One useful technique is to turn monitoring outputs into stories, particularly stories highlighting weaknesses in program implementation and service delivery. For example, it has been said that the first Uganda participatory poverty assessment report was influential not merely because it articulated non-income perceptions of poverty, but because it generated memorable examples of problems with service delivery. Local communities could readily grasp these problems and mobilize around them, forcing government to respond.

The issues that matter most to communities are usually local in nature, and comparisons between different jurisdictions can be very powerful. Citizens are unlikely to be motivated by small changes in national poverty statistics, but may care deeply whether their municipality is performing better or worse than other municipalities. Increasingly, the availability of performance information in this format helps to build local demand for improved services.

Disseminating analysis on government performance helps to channel public dissatisfaction in a positive direction toward social pressure for change. Picciotto (2004) notes that social learning cannot take place if institutions are unable to channel public protest into responsive shifts in public policy. Such channeling is accomplished through the generation, dissemination, and interpretation of information that promotes public understanding of policies and programs. Social learning also demands account-ability and a credible capacity for independent review, according to Pic-ciotto. Public protest and participation transform the energy of disappointment into reform if evaluation lends a helping hand.

While debate and a measure of disagreement is necessary, PRS mon-itoring should not be seen as primarily adversarial in nature. Rather, it is a tool for decision making that is more informed, policies that are better designed, and interventions that are more effective. Governments can also view greater openness and public discussion around development policy as an opportunity to demonstrate their legitimacy. As well as publicizing their own success stories, such openness enables governments to explain to the public the choices and trade-offs involved in development policy.

Linking PRS Monitoring and the Budget

Creating a link between PRS monitoring and the budget process is a crit-ical objective for a PRS monitoring system. The need to access public resources creates powerful incentives across all public agencies and pro-vides the most promising hook for creating demand for effective monitor-ing. Moreover, unless this link is established, the PRS monitoring system will fail to meet its central objective of information-based decision making because budgets are the central mechanism for policy implementation. However, the country studies also demonstrate that this link can be very difficult to implement, especially if budget planning and public expenditure management systems are poorly developed.

In principle, budget priority should be assigned to programs with an impact on poverty reduction that has been demonstrated through the PRS monitoring system. In practice, performance-oriented budgeting is a recent innovation that has been adopted in a limited number of developed coun-tries following major shifts in public sector management practices. It depends upon technically advanced systems for budget planning and public expenditure management, which are a long-term goal in most PRS coun-tries. Among the countries under study, most still use incremental budget-ing and have only recently begun establishing systems to match public spending and PRS priorities. Some lack the financial management sys-tems to ensure that actual spending is aligned with the budget or to report accurately on expenditure.

Budgetary and public expenditure management reforms are necessarily evolutionary. Most PRS countries need to establish compliance (effective control over spending) and macroeconomic stability (the capacity to meet overall spending targets), before they take on the task of increasing the efficiency and effectiveness of public spending; this is a sequence that may take many years to complete. In addition, in many countries, large segments of the budget are devoted to wages and salaries, leaving little room for re-allocation in the short term. Greater alignment and flexibility in budgets thus depend on broader government reforms.

The question is therefore whether it is possible to create an effective link between the PRS monitoring system and the budget in PRS countries given current conditions. Relatively little experience emerges from the country studies on this point.

The most promising strategy identified in the country studies is the introduction in the rules and procedures surrounding the budgetary process of a requirement that spending agencies justify their resource bids according to PRS priorities and the evidence on past program performance. This is more readily accomplished in countries that have successfully introduced an MTEF. While the PRS sets down general objectives and priorities, it is usually the MTEF that provides the framework within which explicit spending choices and trade-offs are made; it therefore represents the ideal opportunity to use monitoring information. PRS monitoring system outputs can be timed to feed data and analysis into annual MTEF updates.

If there is no MTEF in place, there may be other opportunities connected to the annual budget process or the preparation of public investment plans. Monitoring data can influence decisions on which areas receive priority status. Likewise, there may be decision points involved in the selection of target areas and target populations for particular programs, such as social funds, roads, transport, energy, and so on, or in negotiating processes around multilateral or bilateral assistance strategies. In short, wherever line ministries are bidding for resources, the potential exists to use the occasion to encourage the ministries to support their proposals with evidence of the potential impact of the proposals on poverty reduction.

Among the countries under study, only Tanzania and Uganda have made progress in establishment concrete links to budgets, and, in both cases, this has represented the culmination of more than a decade of budgetary and public expenditure management reforms.

In Uganda, there is a technically advanced MTEF and a virtual fund within the budget—the poverty action fund—that protects disbursements in priority subsectors. In Uganda's consultative budget process, line ministries are required to submit budget framework papers to provide a rationale for their medium-term recurrent and capital funding bids. The submissions are supposed to cover achievements and goals linked to the PRSP framework and supported by monitoring data.

In practice, as the country study notes, the link has not yet had much influence on MTEF ceilings. (Under the poverty action fund, some subsectors are presumed to be priorities regardless of their performance, which weakens the demand for performance data.) However, it has provided a noticeable, if uneven, impetus toward more results-oriented policy making within sectors. This has allowed for greater donor alignment through budget support, which, in turn, generates more demand for monitoring information.

A key element in the Ugandan process is the external scrutiny of and dialogue around annual budget submissions. This is performed partly by the Budget Policy and Evaluation Department within the Ministry of Finance, Planning, and Economic Development and partly by the poverty eradication working group, a consultative body involving stakeholders and civil society. The department plays a challenge function within the budget process, that is, it engages the spending agencies in dialogue around their policy choices. Without this challenge function, a purely formal requirement that performance information be included in budget submissions is unlikely to be meaningful. The challenge function needs to be carried out by an agency with both the capacity and the authority to engage with spending agencies at a senior level.

Tanzania also has a functional MTEF and a technically advanced financial management information system. It has recently shifted from a system of protected priority sectors in the budget to a more flexible set of cluster strategies, which are prioritized, pro-poor policies spanning most sectors. As in the Ugandan case, to receive prioritization in disbursements, units must justify annual budget submissions in terms of these cluster strategies. The country study comments:

> In effect, sector policy makers have a material incentive to develop outcome-oriented rationales for what they do with their allocations from public resources. For the first time, they are being given reasons to make use of data on results. (Booth 2004, 6)

However, in Tanzania the challenge function is not well developed, and the incentives are correspondingly weaker. The link is also diluted by the large amounts of off-budget donor spending, which undermines accountability and, thus, the effectiveness of national funds.

The link between the PRS monitoring system and the budget is usually created via rules governing budget submissions. However, the literature suggests that care needs to be taken in setting these rules for a number of reasons:

1. Particularly while the system is under development, PRS monitoring data are not always suitable or sufficiently accurate for preparing programs, defining interventions, and setting expenditures. It takes many years for some indicators to reflect and respond to policy interventions, and these indicators thus may not immediately support annual budget planning. In addition, the information for some areas might be less developed, which could result in the neglect of these areas. For instance, there might be less information on poorer areas or on particular sectors that have received less attention in the past. Finally, there is always a danger that one will focus on those interventions that are likely to result in measurable short-term changes and neglect areas in which results might take longer to materialize or are more difficult to measure.

2. In addition, the attribution of a positive or negative outcome to a particular program is not always possible because changes are often likely to result from a myriad of factors, many of which will be outside the realm of the program. The analysis must be able to identify a counterfactual (the situation that would have taken place without the program) to attribute specific changes in outcomes to individual interventions.

3. Where budget releases are unreliable, particularly in a cash-budgeting system, public sector managers cannot be held to strict account for the performance of programs, since irregular releases may render program implementation erratic. This undermines the link between the PRS monitoring system and the budget. In the case of Uganda, one commentator noted:

> Below budget outturns and uncertainty in the timing of disbursements were justifiably cited widely as seriously impacting the ability of agencies to deliver results. This undermines the ability of and incentive for managers to plan for activities in advance, as they do not know when or whether they will actually be able to carry the activities out. (Williamson 2003, 32)

In these circumstances, a PRS monitoring system needs to track public expenditures to identify situations where budget execution could be negatively affecting program outcomes. Only when the budget and public expenditure management systems become more reliable will it be feasible to base budget decisions directly on PRS monitoring system indicators.

4. While budget rules can mandate the use of monitoring data, creating an effective sanction against those who do not comply is difficult. Generally, it would not be appropriate to cut funding to PRS priority areas simply because the responsible public agencies have performed the monitoring function poorly. For instance, the weakest agencies might not be able to monitor and report on their activities and to make a case for their programs, yet these programs might be the very ones most in need of funding. Nonetheless, a monitoring process unaccompanied by sanctions for nonuse of the monitoring system may generate only token compliance.

5. Perverse incentives represent a danger. If the link between compliance and access to the budget is poorly designed, there may be a disincentive to effective and accurate reporting. Likewise, the selection of indicators may be influenced in favor of those that can be more readily controlled by line agencies, or there may even be an incentive to falsify the results of monitoring or voluntarily to neglect the effective monitoring of these indicators. One study points out that, "if failure to achieve agreed targets has unpleasant financial consequences, there is little incentive to strengthen monitoring systems which have the potential to highlight that failure" (Lucas, Evans, and Pasteur 2004, 38).

For all these reasons, establishing a link between performance data and resource allocation that is too strict may not be feasible or desirable until budget and public expenditure management reforms and the PRS monitoring system have become more developed. However, this does not preclude introducing a more general requirement that public agencies justify their budget bids based on the PRS through the use of evidence on program performance. The lesson seems to be that it may be fruitful to use the budget process to create opportunities for dialogue on program performance, as gauged by monitoring information, between spending agencies and a central body with the capacity and authority to play an effective challenge function.

The Role of Parliaments

In the countries under study, there is very little substantive involvement of parliament in PRS monitoring or, indeed, in the PRSP process as a whole.

This appears to be a missed opportunity both for increasing the impact of PRS monitoring and for building parliamentary capacity. The involvement of parliaments in PRS monitoring has the potential to bring legitimacy, country ownership, and the voice of constituencies into the process.

Parliaments play many different roles, and some of these roles provide critical openings whereby PRS monitoring systems may have a positive impact. Parliaments have a legislative role that involves collaboration with the executive in the formulation and implementation of development policy. PRS monitoring systems are a critical source of information for parliaments and the other actors involved in the design and implementation of sound policies and programs.

Parliaments also have an important oversight role with regard to the executive. In this role, through committee hearings, ministerial questioning, and investigations, parliaments hold government administrations accountable in reaching policy objectives. To carry out this role successfully, parliaments must be able to determine if resources are being used as budgeted and if they are achieving their objectives. PRS monitoring systems should include mechanisms to provide parliaments with such information, thereby ensuring that the checks and balances of good government are maintained. Parliaments may become involved in reviews of the results of monitoring results on a regular basis through public hearings on sectoral strategies or reports on implementation. It is important to note, however, that this role will depend on the relationship and balance of power between parliament and the executive, which is determined by the constitution and the context of the country.

Parliaments have a representative role. They must speak for the needs and interests of their constituencies, especially the poor. They must inform these constituencies about the efforts being undertaken by the government to meet the needs of the constituencies. PRS monitoring systems can provide parliaments with the relevant information. This information can be shared through venues such as public forums and press conferences.

A central role of parliaments is to review and authorize budgets. By understanding how previous budgets were implemented and what the budget expenditures were able to achieve, parliaments will be much better equipped to review current budgets and identify items that require adjustments in expenditure allocations. There are also opportunities to open the budget process to parliamentary scrutiny when budgets are being submitted and to use PRS monitoring systems to give parliaments more scope for making a substantive input into dialogues on the budget.

The low capacity of parliaments in many countries is one reason parliaments are not involved in PRS monitoring systems, particularly in sub-Saharan Africa (GTZ 2004a). Without a developed committee system, analytical capacity, or sufficient institutional resources, it is difficult for parliaments to engage effectively with the executive on policy issues. Parliamentary capacity is also limited because of a lack of understanding of PRS monitoring systems and the opportunities these systems present for parliamentary engagement.

There are several general ways to increase the capacity and ability of parliaments to engage in and effectively use PRS monitoring information.

- Groups within parliament that have a special need for PRS monitoring information should be identified. These groups are in a good position to use and publicize the use of PRS monitoring information because they are able to access more financial and staffing resources than are individual members.
- To ensure that PRS monitoring information is understood by parliament members, the system analysis, conclusions, and recommendations must be presented in comprehensible terms and laid out clearly. It is also important to strengthen the capacity of members of parliament in understanding data, how the information can be used to inform decisions and ensure accountability, and how it can be conveyed to the media and the public.
- Official venues at which PRS monitoring information can be presented should be identified since any information presented at such venues becomes part of the public record. Through this process, one may disseminate the information to the media and among the public, thereby increasing its reach and impact.
- Alliances should be developed between parliament and civil society groups. Civil society groups are a key mechanism through which parliament can disseminate PRS monitoring information to constituencies. These civil society groups may also be important sources of information and independent analysis for parliament. Civil society would in turn gain an additional entry point into the policy process.

4

Organizing Participation

Nongovernmental organizations (NGOs), interdisciplinary research groups, universities, unions, lobbying groups, and other civil society entities can play various roles in monitoring the implementation of a poverty reduction strategy (PRS). They may be suppliers of information and carry out certain monitoring activities. They may also be important users of the information and analysis, which allow them to participate in the policy debate. Civil society participation is therefore a design principle that should be incorporated in all aspects of a PRS monitoring system.

In many countries, the Poverty Reduction Strategy Paper has represented the first attempt at a participatory approach to development policy, and, for many observers, the widening of the political space that has resulted has been as important as the strategy itself. However, participation has a tendency to taper off once a PRS is adopted. Incorporating participatory elements into the monitoring system is a way of sustaining participation.

Among the countries under study, the nature and extent of civil society participation in PRS monitoring and the policy process more generally vary widely depending on the political dynamics. In the Latin American cases, civil society mobilized strongly around debt reduction campaigns during the 1990s and continues to be active in the scrutiny of expenditures related to the Heavily Indebted Poor Countries (HIPC) Initiative. Participation in these cases is focused closely on public accountability. Governments have come under pressure to formalize and even mandate the participation of civil society in the policy-making process, often through quite elaborate mechanisms, in order to sustain popular legitimacy. In

Uganda, there is a high level of civil society participation in the policy process. This has been attributed to the need of the single-party system to sustain its legitimacy in the face of pressures for democratization and has led to a relationship between civil society actors and the government that is considered too close by some (Brock, Cornwall, and Gaventa 2001). In other cases, such as Albania, the Kyrgyz Republic, Malawi, and Niger, where there is a limited tradition of civil society engagement in policy making, it may take considerable time for national NGOs to develop the skills and interest to participate actively in the PRS process.

The challenges of organizing participation are therefore very different in each case. A well-designed PRS monitoring system may, however, help provide civil society with the information it needs to take part in the policy process. The system may also place the relationship between civil society and government on a more constructive basis.

Among the countries under study, it is possible to distinguish different forms of civil society participation in PRS monitoring systems, as follows:

1. *Carrying out monitoring activities.* Civil society may have a comparative advantage in certain monitoring activities, including participatory poverty assessments, service-delivery satisfaction surveys, and citizen report cards. Civil society organizations (CSOs) have also made useful contributions in budget monitoring and analysis and in public expenditure tracking. International NGOs have been active in training and organizing their local counterparts to carry out these activities. It is important to make a distinction between monitoring activities commissioned as part of a PRS monitoring system (as in the case of the subcontract for the participatory poverty assessment that went to Oxfam in Uganda) and those carried out by CSOs on their own initiative, which are more common. Thus, a PRS monitoring system may not explicitly plan for civil society monitoring activities, but may nonetheless draw on the independent contributions of CSOs in the elaboration of annual progress reports and other monitoring outputs.

2. *Participation in PRS monitoring system institutional structures.* In most of the countries under study, civil society representatives are included as members of committees and working groups of the PRS monitoring systems. These representatives are thus given the opportunity to contribute to debates on priorities, indicators, and targets and help in the preparation of sectoral and thematic reports. The value of this form of participation depends on the effectiveness of the committee system.

Organizations with very different interests, agendas, and knowledge may not always coalesce into effective committees and working groups. Active secretariats that prepare meetings well and ensure timely flows of information are key to effective participation. If membership on a committee becomes onerous and does not deliver clear benefits, the interest of civil society in the work is likely to taper off.

3. *Analysis and policy advice.* In some of the countries, independent research institutes, located at universities or NGOs, have become sources of analysis and policy advice for governments. Given the shortage of in-house analytical capacity in many government departments, this may sometimes be a key role for civil society. It is an area in which diversity is recognized as a value. The Tanzanian PRS monitoring system recognizes the dangers involved in investing the full ownership and control of research and analysis within a single or lead agency model. Hence, a conscious choice has been made for a more pluralistic and dynamic engagement in research focused on poverty.

4. *Information flows.* Civil society may also have a comparative advantage in turning monitoring information into products that are suitable for domestic audiences (a role that began in many countries with the production of simplified Poverty Reduction Strategy Papers in local languages). In some cases, civil society is preparing media campaigns and raising public awareness about PRS implementation, including through the creation of local information centers.

5. *Action-oriented monitoring.* Local NGOs may prefer action-oriented monitoring, which can directly feed into concrete improvements, rather than analysis aimed at dealing with broader issues of prioritization and policy design. For example, some NGOs monitor the implementation of selected projects at the local level in order to identify obstacles, and then they attempt to resolve the obstacles through interventions. This is often seen as less confrontational than broad analysis and assessment of government programs, particularly in closed political environments.

Interactions between civil society and governments have become institutionalized most notably in the Latin American cases. For example, *Bolivia* passed a Law on National Dialogue mandating CSO participation in determining, monitoring, and evaluating national poverty reduction policies and programs. The law requires large national conferences to be held every three years. A technical secretariat for national dialogue organized the participatory process. An umbrella group of 53 NGOs created the "social control mechanism," which operates at various levels, is represented on government agencies, and scrutinizes the use of HIPC funds.

Honduras has established a system of social audits, which are community-based accountability mechanisms for development programs. Local communities appoint a commission to monitor the use of HIPC funds by local authorities, and the results are posted in local schools and community centers.

Nicaragua has created a National Council for Social and Economic Planning, which is a communications channel between civil society and the government on development issues. It is mainly a user of PRS monitoring information, but also participates in the dissemination of PRS information and analysis. With donor support, it produced an independent, civil society critique of Nicaragua's first annual progress report.

NGOs do not always wish to play an institutionalized role in poverty monitoring for fear that they will be co-opted and become controlled by government, particularly if they accept government financing for their activities. Many prefer to retain an independent voice, collecting their own information and preparing their own analysis.

A related problem concerns representation and legitimacy. Whenever civil society is invited to participate in public agencies and processes, this raises questions as to how the civil society representatives are selected and whose interests they represent. If the representatives are chosen by government (as in Mauritania), this may undermine their legitimacy. If CSOs and their representatives are selected on the basis of capacity, visibility, or ability to lobby, they may not truly represent the overall population, given that minorities and the poor typically have less voice and capacity to organize. In Honduras, representatives are appointed by a national CSO council, which can improve the legitimacy of the CSOs, assuming the council itself provides space for representative CSOs. There may be tactical advantages if CSOs form networks to pursue shared advocacy strategies, as is the case in Malawi. However, some of the Latin American country studies raise the question of whether it is appropriate to seek a unified voice in civil society or, in contrast, whether CSO networks should be designed to accommodate greater diversity.

5

Conclusions of the Analysis

I t is possible to imagine an idealized, evidence-based policy cycle in which development programs are constantly monitored to assess their impact on poverty, policy makers always make rational decisions after due consideration of sound technical advice, and policies are implemented faithfully through the budget and service-delivery processes. However, this is far from the reality in countries involved in implementing a poverty reduction strategy (PRS). Indeed, there is little evidence that developed countries operate in such a fashion either. In every country, policy emerges as the outcome of multiple forces that are difficult to describe, let alone control. Evidence-based policy making and institutional learning are key objectives of the PRS initiative, but they are notoriously difficult to institutionalize.

However, for all the complexity of political systems, there are always points in time when technical advice is sought and given, when governments and public agencies are held to account for their performance, and when citizens and interest groups have a chance to influence policy through advocacy and debate. At these points in time, information on poverty and the performance of development programs that has been gathered, analyzed, and disseminated through a PRS monitoring system can play an important role. A PRS monitoring system should be designed to link into these various windows and entry points in the policy process.

It may be useful to think of the PRS monitoring system as involving two levels of activities. One is an inner circle of activities that take place largely within the government administration and that encompasses the selection of indicators and monitoring priorities, the coordination of monitoring activities, analysis, evaluation, and the dissemination of outputs. The other is an outer circle of activities that revolve around the connections between the PRS monitoring system and government processes and external stakeholders.

For planning purposes, it is useful to think of the inner circle of activities as a unified monitoring system. However, at the outset, many of the actors involved will not perceive the inner circle in this way. They are likely to resist the rationalization and coordination required to operate the system. In the fragmented public sphere that characterizes many PRS countries, it is rarely feasible to establish a new and complex system purely by decree, and attempts to do so have failed to increase cooperation and compliance.

The second circle of activities may be thought of as an open-textured network rather than as a system. This network links the PRS monitoring system to other systems throughout government and democratic institutions. To be effective, a PRS monitoring system must ensure that its outputs have been adapted to the needs of and are accessible to as many actors as possible both within and outside government.

Because the buy-in from stakeholders is critical, the process of the development of a PRS monitoring system may be as important as the institutional design. Effective systems are not static "ideal" structures, but rather they need to encourage and evolve with broader processes of change. The design process and the resulting system are likely to be very different in each country. Nonetheless, the following elements have been identified as important in the country studies:

- a process design that brings stakeholders together to discuss joint objectives and common problems and enables the design of the system to emerge as an organic solution to practical challenges
- a process design that builds on existing systems and activities to prevent duplication and competition with other systems, particularly the statistical system
- flexibility in the institutional design to allow the emerging system to evolve as changes occur in the political and institutional context and in the capacity of the various actors
- effective advocacy throughout the government administration carried out by system champions and supported by senior political leaders to emphasize the need for PRS monitoring
- a system built with the central objective of providing timely, relevant information to stakeholders at the various entry points of decision-making processes, including the parliamentary process

- coordination mechanisms that minimize the burden on participants and develop incentives for participation and compliance
- clear roles, responsibilities, and expectations, including ensuring that monitoring responsibilities are written into budgets, organizational charts, and job descriptions
- appropriate support by a secretariat for working groups and committees and well-targeted strategies for building monitoring and analytical capacity through the government administration
- effective information flows among actors, including a solid dissemination strategy that reflects an appreciation of the needs and abilities of various users
- opportunities for participation by civil society and donors to ensure that their needs will be met by the PRS monitoring system—including through the consideration of their inputs—and to develop their confidence in the system, leading, in turn, to their greater use of the outputs of the PRS monitoring system
- commitments by donors to maximize the incentives for coordination by aligning their reporting requirements to the PRS monitoring system and to support the PRS monitoring system as a whole rather than simply supporting discrete system activities in an uncoordinated fashion.

Two

Diagnostic and Guidance Tools for the Practitioner

Part II provides two tools for practitioners. Chapter 1 is a diagnostic tool that provides pointers for designing or reviewing a poverty reduction strategy monitoring system. This checklist covers the issues that should be considered in the design and implementation of a system for monitoring the execution of a poverty reduction strategy. It will help practitioners identify the opportunities, limitations, and options for building and strengthening a realistic poverty reduction strategy monitoring system. Chapter 2 offers principles and guidance for policy makers and their advisers who are engaged in the design and implementation of a poverty reduction strategy monitoring system. These have been derived from the analysis and synthesis presented in Part I.

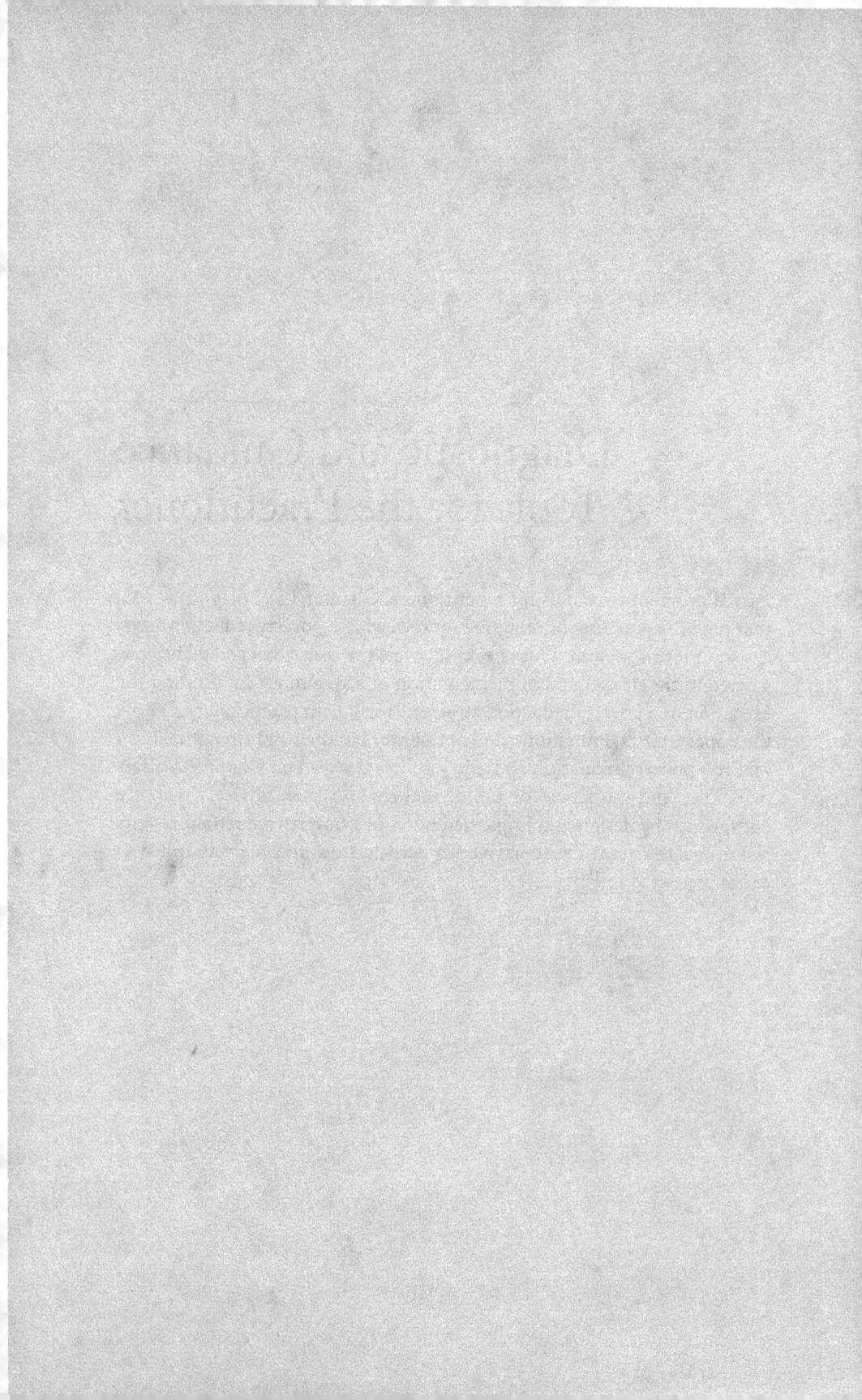

Diagnostic Tool: The Institutional Dimension of PRS Monitoring Systems

The following checklist is a diagnostic tool. It presents in schematic form the issues that should be considered in the design and implementation of a system for monitoring the execution of a poverty reduction strategy (PRS). The checklist is intended to generate country-specific information that maps out the current PRS monitoring system and the demands, activities, and capabilities of key stakeholders. By addressing the issues in the checklist, one should be able to identify the opportunities, limitations, and options for building and strengthening a realistic PRS monitoring system.

The checklist is broken down into three components. These components are interrelated; some questions may therefore appear under more than one heading.

The first component—*the institutional context and design of the PRS monitoring system*—is geared toward understanding the key stakeholders and agencies involved in PRS monitoring, the way they interact with each other, and their interests and abilities with regard to participation in the PRS monitoring system.

The second component—*the ability of the PRS monitoring system to supply information*—focuses on the activities, capabilities, and resources of key actors and agencies on the supply side of the PRS monitoring system. The goal is to understand the capacity of the system to supply the data and analysis needed to monitor the PRS effectively.

The third and last component—*the demand for and use of PRS monitoring system information*—focuses on the assessment of the information needs of key stakeholders and on mapping the processes and systems through which the monitoring information is used. The aim is to understand the demand side, that is, the need, uses, and incentives for PRS monitoring outputs.

Institutional Context and Design of the PRS Monitoring System

What is the design of the existing PRS monitoring system? What is the institutional context surrounding the PRS monitoring system? For example, what is the context in terms of coordination, leadership, legislation? In what ways does the institutional context support the PRS monitoring system?

The design process for the PRS monitoring system

- Is there a single PRS monitoring strategy or master plan? What is its status? Is it being implemented?
- Did the design process include a diagnosis of existing monitoring arrangements? Were monitoring systems already in place that could be used for the monitoring and analysis of progress in terms of PRS inputs, outputs, and outcomes? Were these systems incorporated into the PRS monitoring system?
- Did the design process include a stakeholder analysis? Were existing and potential stakeholders of the PRS monitoring system process identified?
- Did the design process include a needs assessment? Were the various stakeholders, including institutions, consulted about their needs? How was this concern incorporated into the system?
- Did the design process include a data diagnostic? Were the various data needs for the PRS monitoring system mapped out? What data sources existed? Were these incorporated into the system? How was this done?
- Was the design process participatory? Were stakeholders invited to participate in the process of designing the system? In what ways did they help design the system?

Institutional leadership

- Does the government have a political commitment to the PRS monitoring system? Has there been explicit support at a high political level? Are there champions actively making the case for a common monitoring system across the administration?

- Which agency leads on the design, coordination, and implementation of the PRS monitoring system (for example, the ministry of finance, the ministry of planning, the office of the prime minister, president, or vice-president)?
- Is the choice of locus of leadership conducive to providing actors with incentives to participate in the PRS monitoring system (that is, close to the budget and planning processes)? Does it effectively play its role?

Coordination

Coordination mechanisms

- Which mechanisms, such as committees or working groups, have been established to facilitate coordination among agencies and stakeholders?
- Is their composition stable?
- Are various stakeholders represented at an appropriate level to reflect and ensure their commitment?
- Is there a functioning secretariat of the PRS monitoring system?
- Are the meetings organized in a way that supports coordination?
- Are the information flows adequate to support coordination?
- Is the burden on participants excessive?

Oversight

- Is there a high-level body able to provide oversight and encourage compliance within government administration?
- How active is this body?

Liaison with local government

- Where this might be relevant, are regional and local governments represented within the coordination mechanism of the PRS monitoring system?
- Are local governments participating actively in the system? Do incentives support or hamper effective coordination?
- Is the institutional design of the system too elaborate for the capacities of local governments?

Liaison with line ministries

- How do liaisons with line ministries and other agencies function in the PRS monitoring system? How does the system relate to the monitoring arrangements of line ministries?

- Do line ministries take the liaison function seriously? Do they participate actively in the monitoring system? Which incentives support or hamper effective coordination?
- Is the requirement to monitor inscribed in the budgets of line ministries? Within the organizational structures of line ministries? In the job descriptions issued by the ministries?
- Is the institutional design of the monitoring system too elaborate with respect to the capacities of line ministries?

Liaison with civil society

- Is civil society participating in the working groups and committees of the PRS monitoring system?
- Are these civil society groups participating actively in the system? Which incentives support or hamper effective coordination?
- Is civil society represented in an appropriate manner? Who selects the civil society representatives?
- Have civil society organizations been adequately consulted about the roles they may wish to play? Are they able to fulfill these roles?

Liaison with development partners

- Are development partners providing incentives and other encouragement to government agencies to use PRS monitoring information?
- Are development partners using the PRS monitoring system?
- Are development partners supporting or crowding out national accountability mechanisms?
- To what extent is the demand for monitoring data from development partners coordinated? To what extent is the demand from development partners uncoordinated? What is the resulting impact on the functioning of the PRS monitoring system and the related actors? Do the differing monitoring requirements of development partners contribute to a sense of territoriality among government agencies and thereby discourage coordination?

Legislation and regulation

- Are the roles and responsibilities of various actors clearly set out? Is this supported by a legal framework? What is the nature of this legal framework? Has the framework been implemented?
- Is the lead agency within the PRS monitoring system explicitly charged with the compilation and dissemination of the outputs of the system?

- Is there legislation regulating the access to and dissemination of information and data in the country? Does it provide incentives to disseminate information widely or does it restrict information flows? Are the data producers effectively required to provide their information to other users within and outside government?
- Have quality standards been set for data?

Outputs and links to policy-making processes

- Are the outputs of the PRS monitoring system designed within a perspective on how they are to be used in policy making? Have the relevant policy-making processes been mapped out? Have the entry points for system outputs been identified? Have system activities been defined accordingly?
- Do mechanisms exist for consulting users within or outside government on the relevance of the outputs, emerging needs, and priorities that the PRS monitoring system should address? Do these consultations influence the functioning of the system? How?
- What are the institutional links between the PRS monitoring system and policy-making processes? Are outputs produced in a timely fashion to affect particular events, including budget preparations, parliamentary hearings, planning sessions, budget approvals, reporting, and so on? Are these links effective? Are there other channels through which the information produced by the system may influence policy?
- Is there evidence that information produced by the PRS monitoring system has been used by the government during various decision-making cycles such as for budgets, sectoral plans, investment planning, and so on? Is monitoring information circulating beyond government and stimulating public debate on policy choices?

National statistics

- Is there a functioning national statistical system where various data producers may coordinate their activities, common standards and principles are issued, and so on? Is there a national statistics institution? Is there a national statistical master plan?
- How well are the PRS monitoring system and the national statistical system integrated? Are there overlaps between the two systems? Poten-

tial rivalries and conflicts? Is the PRS monitoring system consistent with other plans and processes for the development of the statistical system?

- What roles does the national statistics institution play in the PRS monitoring system? A standard-setting, technical-assistance, or capacity-building role? Does the national statistics institution have the resources to fulfill its roles?

Ability of the PRS Monitoring System to Supply Information

Is the PRS monitoring system able to supply the data and analysis needed by users? Is the framework able to provide adequate resources for the monitoring processes?

Capacity for data production

Are data relevant to the elaboration and monitoring of the PRS generally available? Are data deficient in particular areas? Where are the gaps?

On each type of data, including data that are missing or are low in quality, the sets of questions listed below may be used to characterize the agency that produces or should be producing the data. These agencies will typically include the national statistics institution, the ministry of finance, the ministry of planning, the central bank, line ministries, local governments, local agencies, development partners, and civil society. (For a more thorough analysis of the quality of data in a particular country, go to the sources described at the end of this diagnostic tool.)

Definition

- How are the data collection and computation activities of the agency determined?
- Are users and other experts and specialists consulted on issues, gaps, emerging needs, and priorities?
- Do the outcomes of these consultations influence the process of data collection and compilation and the work program?

Sources

- What are the main sources of the data? Administrative records? Budgets? Population censuses? Household surveys? Others?
- Who is responsible for collecting and compiling the data?

Relevance

- What is the frequency or periodicity of data collection on particular issues (monthly, quarterly, annually)?
- What is the length of time between the reference period and the distribution and use of the data? Is this lag too long, thereby limiting the uses of the data for decision making?
- What level of disaggregation is available (geographic, gender, socioeconomic status)?

Standards

- Do processes and procedures in data compilation adhere to professional and ethical standards?
- Is an agency, such as the national statistics institution, responsible for enforcing the standards? Does it effectively play this role?
- Is the data consistent internally and with other data sets? Are there processes in place to check the accuracy and reliability of the data?
- When discrepancies are found, are they investigated?

Coordination

- Are the data collection activities of the agency, its technical platform, its standards, and its definitions coordinated with the other activities of the PRS monitoring system? In particular, how is the PRS monitoring system linked to the monitoring units and other arrangements in line ministries? In local level agencies?
- Are there issues of incompatibility (differing definitions, systems, geographic coverage, and so on)?

Manpower

- Does the agency have a dedicated monitoring unit?
- What is the capacity of the agency or the agency's monitoring unit in terms of the number and qualifications of the staff? In terms of staff turnover?
- Are monitoring burdens excessive for the capacity of the agency or monitoring unit?

Resources

- What resources, including physical infrastructure, are available for the collection and compilation of monitoring data?
- To what extent is data gathering financed by external development partners? How sustainable and predictable are these funds?

Dissemination

- Are the data understandable and clearly presented?
- Are the processes and procedures for data compilation transparent?
- Are the data published or otherwise available to the public? In what forms are they available? How are they disseminated?

For public expenditure data

- Are systems in place to track poverty-related expenditures?
- How is the PRS monitoring system linked to the development of budgetary and public expenditure management systems?
- If accurate expenditure data are unavailable, are other techniques being used to monitor expenditure (such as public expenditure tracking surveys and public expenditure reviews)?

For regional government data

- What are the roles of central and subnational governments and agencies in monitoring decentralized services? What sorts of data are collected by each actor?
- How are the data aggregated and analyzed? Who performs these functions?
- Are there multiple systems for monitoring and reporting? Are these systems compatible?
- Are there incentives to distort the data?

Capacity for analysis

- Which agencies and units inside and outside government are responsible for analyzing monitoring information (ministry of finance, ministry of planning, local governments, local agencies, line ministries, the central bank, the national statistics institute, civil society, development partners, universities, research centers, and so on)?
- What is their capacity? How are these agencies and units funded? Are the government agencies and units effectively mandated and resourced? How reliable are the funding arrangements of the agencies and units?
- How is the work program of these agencies and units determined? Is there a mechanism to define activities in light of the needs of the end users?
- What is the quality of this work? Are the analysts considered objective? Is the quality of the analysis limited by data constraints? What is the level of the demand for the work of the analysts?

- Are the analysts able to communicate their analyses effectively to end users in an appropriately adapted format?
- What types of analyses (regular or one-off) have been effectively produced? Are these sufficient to fulfill the needs of system users? What are the gaps in analysis?

Capacity for evaluation

- What are the requirements and procedures for evaluating PRS programs? Are the data and information gathered through monitoring activities used to support evaluations?
- To what extent are evaluations and reviews undertaken or commissioned? What types of evaluations and reviews are carried out? Expenditure tracking surveys? Participatory monitoring and evaluation? Rapid reviews? Impact evaluations? Performance audits? How frequently are the evaluations and reviews performed? What is the quality of the output?
- Who are the main actors who undertake or commission the evaluations and reviews? Are these evaluations and reviews undertaken on the actor's or agency's own initiative? To what extent do government ministries undertake or commission evaluations and reviews of their own performance?
- Are evaluations and reviews that are commissioned by development partners the main source of this type of work in the country? Are any of these evaluations and reviews conducted jointly with the government? If so, what is the level of government input?
- Are evaluations and reviews commissioned by the government from civil society groups such as universities and interdisciplinary research groups? Does civil society provide policy advice to the government during these evaluations and reviews?
- Are the findings of evaluations reported? To whom are they reported? Parliament? Development partners? How are the findings reported or published?
- Do any particular actors or agencies follow good practices?

Outputs and dissemination

The questions below are linked to the set of questions in the section on the design of the PRS monitoring system and the institutional context. Those questions focus on the definition of outputs and the links between the production of outputs and decision-making processes. The questions in this section focus only on the outputs themselves.

- Is there a catalog of outputs? Does it include all the data and analytical products? Is it widely available and updated regularly?
- Is there a calendar schedule of outputs? Is it advertised?
- Are outputs simultaneously released to all interested parties? Do all users have equal access?
- Are the sources, methods, and procedures related to the production of outputs published and available to all users?
- Are the products available in various formats for users who have different levels of familiarity with and literacy in the topics covered, different needs in terms of the depth of information, and so on?
- Is there a dissemination strategy? A communication strategy? Are selected actors in the monitoring system in charge of these activities?
- Do systems exist to maintain and disseminate information? Are they user-friendly?

Capacity building and funding

- Are specific budgetary resources allocated for PRS monitoring? For central activities (such as the secretariat)? For the various components (for example, line ministries, universities, and so on)? Are the resources sufficient, and is the funding predictable and sustainable?
- Is there financing for the sustained operation of data systems?
- Is there an overall capacity-building program or plan? Does it identify needs and gaps? Is it clearly prioritized? Is it costed and funded?
- Are development partners key funders? What are their funding trends? How sustainable and predictable is their funding? Are they supporting the overall system or only selected activities by certain actors? Is the government providing guidance to development partners on supporting capacity development?
- Are development partners funding technical assistance in the design and strengthening of the PRS monitoring system? Are skills being transferred to the country as a result of this assistance?
- Are substantive capacity-building efforts in monitoring, analysis, and evaluation currently under way in the country? Are they directly related

to the PRS monitoring system? Are they at the national, sectoral, or project levels?
- How sustainable are the capacity-building efforts and the ability to retain the capacity created over the medium to long term?
- Does the lead agency of the PRS monitoring system possess the required physical infrastructure to implement the system? If not, is there a plan and resources to acquire this infrastructure?
- What is the potential for in-country universities and other training organizations to provide training in data collection, monitoring, analysis, and evaluation to various actors in the PRS monitoring system?

Demand for and Use of PRS Monitoring System Information

Are the goals of the PRS monitoring system clearly defined? Are the needs of the stakeholders clearly understood? How are the outputs of the system used and incorporated within the government and beyond?

Poverty reduction strategy

- What types of data are needed for the PRS indicators?
- How would you assess the PRS in terms of its treatment of indicators?

 a. relevant to the subject and PRS objectives
 b. consistent with PRS policy priorities
 c. sufficient as a basis for assessing performance
 d. clearly defined
 e. accessible at a reasonable cost
 f. can be independently validated
 g. time bound

Budget and planning

- Are agencies required to present monitoring information in support of their budget and medium-term expenditure framework submissions? Are there any incentives to encourage this? Are there incentives likely to distort the quality of the data?
- Does the ministry of finance or other agencies engage line ministries in dialogue on their policy choices based on performance information?

- If yes, what information is required when submitting budget proposals?

  a. retrospective and prospective information on ministry spending
  b. information on ministry outputs
  c. information on sector outcomes and impacts
  d. results of formal evaluations and reviews

- Is a separate body responsible for national planning? If so, what types of information does it require for submissions on sectoral inputs to national plans?

  a. retrospective and prospective information on ministry spending
  b. information on ministry outputs
  c. information on sector outcomes and impacts
  d. results of formal evaluations and reviews

Local government and agencies

- Is there evidence of a demand for monitoring and evaluation data among local governments and agencies? What forms of data are being requested or would be relevant to local agencies and governments?
- Does the PRS monitoring system provide feedback and information flows to local governments and service providers? What is the dissemination strategy?
- Is such information used at the local level (such as for an incentive system to improve the performance of service providers)?
- Are the timing and form of the outputs provided to local governments and agencies adapted to the needs of these entities?

Line ministries

- Do sector ministries use information as a basis for their own planning and management? Is there any specific evidence of the use of data to inform poverty-related policy at the sectoral level?
- Do line ministries have the capacity to produce such information? Do line ministries have strategies to disseminate monitoring information and outputs within their sectors? Are data quality and relevance an issue?
- Do line ministries rely on the PRS monitoring system? On information produced by other agencies? Are the timing and form of outputs produced by the monitoring system appropriate to the needs of the ministries?
- Do line ministries communicate their needs to system management?

Parliament

- Does the PRS monitoring system embrace a strategy for disseminating monitoring outputs on poverty to parliament? Does the system provide for parliament as one of the users? Are the timing and form of outputs appropriate to the needs of parliament?
- How does parliament use the information provided by the monitoring system, the finance ministry, or sector ministries? Use it in formal hearings among parliamentary committees? In other ways?
- Does parliament communicate its data needs informally or formally through legislation requiring particular information?
- Does parliament have the capacity to use monitoring information effectively?

Development partners

- What are the monitoring and reporting requirements of development partners?
- Are development partners using the PRS monitoring system for their own monitoring and reporting needs? What other mechanisms are they using (other project and program monitoring systems, internal systems, and so on)?
- Is the demand for monitoring and evaluation among development partners the main source of demand in the country? If yes, is this because existing national capacity cannot serve development partners and domestic clients at the same time or because there is little domestic demand?
- What is the impact of the demand by development partners on agencies that produce data and information?
- Have development partners coordinated their monitoring requirements?

Civil society

- Are strong pressures exerted by civil society—the media, nongovernmental organizations, universities, interdisciplinary research entities, and so on—on government for information about the performance of government in reducing poverty?
- Does the PRS monitoring system have a strategy for disseminating monitoring outputs to the general public? Are the timing and form of

the outputs appropriate to the needs of the various audiences among the public?

- Is monitoring and evaluation information published widely in the media?
- Does civil society communicate its data needs formally to the PRS monitoring system?

Additional Resources on Data and Statistical Systems

- The *Data-Quality Assessment Framework* (DOAF) proposes a procedure for assessing the dimensions of statistics programs and data-producing agencies with a view to strengthening capacity. This encompasses the quality of the statistical products and the effectiveness of the agencies. It represents a framework for assessing high-quality economic and social data. It helps determine the extent to which country statistics offices follow good practices and international standards. It reports on observations of procedures and practices with respect to good practice. See http://www.imf.org/external/np/sta/dsbb/2001/supp.htm.
- The *General Data Dissemination System* (GDDS) is a macroeconomic and social framework for statistical development and capacity building in developing countries. It documents current practices and sets priorities for improvements in statistical methods and data dissemination. It presents information on how statistical systems function, the principal agencies responsible for compiling and distributing data, the methods used to calculate indicators, and the rules governing public access and data integrity. See http://dsbb.imf.org/Applications/web/gdds/gdds home/.
- The *Guide to Designing a National Strategy for the Development of Statistics* (NSDS) provides a country's national statistical system with a strategy for strengthening statistical capacity. The guide has been prepared primarily to assist developing countries in designing national statistics strategies, but is also helpful for development partners in supplying technical and other forms of assistance to countries in improving the quality and use of statistics to enhance management and achieve better development results. The guide is broad and sufficiently general to offer an introduction for a team designing a national strategy for the development of statistics and encountering some of the related concepts for the first time. The guide is underpinned by practical advice, case studies, and country experiences as disseminated in the knowledge base

on the national strategy for the development of statistics. See http://
www.paris21.org/pages/designing-nsds/NSDS-reference-paper/index.
asp?tab=doc.

- *Statistical Capacity-Building Indicators* (SCBI) provide an overview of a
country's statistical capacity and needs and ways to facilitate capacity
building. Statistical capacity-building indicators can help in identifying
strengths and weaknesses, in planning toward specific goals, and in
monitoring activities leading to these goals. They can also facilitate
communication and coordination among the organizations involved in
technical assistance by providing common measuring rods of a country's capacity needs in statistics. The indicators can help track development in statistics over time. This involves collecting information through
16 quantitative indicators that cover resources, inputs, and statistical
products and 18 qualitative indicators that focus on relevant aspects of
the institutional and organizational environment, core statistics processes, and statistics products. See http://www.paris21.org/documents/
1024.pdf.

Guidance on the Institutional Dimension of PRS Monitoring Systems

This chapter is intended to assist policy makers and their advisers with the design and development of a system for monitoring the implementation of a poverty reduction strategy (PRS). It focuses on the institutional rather than the technical dimensions of PRS monitoring, that is, how to organize a coherent system for monitoring across the various sectors covered by the PRS and how to encourage the use of the information derived from monitoring in the development of PRS programs. The chapter extracts practical guidance and lessons from the 12 country studies summarized in Part III.

Given the complex dynamics of the political and institutional environment that surrounds the policy process in any system of government, this subject does not lend itself to purely technical solutions or the straightforward application of international best practice. A PRS monitoring system needs to attract willing participation from a wide range of stakeholders, as well as generate a demand for system outputs among policy makers. Experience suggests that the practical obstacles are substantial and that the solutions will vary widely in different contexts. This chapter provides possible strategies to address these issues.

What Is a PRS Monitoring System?

A PRS monitoring system provides the information required to generate an overview of PRS implementation. A PRS monitoring system incorporates the periodic measurement and analysis of priority welfare indicators, as well as the monitoring of outputs on PRS implementation. It therefore usually includes the following functions, each with somewhat different institutional leads:

1. *Poverty monitoring* tracks the overall progress in poverty reduction against national targets and international measures such as the Millennium Development Goals. This is usually accomplished through censuses, surveys, and other research tools.
2. *PRS implementation monitoring*: The system should support the monitoring and evaluation of PRS programs by tracking the most important inputs, activities, outputs, and outcomes across different sectors and priority thematic areas. It depends on administrative data systems in a wide range of agencies.
3. *Expenditure tracking*: Although conceptually part of implementation monitoring, the tracking of budgeting and expenditure is institutionally distinct and is usually achieved under the leadership of a ministry of finance. Reliable and timely data on expenditure are indispensable to an effective PRS monitoring system, but depend on parallel progress in budget and public expenditure management reforms.

A PRS monitoring system should deliver timely and reliable data and analysis to feed into the PRS policy process. To accomplish this, it must include a range of functions that are specifically institutional in nature, including coordination among data producers to establish a common set of indicators and eliminate gaps and redundancies; the development of common standards, procedures, and platforms; a strengthening of monitoring capacity across the government administration; the organization of information flows among stakeholders inside and outside government; the compilation and analysis of data from various sources; data analysis and PRS program evaluation; the generation of annual progress reports and other outputs; the provision of advice and support to policy makers; the dissemination of outputs across government and to the public; and the organization of the participation of civil society.

Conceptually, these elements all form part of the PRS monitoring system. However, it is important to recall that, at the outset, most of the actors involved will not recognize their activities as part of a national system. Whether they will participate vigorously in making the PRS monitoring system operational depends largely on their interests and incentives. The rules, both formal and informal, that govern these incentives are therefore a key dimension of the PRS monitoring system. Examples of rules that influence monitoring incentives, particularly rules regarding the budget process, are discussed below.

The Supply Side: Designing and Implementing a PRS Monitoring System

A PRS monitoring system does not begin with a blank slate. Most countries already have a range of monitoring mechanisms and information systems in place. Typically, these have emerged as a result of discrete donor interventions at different times and operate in isolation from each other even in cases in which they involve the same actors. A lack of strategic oversight causes a range of problems, including duplication and redundancies in data collection, excessive administrative burdens, neglect of areas that have not been a focus of past donor programs, data incompatibility, and inadequate information flows.

Whatever the limitations of the existing mechanisms, it is rarely appropriate to bypass them. Experience shows that adding new monitoring arrangements, even where technically superior, is unlikely to be helpful unless steps are taken to eliminate redundancies and minimize the overall burden of monitoring. The existing mechanisms are therefore the primary building blocks of the PRS monitoring system, and the agencies that "own" them have to be persuaded of the benefits of participating in the new system.

The key supply-side challenges of developing a PRS monitoring system are therefore the rationalization of existing monitoring activities according to the priorities set out in the PRS and the definition of the working relationships among the various actors in the system, including allocating responsibilities, developing modalities for cooperation, and mapping and organizing information flows.

Experience suggests that there are often strong disincentives to effective rationalization and coordination. Agencies tend to defend their autonomy in the monitoring sphere because this autonomy is typically associated with resources. In the face of these disincentives to cooperation, the principal risk (borne out by a number of the country case studies in Part III) is that the PRS monitoring system will remain merely a creation on paper and will not change the bureaucratic reality.

Guidance Note

Managing a successful design process

Buy-in by stakeholders is a key condition for a successful PRS monitoring system. Achieving buy-in may depend as much on the design process as on the final design of the system.

So far, not much attention has been paid to design processes. Most countries have produced a PRS monitoring strategy or a master plan, often two or three years after the first Poverty Reduction Strategy Paper (PRSP) and usually with the help of external consultants. There has generally been a limited survey of existing monitoring mechanisms and some degree of consultation, but formal stakeholder analysis and participatory design processes have been rare. As a result, new monitoring systems have a distinct tendency to run out of steam within a short time for want of active support from stakeholders.

To attract greater buy-in, the design process might include a map of existing monitoring arrangements that identifies the main stakeholders and analyzes strengths and weaknesses; a clear statement of political commitment to effective PRS monitoring; champions who are able to advocate the value of a shared monitoring system across the government administration; and a structure for consultation and facilitation to assist stakeholders in articulating their needs and expectations.

There is no single solution to the problem of territoriality within the bureaucracy and its tendency to impede the establishment of a unified monitoring system. There are two important strategies emerging in practice. One is to review existing donor funding of monitoring mechanisms at the program or sectoral level and involve donors in identifying and minimizing any financial disincentives to the creation of a unified system. The other is to ensure that the design of the PRS monitoring system emerges out of a mutual commitment to successful PRS implementation. Some countries have found that a rigorous and participatory process for selecting indicators has the effect of encouraging different agencies to review their strategies and their institutional structures with the aim of becoming more results oriented. This leads these agencies to recognize the value of a more systematic approach to monitoring, particularly in relation to cross-sectoral and thematic issues.

In most cases, the initial monitoring plan is quite open ended and contains a broad allocation of responsibilities and a conceptual mapping of information flows. Detailed modalities for cooperation then need to be worked out in practice. The design therefore usually provides for the formation of interagency committees or working groups to elaborate additional details. The design of the PRS monitoring system may change substantially during this extended design phase, and it may be appropriate to delay codifying the system until the design has been finalized.

Most existing monitoring strategies or plans do not have any legal status. Some observers have called for greater use of regulatory frameworks to reinforce accountability and bolster compliance. Experience suggests that legal obligations alone are unlikely to make the system operate effectively in the absence of stakeholder buy-in, but may help to increase predictability once the system begins to function.

Issues in institutional design

Among the PRS monitoring systems developed to date, most contain the following features:

1. A high-level *steering committee* to provide political support and oversight and supply a formal link to the cabinet. It may set monitoring priorities and approve annual progress reports.
2. A *coordination unit* responsible for coordination throughout the system. The unit may act as a secretariat for interagency committees and working groups, compile data, and draft reports. It is usually made up of a small number of dedicated staff within the office of the president or prime minister or in the ministry of finance or planning. It is usually linked to a broader PRS implementation structure.
3. One or more *interagency committees or working groups*, sometimes with sectoral or thematic mandates, that facilitate interagency cooperation and dialogue. They may be responsible for defining indicator sets and monitoring priorities, preparing sectoral reports, and advising policy makers. They often include representatives of civil society and donors.
4. The *national statistics institute* is usually a key actor in the system. As well as being an important data producer, it may be responsible for compiling administrative data from line ministries, setting overall standards, developing information technology platforms, and providing technical assistance to other producers.
5. *Line ministries* are usually required to nominate a point of liaison with the PRS monitoring system. This may be an individual officer (such as a director of planning) or a dedicated monitoring and evaluation or

statistical unit. It is responsible for ensuring the production and delivery of sectoral data.

While the basic elements tend to be similar across countries, the performance of the system is strongly influenced by the power relations and diverse capacities among the various institutional actors. The following factors should be taken into consideration in the design.

Leadership: Experience suggests that the choice of the institutional leadership for the system is critical. The leadership function should be located close to the center of government or the budget process, depending on where effective authority over the PRS process lies. Care should be taken to avoid entangling the PRS monitoring system in existing institutional rivalries. In some countries, the allocation of system leadership to the ministries of finance has helped to link the PRS monitoring system to the budget, increasing the profile and authority of the systems. When leadership resides within the planning agency, on the other hand, the systems may benefit from closer links to the planning process. In practice, the choice of the institutional leadership is often influenced by the location of those individuals who champion the systems, although tying institutional choices too closely to a single champion may leave the system vulnerable to political changes. The leadership role needs to be taken seriously within the nominated institution and to benefit from dedicated staff and resources. Committees that meet only once or twice a year do not provide effective leadership.

Coordination: Organizing effective coordination among different agencies is one of the most difficult challenges in the creation of a PRS monitoring system. Some observers are skeptical that simply bringing different actors around a table is sufficient to overcome the disincentives to real coordination. Interagency committees often produce superficially plausible solutions, such as ambitious new training programs, without addressing the real problems. Effective secretariat support is key in ensuring that meetings are focused and substantive. The secretariat should be both conversant with PRS priorities and skilled at mediating among the stakeholders by helping them to find common ground. The secretariat is usually a small unit located at the central level within the presidency or ministry of finance or within a national PRSP committee. It needs strong and stable staffing to function effectively. When designing interagency committees and working groups, one should recognize that good committee work requires a substantial commitment of time from the participants. Care should be taken to avoid that the structure becomes too elaborate or burdensome. Donor alignment is another condition of effective coordination. If donors impose separate project-level monitoring and reporting requirements (and provide the resources to fund these), this creates strong disincentives to coordination. While the information needs of donors are not necessarily the same as those of governments, it should be possible to support both through the PRS monitoring system. Governments need to be proactive in encouraging donors to articulate their monitoring needs during the design of the system and to ensure that their systems and procedures are adapted to the PRS monitoring system.

Liaison with line ministries: This works best where the nominated liaison point is substantively engaged in monitoring and evaluation for sectoral policy making and management purposes. If the points of contact lack the authority to represent and make commitments on behalf of the line ministries or if they change regularly, this will weaken the system. In practice, a PRS monitoring system is dependent on the quality of sectoral information systems. The PRS monitoring system may need to incorporate strategies for encouraging monitoring and evaluation among line ministries, such as through rules requiring monitoring and evaluation functions to be incorporated in departmental budgets, work plans, and job descriptions. Where the monitoring capacity of line ministries is too weak to be reliable in producing the data needed by the system, a program of capacity strengthening should be designed.

Links to the national statistical system: Care should be taken to ensure complementarity between the PRS monitoring system and similar structures in or strategies for the statistical system. National statistics institutes are often given responsibility for setting quality and technical standards for administrative data producers and for providing technical support or capacity building. In practice, they have usually been slow in taking up this role. The problem may relate to funding modalities for national statistics institutes, which cause them to prioritize large surveys and statistical operations over participation in a PRS monitoring system. It may therefore be appropriate to discuss with donors the possibility of basket funding arrangements for national statistics institutes so as to avoid distorting the priorities of the institutes.

Involvement of local governments: PRS monitoring in an environment of decentralized service delivery poses complex problems, on which the experience to date provides relatively little guidance. The design of local monitoring arrangements necessarily depends on the structure of government and particularly on the degree of fiscal and policy autonomy given to local governments. A few countries have tried to encourage local governments to develop their own monitoring arrangements, which may support the objective of decentralization to bring the development policy process closer to the communities it affects. Other countries have recognized that the process of decentralization might exacerbate regional inequalities and foster the local capture of services or development funds; these have followed the opposite strategy of strengthening the central government monitoring of local authorities. The relevant mechanisms include retaining central controls over local budgeting and expenditure and using surveys to check on local government performance on a sample basis.

While the literature is quite pessimistic about the prospects for effective local monitoring, a number of strategies have been proposed, including the careful selection of indicators for monitoring at the local level in order to minimize the administrative burden; the development of quality control mechanisms linked to targeted technical support and capacity-building programs; the use of secondary monitoring methods (such as public service satisfaction surveys) to triangulate local administrative data and identify biases in reporting; the provision of feedback to local governments and service-delivery units about monitoring results at a level of disaggregation that is meaningful to them; and the stimulation of information flows between local governments and their communities.

The Demand Side: How Are PRS Monitoring Data Used?

Ideally, a PRS monitoring system supports a number of distinct objectives within the development process.

1. It supports government decision making on pro-poor policies and programs, including setting budget priorities and annual updates of the PRS.
2. It supports accounting for development expenditures.
3. It supports government accountability to the public for policy choices and their impact on poverty.
4. It promotes evidence-based dialogue between the government, civil society, and donors, thereby strengthening development partnerships.
5. It provides a means of institutionalizing direct civil society participation in the policy process beyond the phase of PRS formulation.
6. It feeds the monitoring, reporting, and accountability requirements of donors, particularly in connection with programmatic support.

To contribute to this ambitious set of goals, a PRS monitoring system needs to strengthen the demand side, in addition to the supply side, of the monitoring equation by promoting the use of monitoring information and analysis in policy making. Effective demand depends on many factors outside the scope of the PRS monitoring system and cannot easily be institutionalized. Politics is an untidy process, and evidence-based policy making—where policy choices are founded on a rational assessment of options—tends to be the exception in developed countries as much as in the developing world.

However, in any political system, there are points at which technical advice is sought and given and governments and public agencies are held to account for their performance. These represent entry points where monitoring information may be influential. They might include decisions on priorities in the budget, annual reviews of medium-term expenditure frameworks or public investment plans, periodic reviews and updating of the PRS, scrutiny of government policy by parliament and parliamentary committees, the setting of priorities for targeted programs or investment plans, the development of budget-support agreements and policy matrices with donors, and the development of multilateral and bilateral assistance strategies.

During the design of a PRS monitoring system, mapping these various entry points is useful. For some of these entry points (such as the budget process), a formal link could be created with the PRS monitoring system (for example, through rules governing budget submissions). The PRS monitoring system can support others indirectly by ensuring that monitoring information and analysis are readily available in the appropriate form and at the proper time. If policy capacity is strong and poverty reduction features high on the political agenda, the opportunities to formalize the use of monitoring information will be more numerous. Conversely, in more difficult political and institutional environments, the best strategy may be to propagate basic information in the public domain in order to strengthen popular demand for pro-poor policies.

Analysis and evaluation

If they are to be influential in the policy process, monitoring data must be analyzed and used to evaluate the effectiveness of policies and programs. If these practices are still in their infancy, a monitoring system may introduce them in distinct phases: the collection of quality data followed by capacity building for the analysis of the data and, finally, the institutionalization of the practice of using the data to evaluate specific policies and programs.

Analysis and evaluation have been a real deficit in PRS monitoring systems so far. In many cases, data collected through the PRS monitoring system are only edited into the annual progress report format. As a result, it is difficult for stakeholders to see any concrete benefits from the system.

Some countries have tried to institutionalize data analysis by establishing a central analytical unit located in the presidency, the ministry of finance or planning, or the national statistics institute. These analytical units have been most successful when they have remained small and close to government and have focused on analytical tasks exclusively. When the attempt has been made to expand the role of these units into either data collection or policy making, they have become competitive with other agencies and ceased to be effective. It is important to find funding modalities that help ensure that these units remain responsive to the needs of government and national stakeholders.

Joint analytical exercises by government and donors have also emerged as a useful tool for stimulating the capacity for and interest in analysis. Joint public expenditure reviews are particularly useful if financial information systems are weak, and such reviews are being conducted in a number of countries on an annual basis. If poverty and social impact analysis is introduced as a requirement for new programs, this encourages public service managers to consider analysis as a means of achieving their own objectives rather than as an external requirement. Similar dynamics can be seen within sectorwide approaches. Overall, donors should be taking every opportunity to encourage governments to defend their policy choices on the basis of evidence and analysis.

Outputs and dissemination

Monitoring information and analysis must be compiled into outputs and distributed as widely as possible both within and outside government. A good monitoring system will produce a range of outputs appropriate for different audiences and purposes and include a strategy to disseminate the outputs actively to intended users.

This is not currently being done effectively. Most PRS monitoring systems are focused mainly, if not exclusively, on the production of annual progress reports. These reports are supposed to represent an opportunity to review and update the PRS. In practice, however, they are often viewed as an external reporting requirement and not part of the national policy cycle. Annual progress reports are typically not distributed widely and are poorly suited to domestic audiences. In designing a PRS monitoring system, one should seek to ensure that annual progress reports serve the government's own needs and, if appropriate, introduce additional outputs to meet specific needs or fulfill specific steps in the policy cycle.

Making information available to civil society organizations (CSOs) and the media is also a key objective if the PRS monitoring system is to support public accountability. This has also been widely neglected. There are a few cases in which annual progress reports have been circulated in draft form for public comment or monitoring data and reports are published on official Web sites. However, there are very few examples of the production of monitoring reports in a style or format aimed specifically at the public. Presenting monitoring data in a form meaningful to domestic audiences is a new skill for governments, and it might be useful to involve civil society partners in such efforts.

Monitoring outputs that are designed for the general public need to focus on issues of relevance to local communities and enable these communities to assess the performance of their own local authorities. Disaggregated data that permit ready comparison among various jurisdictions can be a powerful tool. While citizens are unlikely to be motivated by small changes in national poverty statistics, they may care deeply whether their municipality is performing more effectively or less effectively than others.

Linking PRS monitoring to the budget

Creating a link between the PRS monitoring system and the budget process is a powerful way of generating demand for monitoring. When agencies bid for public resources, this is an important opportunity to require them to justify their policies and plans based on evidence provided by monitoring data. However, this link has proved difficult to establish.

Many PRS countries are still at an early stage in budget and public expenditure management reforms and are not yet able to provide accurate and timely information on expenditure or relate expenditure to particular programs. Because of the slow and evolutionary nature of public expenditure management reforms, it may be many years before these countries are in a position to introduce performance-based budgeting as this is understood in developed countries. Nonetheless, it may be possible to introduce a more general requirement that spending agencies justify their resource bids on the basis of PRS priorities and the evidence of past performance. This is most effective in countries with a successful medium-term expenditure framework, since PRS monitoring system outputs can be fed into annual updates. Opportunities may also arise during the preparation of annual public investment plans or annual budgets.

In a few countries (Tanzania and Uganda, for example), rules on budget submissions have provided a noticeable, if uneven, impetus to more results-oriented programming and planning. This approach has worked best where a structured dialogue has been instituted in connection with budget submissions. This requires a central body, whether within the ministry of finance or close to the cabinet, with the capacity and authority to challenge line ministries on the substance of their plans. Without this challenge function, compliance may be purely token.

In linking the PRS monitoring system to the budget, care needs to be taken to avoid perverse effects. Monitoring data are not always sufficiently accurate or suitable for setting annual expenditure priorities, and the attribution of the results to spending can be difficult when multiple interventions jointly influence results and outcomes and when some of these interventions are implemented outside the budget. If budget releases are unreliable, it is also difficult to hold public sector managers accountable for their performance. Finally, sanctions may be difficult to enforce since they might lead to cuts in funding for some programs simply because the responsible institution has performed poorly at monitoring, irrespective of the actual performance, impact, and importance of the program.

For all these reasons, the creation of a link between performance data and resource allocation that is too strict is unlikely to be feasible until budget and public expenditure management reforms are well advanced. However, this does not preclude building into the budget a more general challenge function based on performance monitoring.

The role of parliament

Parliaments should be a key user of monitoring information. In practice, however, they have not been involved very heavily in PRS monitoring systems. This is partly explained by the low capacity of parliaments in many PRS countries. Without a strong committee system supported by analytical and research staff, these parliaments are generally unable to engage effectively with the executive on policy issues. This appears to be a missed opportunity for increasing the impact of PRS monitoring and for building parliamentary capacity. Public committee hearings on PRS implementation, based on annual progress reports or other outputs, would help to raise the profile of a PRS monitoring system. This process could be enhanced if a role for parliamentary committees is institutionalized within the PRS monitoring system or if financial and technical support is provided to parliaments in this area. To assist in interpreting data, parliamentarians may draw on expertise within civil society, thereby helping to forge useful alliances and broaden the inputs into the policy process.

Organizing Civil Society Participation

CSOs can play various roles in PRS monitoring systems both as producers and users of monitoring information. In many countries, the PRS has represented the first attempt at a participatory approach to policy making, and, according to many observers, the political space that has resulted has generated important benefits. A PRS monitoring system may therefore provide an opportunity to sustain participation over a longer period.

The extent and nature of civil society participation in a PRS monitoring system vary considerably. Where civil society is already highly mobilized around development issues (for example, in Latin America following the debt-relief campaigns of the past two decades), popular participation in development policy tends to be well institutionalized and sometimes legally mandated. Where there is little tradition of civil society involvement in the policy process, building up interest and capacity in such involvement must be a longer-term goal.

Among the countries that are the subject of the studies summarized in Part III, diverse forms of civil society participation are evident.

1. *Carrying out monitoring functions*: CSOs have a comparative advantage in certain types of monitoring, particularly qualitative techniques such as participatory poverty assessments, service-delivery satisfaction surveys, and citizen report cards. They can also make a useful contribution to budget analysis and public expenditure tracking. CSOs may be commissioned to carry out monitoring as part of a PRS monitoring system or they may prefer to undertake their own activities outside the system.

2. *Participation in the institutional structures of a PRS monitoring system*: Most PRS monitoring systems include representatives of civil society on

committees and working groups, thereby giving civil society an opportunity to contribute to debates on the priorities and results of monitoring. Note, however, that committees made up of organizations with very different interests, agendas, and knowledge do not always work together effectively. Active secretariats and good information flows are key. If participation becomes too onerous and does not appear to offer civil society a real input into the policy process, the interest of civil society participants is likely to taper off.

3. *Analysis and policy advice*: Some systems draw on independent research institutes, universities, or nongovernmental organizations to contribute analysis and policy advice. Flexible funding that allows research and advocacy organizations to retain their independence is therefore a useful contribution to PRS monitoring systems.

4. *Information flows*: Some CSOs have a comparative advantage in turning monitoring information into products suitable for a range of domestic audiences. In some countries, CSOs have prepared media and public education campaigns on PRSP implementation.

5. *Action-oriented monitoring*: In countries with low literacy levels, CSOs may prefer to couple monitoring with direct interventions. For example, CSOs may track the implementation of PRS programs at the local level in order to intervene with targeted capacity building or mediation efforts whenever the need arises. In difficult political environments, this may be less confrontational than producing reports critical of a government.

It is important to consult civil society actors on the role they wish to play in the PRS monitoring system. In some countries, CSOs prefer to remain outside the system for fear of co-optation and control by the government, particularly if participation requires accepting government funding. There may be good arguments in favor of the retention by civil society of a fully independent voice, and donor funding modalities should respect this choice.

Problems of representation and legitimacy—who really speaks for the poor?—are likely to arise if particular organizations or individuals are chosen to represent civil society. In some countries, civil society networks are well organized and thus facilitate representation. However, it may not always be appropriate to attempt to represent a single civil society voice within the monitoring arena. The design of the participatory process may need to accommodate a diversity of voices. This issue should be discussed explicitly with civil society during the design phase.

Concluding Observations

It may be useful to think of a PRS monitoring system as two concentric circles: an inner circle of activities that take place largely inside the public administration and that ensure the production of data on a set of priority PRS indicators and an outer circle of connections between the monitoring system and key points in the policy-making cycle and the democratic process.

Within the first circle, the actors must be persuaded to participate actively in the PRS monitoring system if this is to function effectively. In achieving this buy-in, the process of design and implementation may be as important as the final institutional structure. Data producers need to be convinced that the monitoring system is a solution to common problems and not a mere bureaucratic requirement. Once this is achieved, the system can be formalized and placed within a regulatory framework.

The second circle of activities may be thought of as an open network that connects data producers to other systems in the government and to the public. It works by creating links and improving information flows rather than through hierarchies or predetermined roles. The more links that are created, the more chance of stimulating evidence-based policy. The primary audience for monitoring information will be the elected officials and public sector managers who are directly responsible for the development and management of PRS programs. The PRS monitoring system must first of all meet the needs of these individuals for timely, accurate, and useful information and analysis. However, to reinforce demand, these officials should also be subject to a challenge function, that is, external actors should hold them accountable for their policy choices and their performance. The types of actors that are able to play this challenge function will vary in each country, but may include the cabinet, the ministry of finance, parliamentary committees, opposition parties, the media, CSOs, and donors. While these processes are much broader than the PRS monitoring system, the system can help support them by disseminating information and analysis on poverty and PRS implementation widely in the public sphere.

The experience of the 12 countries under study teaches us that, in elaborating and implementing a PRS monitoring system, one should build on existing elements; recognize that change will be gradual; aim at starting a process of change rather than at designing a "perfect" system; focus on building flexible arrangements that can be adapted to change; define relationships, incentives, and activities clearly; identify entry points in decision-making processes, particularly in the budget process; and adapt the various outputs to the needs of the intended users.

Three

Country Studies

Institutional Arrangements for PRS Monitoring Systems

Part III summarizes the situation in 12 countries in Africa (Malawi, Mali, Mauritania, Niger, Tanzania, and Uganda), Latin America and the Caribbean (Bolivia, Guyana, Honduras, and Nicaragua), and Europe and Central Asia (Albania and the Kyrgyz Republic). It is based on studies undertaken in the second half of 2004. Most of these studies have been partially updated to reflect conditions in the summer or fall of 2005.

Although substantial changes may have occurred in some countries that are not reflected in this chapter, the historical situation is instructive on some of the problems faced early on in the process of designing systems for monitoring the implementation of poverty reduction strategies (PRS). Readers are encouraged to seek additional information if they wish to focus on particular countries.

These studies have been drawn on extensively in identifying the more general lessons presented in the main body of this volume. The authors believe that they may also be used to gather other useful information and insights and have therefore elected to include summaries of the studies in this volume.

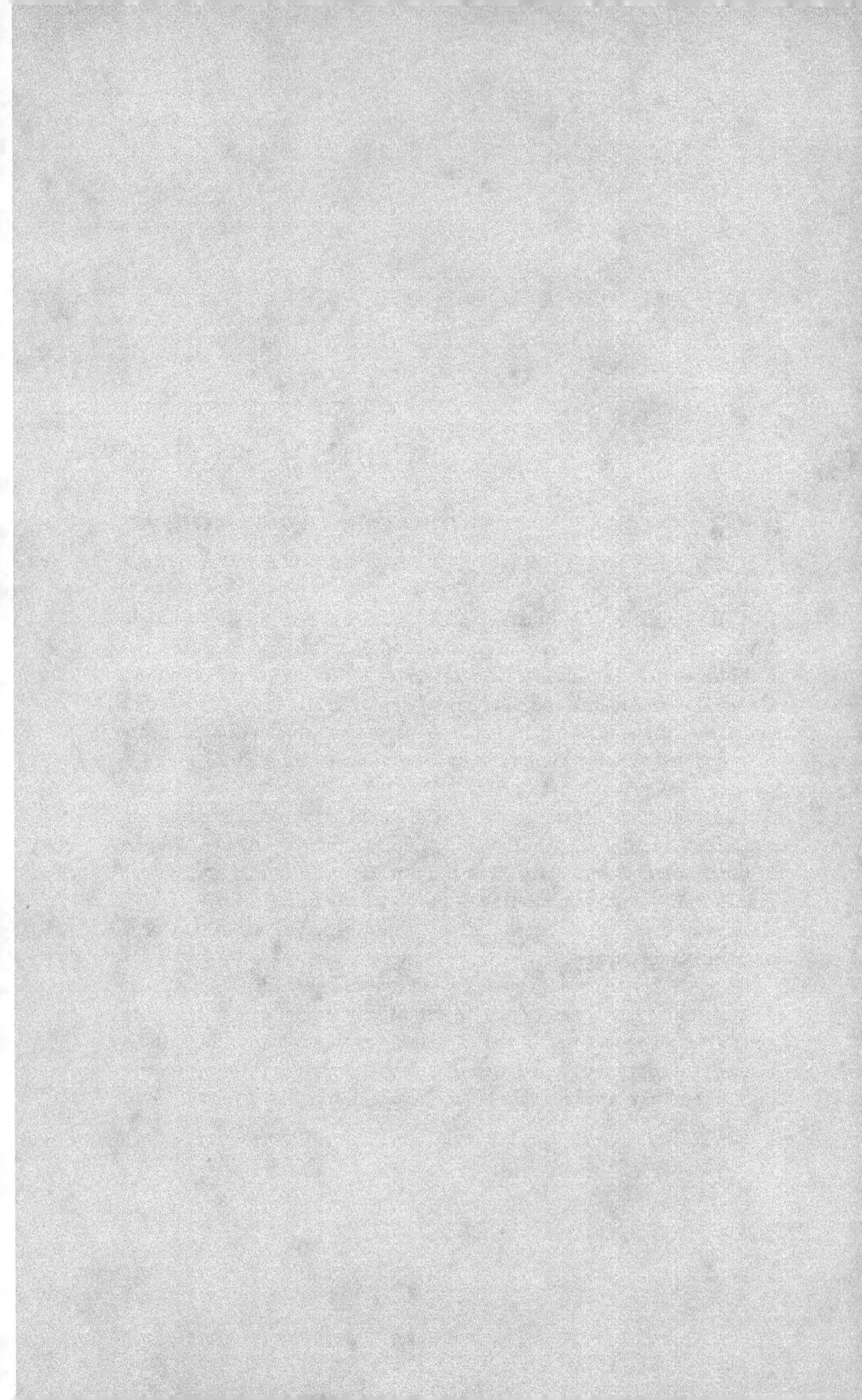

1

Albania

ACRONYMS AND ABBREVIATIONS

DPDC	Department for Policy Development and Coordination (Council of Ministers)
GNAP	Government National Action Plan
IMWG	interministerial working group
INSTAT	National Institute of Statistics
LSMS	Living Standards Measurement Survey
MTBF	medium-term budget framework
NSSED	national strategy for socioeconomic development
SAp	Stabilization and Association process (European Union)
TSWG	technical sector working group

This chapter is based on a background country report by Ivy Papps and Shkelzen Marku (2004) and on extensive inputs by Alia Moubayed and Andrew Dabalen. The study was undertaken in the second half of 2004 and has been partially updated to reflect conditions in the summer of 2005. Substantial changes may have occurred that are not reflected in this chapter, and readers are encouraged to seek additional information if they wish to focus on the system of this particular country.

History and Context

The national strategy for socioeconomic development (NSSED) is the main strategy document of the government of Albania. It emerged from a process initiated in June 2000, when the interim Poverty Reduction Strategy Paper was presented to the Board of Executive Directors of the World Bank and the Board of the International Monetary Fund. In November 2000, the full poverty reduction strategy (PRS) process was launched with the creation of sectoral working groups (led by line ministries) and civil society advisory groups. A technical secretariat was established to support the minister of finance in coordinating the PRS process. The final version of the strategy, the NSSED, was launched in November 2001. In June 2002, the NSSED was transmitted to the boards of the World Bank and the International Monetary Fund.

The incorporation of Albania's PRS in the NSSED aims to make the PRS part of the overall development agenda and to increase ownership of the PRS. In practice, however, there are three separate monitoring frameworks, and the NSSED has not fully become the single national strategic framework.

First, there is considerable overlap with the Government National Action Plan (GNAP), which is used to evaluate ministry performance. The government operates on the basis of a three-year GNAP. Ideally, the GNAP should incorporate all priority actions in the NSSED. In fact, there is considerable overlap and incomplete consistency, and the monitoring arrangements differ.

Albania has also signed on to the Stabilization and Association process (SAp), which sets out the principles according to which the western Balkan countries may eventually join the European Union. The SAp offers strong incentives to Albania to undertake policy reform, but places demands on the country's resources that compete with the goal of poverty reduction. Although there are relatively fewer areas of overlap between the NSSED and the SAp, these are still substantial and would justify coordinated monitoring mechanisms that currently do not exist.

Despite these caveats, the NSSED has gained a national character, not least because of the participatory approach it embodies. Still, though sectoral strategies have been aligning with the NSSED, there are no standards for assessing how functional this alignment is. The fact that sectoral and cross-cutting strategies are still being submitted without a costed implementation plan suggests that policy prioritization is limited. This could be an obstacle in achieving PRS objectives and does not make the case for an efficient monitoring system sufficiently pressing.

Description of the PRS Monitoring System

Origins of the system

In early 2002, the government reviewed the institutional location, status, and functions of the technical secretariat for growth and the PRS in the Ministry of Finance, and the secretariat was upgraded to a directorate in the ministry. In September 2002, the institutional structures for NSSED monitoring were set up. The Council of Ministers established the NSSED steering committee and mandated the creation of an interministerial working group (IMWG), as well as technical sector working groups (TSWGs) and monitoring and evaluation (M&E) units in line ministries. This structure was developed partly to emphasize that the NSSED is the key national poverty policy framework and combat the perception that it is a separate, externally driven poverty strategy. The changes were also designed to give the Ministry of Finance a greater role in coordinating national policy planning and more resource control.

The NSSED monitoring system exists in parallel with other monitoring systems. Some of the M&E units are responsible for monitoring the GNAP and the SAp. Despite the intention to synthesize reporting requirements, each of the three principal strategies has a separate monitoring framework with a distinct reporting mechanism. In the case of the GNAP, the Department for Policy Development and Coordination (DPDC) at the Council of Ministers maintains a management information system database based on semiannual reports of the line ministries. This system was piloted in the Ministry of Agriculture and Food through a project financed by the United Nations Development Program and has been rolled out to other line ministries. In the case of the SAp, line ministries report to the Ministry of European Integration.

Main institutional actors

The *steering committee* is chaired by the prime minister and represents the highest level of decision making in the NSSED monitoring process. It is in charge of guiding NSSED implementation, approving action plans, and assessing results. Representatives of donors, civil society, the business community, and local government may be invited to attend meetings.

The *interministerial working group* was set up by the steering committee. Initially, it included deputy ministers in 12 line ministries, but the Council of Ministers expanded it to all 16 ministries and the National Institute of Statistics (INSTAT) in June 2003. The IMWG is chaired by the minister of finance as national coordinator of the NSSED. It is responsible for coordinating all institutional operations in the implementation of the strategy. The IMWG meets several times a year and reports to the NSSED national coordinator on the fulfillment of objectives contained in the NSSED, the fulfillment of obligations that result from the Poverty Reduction Strategy Credit, comments regarding the action plan to be implemented in monitoring, problems in the M&E units, and issues of harmonization of the medium-term budget framework (MTBF) and the NSSED.

The *NSSED Department* in the Ministry of Finance has a director and four staff members and is responsible for supporting the development and review of the NSSED, coordinating the NSSED monitoring system, providing general guidance to the M&E units, and preparing reports to the government, civil society, and donors. It is accountable for an annual progress report on the achievement of NSSED objectives. This includes coordinating the contributions of the line ministries, checking the quality of the contributions, ensuring adequate civil society consultation and participation, and acting as IMWG secretariat.

The *technical sector working groups* are ad hoc working groups within each ministry that are responsible for contributing to the NSSED. They are chaired by the deputy ministers (or other appointees in the case of central agencies reporting to the Council of Ministers, such as INSTAT). They consist mainly of directors of departments with decision-making influence in the ministries. They deal with sectoral issues, providing information and making proposals on plan implementation and suggesting measures to the ministers. The TSWGs draft the contributions to the NSSED progress report. As part of the consultation process for NSSED development, the TSWGs may include civil society representatives.

Monitoring and evaluation units have been established in all 16 line ministries and INSTAT. They are responsible for reporting on progress and advising on changes in sectoral strategies. They are intended to play a major role in the decision-making process. It is proposed that the units conduct reviews on quantitative and qualitative data to check progress against sectoral goals specified in the NSSED. The M&E unit in the Ministry of Labor and Social Affairs is especially tasked with monitoring poverty and conducting reviews on the causes of poverty. However, its activities are limited to data collection, reporting on unemployment, and the distribution of economic assistance. The units are responsible for periodic reporting to the NSSED Department on the sectoral reviews they undertake. Indicators have been developed for the action plans of the ministries. In addition, each unit is supposed to cooperate closely with the Budget Department in the Ministry of Finance on the preparation of the MTBF to ensure that allocations match priorities specified in the NSSED. Each unit is also responsible for the following:

- coordinating the development of appropriate indicators and targets
- establishing a data collection system and maintaining a database of indicators
- cooperating with and coordinating the activities of experts in other technical departments for the development of appropriate objectives, indicators, and targets
- improving indicators and proposing appropriate methodologies for data collection
- preparing periodic reports and other specific reports requested by government structures related to policy monitoring or specific indicators
- cooperating with experts of the ministry in formulating and revising policy frameworks, the production of specific studies, and the management of related expenses
- cooperating with institutions outside the ministry in the production of policy analysis
- promoting wider use of M&E results in policy formulation and updating the process

The *National Institute of Statistics* is an important source of information for NSSED and poverty monitoring. It collects and provides data on the gross domestic product, consumption, investment, exports, imports, and prices. Information on poverty, living conditions, and social indicators is generated through the 2001 Population and Housing Census and the three waves (2002–4) of the Living Standards Measurement Survey (LSMS). INSTAT also makes these sources widely available and provides estimates of measures of poverty upon request. INSTAT has led capacity building efforts. For instance, in preparation for the LSMS, INSTAT coordinated a data users group made up mainly of line ministry representatives who were invited to participate in questionnaire design and introduce questions relevant to policy. It has also trained data users in line ministries, civil society, the media, and interdisciplinary research entities in the context of its dissemination activities. Finally, INSTAT produces research reports.

Challenges recognized by the government and proposed changes

As part of envisaged improvements over the short and medium term, the government will strengthen ownership by promoting the NSSED as a single strategic planning framework that encompasses competing frameworks. A technical secretariat including representatives of central policy-making institutions has been established to formulate a concept for the harmonization of these frameworks. This should assist in enhancing links between the NSSED and the MTBF. Moreover, it would strengthen the lead of the NSSED in demanding explicit information about the expenditure implications of priorities set by line ministries. The integrated planning system adopted by the government in April 2005 aims at improving the overall strategic planning framework through an emphasis on aligning the NSSED with the medium-term budget program and the annual budget and improving the management and coordination of external assistance. The integrated planning system proposes a robust monitoring framework to orient the budget program toward more informed resource allocation. System implementation is a daunting task and will face many challenges. However, if the integrated planning system is implemented at a measured pace over the next three to five years, a more coherent and stable policy environment and a solid framework for monitoring results will emerge.

Donors are directly supporting the NSSED Department. Through the management of a multidonor Poverty Reduction Strategy Trust Fund, the World Bank supports activities to refine indicators and introduce results-based management and qualitative poverty monitoring. The U.K. Department for International Development focuses its support on strengthening the analytical capacity of the NSSED Department to monitor and evaluate and, in general, to mainstream the role of the NSSED in the policy process. Part of this support is channeled toward capacity building in policy analysis in the M&E units of two line ministries.

Based on its five-year action plan, INSTAT has a vision for enhancing its work. A new law on statistics was to be submitted to Parliament in 2005. The law envisages regular labor force and household budget surveys, a five-year cycle for the LSMS, and, most importantly, obtaining the government's commitment to use budget resources to finance these activities.

Overall Status

Though the machinery necessary for the effective functioning of the policy cycle is in place, the actual operation of the system does not reflect the intentions. This is mainly because of gaps in the organizational arrangements and considerable capacity constraints, as follows:

- The TSWGs are loose, ad hoc groups inside each ministry that are not demanding information, and M&E staff do not feel positioned to undertake such tasks. Furthermore, despite identified membership, TSWGs convene rarely and usually only meet deadlines imposed by the NSSED annual reporting timetable.
- The Council of Ministers established a monitoring system through M&E units in all 16 line ministries that displays all the necessary features for the operation of an effective policy cycle. However, despite this legal framework, the system has not yet achieved full capacity.
- The M&E units have relatively low status within the line ministries, and, although they formally report to the TSWGs, the real recipient of the information is the NSSED. As a result, M&E units do not yet have much impact on policy formulation within their ministries.
- The demand for the tasks done by M&E units and their outputs seems limited. If ministries are not required to justify their annual requests through rigorous policy analysis or to analyze the impact their spending has on outcomes, then they do not have the incentive to staff their M&E units nor to use the outputs of the units.
- In most cases, the M&E units do not have adequate resources. For the most part, no resources were diverted to establish the M&E function. Monitoring is often not the only or even the primary task of M&E units. M&E tasks have simply been added to existing staff positions in the ministries. Moreover, the units frequently do not have a fixed location in the ministries.

- Although some staff have received training in aspects of M&E (project management and statistical methods), this has seldom been followed through to the practical level required to boost confidence in the use of these skills. Moreover, no training in policy analysis has taken place, and skills in this area are extremely limited.
- Inputs of civil society organizations to focus monitoring activities are limited. Weaknesses include low participation at the grassroots level, problems in identifying stakeholders, preferential links with specific groups, inadequate participation, and poor use of the media. The rudimentary involvement of Parliament and elected local government leaders is a concern.

Key Topics

Leadership of the system

System leadership resides with the NSSED steering committee, chaired by the prime minister. Despite its high profile, the committee meets only occasionally, mostly for the purpose of discussing progress reports.

The steering committee set up the IMWG, which includes all deputy ministers and INSTAT. The IMWG is chaired by the Minister of Finance and is responsible for piloting and implementing the strategy. It meets several times a year. Weak when first established, the IMWG has recently become more active. For example, it became a forum for assisting the Ministry of European Integration in the formulation of priorities for the 2004 European Union Community Assistance for Reconstruction, Development, and Stabilization Program. The IMWG has also become a forum for advancing issues such as the link between M&E units and SAp negotiators in line ministries.

Coordination

Albania has opted for a decentralized system with M&E units in individual line ministries. An examination of the organization of the M&E units in six line ministries emphasizes two key system features. First, there are a variety of approaches to organization and responsibilities. Second, given the level of responsibilities, coupled with the fact that staff are not allocated full-time to M&E activities, there is an insufficient number of people engaged in NSSED M&E tasks.

Within each ministry the information flows in a single direction, from technical departments to the M&E unit, to fulfill reporting requirements for central government agencies. The demand from technical departments to their M&E units for information on NSSED progress and the evolution of indicators remains low. The main sources of requests are the deputy minister and, more rarely, the minister. The number of data users inside ministries is limited. M&E units also have to address requests from the NSSED Department and the Budget Department at the Ministry of Finance, the DPDC, and the Ministry of European Integration. These requests are usually similar in coverage, but use different formats, often resulting in a duplication of effort.

The TSWGs are only active during the preparation of the NSSED progress reports. Once reporting obligations are complete, TSWGs dissolve, and contact with the M&E units ceases. This shows that participation is viewed as a bureaucratic obligation and not part of a process to review and improve policies. Formal relations with INSTAT have not yet been established.

Capacity

There is insufficient staff in the M&E units to undertake all tasks. Many of the staff are new; some posts are vacant; and most staff do not have the range of statistical and analytical skills required to fulfill their roles. The use of data is thus limited at best to administrative data, despite an ambitious program led in recent years by INSTAT to collect household survey data. Most of the staff of the M&E units have received training, but this has not been effective partly due to the lack of support in the use of the skills learned.

Participation

The fact that the NSSED process is open and participatory, combined with frequent reference to it by political leaders, has helped to build its appeal nationwide. The NSSED Department is committed to boosting participation, and steps have been taken to formalize participation. Interest groups were given time to contribute to the 2003 progress report. With support from the Organization for Security and Co-operation in Europe, the department hosted regional meetings. Consultations were held with members of Parliament, and the parliamentary committee on economy, finances, and privatization has become part of the NSSED M&E process.

Certain ministries have amended their progress reports on the basis of comments and suggestions by civil society. These include the Ministry of Health, the Ministry of Labor and Social Affairs, the Ministry of Education and Science, the Ministry of Local Government and Decentralization, the Ministry of Economy, and the Ministry of Environment.

However, weaknesses in the participatory process remain. While there have been attempts to undertake participatory monitoring, the formal monitoring outputs by the M&E units have not triggered wider debates. Participation is weak at the grassroots level, and marginalized groups are not always aware of the NSSED. More effective identification and balancing of the interest groups are also required to reduce the risk that personal agendas will dominate the consultations. Actors are not always provided with adequate, timely information. Finally, discussions are often general, and feedback on draft policies is weak.

Decentralization

Considerable effort has been made to introduce regional socioeconomic development strategies and to align these with the NSSED. Two regions (Kukes, Fier) have completed their strategies, while three others have prepared regional Millennium Development Goal (MDG) reports (Berat, Elbasan, Shkoder). With the support of the United Nations Development Program, the aim is for all regions to submit their regional socioeconomic development strategies by the end of 2005.

Serious obstacles remain, particularly the fragmentation of local government units, the undefined roles of regions, the lack of definition in responsibilities, and an insufficient local revenue base. The region is the weakest link in the ongoing reforms. Regional councils have started to take on their official roles in formulating development strategies, but their role in the budget process, implementation, and monitoring needs strengthening. The role of regional councils in poverty reduction will expand as the implementation of the 1999 national strategy for decentralization and local autonomy advances in education, health, and infrastructure.

Indicators and data sources

Most of the information used by line ministries derives from *administrative data* collection systems, essentially the work of the statistical departments or other technical departments in ministries. The sophistication of these systems varies, and there are concerns about their quality and relevance for policy purposes. Often, the activities of M&E units include responsibilities for project monitoring, which involves the provision of data on inputs and, to a lesser extent, outputs and outcomes. Multiple donor reporting requirements are also a concern, as they divert staff resources.

Until 2001, the ability to analyze social conditions in Albania through *survey data* was limited. Some surveys during the 1990s allowed some poverty analysis, but data limitations (for example, the absence of reliable estimates of the consumption of goods produced by households) and the lack of a solid sampling frame made the results difficult to use for policy purposes.

In 2001, the Population and Housing Census was undertaken. The 2002 LSMS was designed to provide information for the targeting, implementation, and monitoring of the social services delivery project supported by the World Bank and the U.K. Department for International Development. Despite heavy investment, there is still distrust of survey data. In particular, ministry officials criticize the inability of the LSMS to produce estimates at the regional level, which suggests a lack of understanding of the purpose of survey data. This may result from the fact that dissemination seminars are only attended by junior staff, while decision-making authority to invest resources in data analysis resides with more senior staff. It is evident that the information contained in the LSMS has been underutilized despite its accessibility.

Ad hoc household surveys continue to be undertaken. For example, in the context of the Poverty and Social Impact Assessment of water privatization, a household survey component collected data on customer satisfaction, perceptions of changes in water quality, the impact of metering, and willingness to pay. The United States Agency for International Development funded a project on citizen report cards. Households have been surveyed in mountainous areas of southeastern Albania, as well as in Tirana, to assess the provision of public services to urban communities. The United Nations Children's Fund has carried out a survey of knowledge, attitudes, beliefs, and practices on reproductive and family health issues.

A variety of sources have provided *qualitative data*. In some instances, there have been attempts to obtain a more rounded picture of social conditions in Albania, as was the case with the Vulnerability Needs and Institutional Capabilities Assessment Report (2000) and the World Bank Qualitative Poverty Assessment (2002).

The limited understanding of data is also reflected in the choice of *monitoring indicators*. The final and intermediate indicators in the NSSED are relatively clear, but there has been limited guidance as to what the NSSED should actually be reporting. Few processes have been initiated to adjust what is measured to what needs to be monitored. Experience suggests that the emphasis should be on a short list of outcome and impact measures, but the response of line ministries has been erratic. In ministries that are more experienced with M&E activities, such as the Ministry of Agriculture and Food and the Ministry of Labor and Social Affairs, the intermediate indicators selected are more relevant for poverty reduction and more closely related to the final indicators. However, other ministries report on too many indicators (emphasizing input indicators), lack a baseline, and have little control over the accuracy of administrative data. Reporting is often on indicators that are not specific, measurable, attainable, relevant, or time bound.

Analysis and evaluation

Data analysis in ministries is limited. As a rule, administrative data are processed in statistical departments and analyzed in technical departments. M&E units typically collate evidence from various subsectors into consolidated reports. NSSED progress reports should be the main dissemination channel for communicating on goals and policy evaluation. However, though survey data have been used in report preparation, they have been analyzed mainly through donor activities. Line ministries report on input and output indicators, which do not shed much light on the links between policies and outcomes. Indicators are biased toward processes.

Most analysis relevant to policy development is carried out by local consultants on behalf of donors in the context of projects, such as the Human Development Reports in 2000 and 2002. INSTAT has been more successful in involving its own staff in producing analytical reports. This is particularly the case in three significant LSMS-based studies, which include a substantial attempt to combine census and LSMS data to produce a poverty ranking of municipalities and communes.

The lack of an understanding of the links between policies and outcomes compromises attempts to undertake policy analysis based on the poverty monitoring system. The weak statistical and *analytical capacity* within the line ministries and the NSSED Department means that there is a tendency to report on figures rather than to analyze them. The reports are thus of limited use in gauging recent experience or in guiding future policy. Most M&E units do not fulfill their responsibility for policy analysis. There is thus no firm basis for policy decisions, and target outcomes risk becoming unrealistic, which further undermines meaningful monitoring.

Steps are being taken to align strategic frameworks and incorporate them into the MTBF to foster links between policies and the budget, but the critical link between monitoring and policy formulation does not exist.

Dissemination

The annual progress reports are the main vehicle for reporting and dissemination. Dissemination seminars are typically attended only by junior staff.

Links to the policy process

Government priority actions under the GNAP are monitored by the DPDC. To help monitor GNAP implementation, a Web-based management information system describing each ministry's objectives, activities, and outputs was piloted in the Ministry of Agriculture and Food in 2002, and has since been expanded to all line ministries. Since July 2004, it has been officially approved by the Council of Ministers as the tool for monitoring the GNAP. Although there is an effort to classify priority measures according to the major frameworks to which they belong (NSSED, SAp, MDGs, the North Atlantic Treaty Organization accession, and the anticorruption strategy), the process is not yet complete.

Twice yearly, line ministries must report information to complete the system matrices. The management information system may then be used to create reports on priority measures (policy and program actions), outputs (achieved and planned), activities (implemented or to be implemented), key factors affecting implementation, and recommendations on actions required by the Council of Ministers. Each report may be presented according to program, sector, group of sectors (for example, social sectors, infrastructure), or policy framework (NSSED, SAp, MDGs, and so on). In many cases, the responsibility for submitting the reports to the DPDC lies with the M&E units.

Using the management information system, the DPDC could provide inputs to both the NSSED Department and the Ministry of European Integration, allowing them to focus their efforts on studying the impact of government actions relative to goals. It is hoped that the management information system will eventually become the single monitoring system to which line ministries report outputs. Providing resources for M&E units and the NSSED Department will assist the focus on monitoring outcomes and the evaluation of the impact of policies.

Budget preparation and policy implementation

NSSED progress reporting should include consideration of ongoing policies so as to assess whether they contribute to the achievement of long-term goals. Indeed, it should open up a debate on alternative ways to achieve the goals. The ultimate aim is to provide strategic guidance in medium-term budget programming regarding the allocation of resources across sectors.

The MTBF process operationalizes policy priorities over a three-year period on a rolling basis. While the initial years of the MTBF focused on creating a framework for prioritization, the current focus is increasingly on strengthening the link between budget and policy. A key objective is to improve the integration of the NSSED within the budget process so that the MTBF becomes the tool through which the NSSED is delivered.

No close link exists yet, and line ministries do not generally consider their NSSED reporting requirements in relation to the resource allocation process. Policy formulation and budgeting functions remain disjointed in several line ministries. This is an obstacle for monitoring units within ministries.

Lessons

The institutional structure of the poverty monitoring system made considerable progress in 2003 and 2004. A number of key lessons have emerged.

Development of M&E units

The structure of M&E units should be harmonized so as to consolidate planning, budgeting, and monitoring functions. Organizational issues relating to monitoring activities should be clarified. There should be a greater understanding of the roles within units and relative to the entities with which the units interact. The capacity of the M&E units should be raised to ensure that the units are adequately resourced in staff, training, facilities, and equipment. A database of NSSED indicators should be established, and training should be provided on its use. The reporting of monitoring results across line ministries needs to be streamlined. Direct links among the results of M&E, policy formulation, and the budget planning process are required. Two possible actions for achieving this are (1) the hiring of the qualified staff necessary in the M&E units and (2) the requirement by the Ministry of Finance, the Council of Ministers, or Parliament that all line ministries justify expenditure decisions and priorities or that any significant shifts in expenditure allocation within the line ministries be based on sound policy analyses.

Policy cycle

The need to strengthen the link between data and policy analysis is a key lesson. Household survey data are not useful without a capacity for analysis. Although statistical techniques and software training were delivered to staff in INSTAT and key line ministries, this appears to have had little impact. Line ministry staff do not receive support or guidance on using the data for policy analysis. This highlights the need for senior staff training in the line ministries on how to request policy analysis and how to use the results in order to improve the policy formulation process.

Demand for M&E must be created at the policy level, but there are also other dimensions of the role of M&E in the policy cycle. One is the absence of results-based strategic planning in the executive branch. NSSED objectives remain general, which makes the identification and measurement of specific indicators difficult. Another dimension is the lack of accountability in public spending. Low civil society participation in assessing the results of public spending is another important barrier.

Coordination and cooperation

The fragmentation of the system highlights the importance of coordination and cooperation. Actors have different levels of capacity, motivation, and willingness to participate in M&E activities. There must be stronger leadership to improve relationships among actors in NSSED monitoring, especially the M&E units, statistical departments in line ministries, and INSTAT. There is considerable duplication in monitoring for different strategic frameworks. Monitoring systems and processes should be harmonized.

Finally, the Albanian experience highlights the importance of feedback in the policy cycle and the public expenditure management cycle. Only when data are used systematically to evaluate policies is there likely to be a demand for a high-quality monitoring system.

Bolivia

CISE   Comitado Interinstitucional para el Seguimiento y la Evaluación (Interinstitutional Committee for Monitoring and Evaluation)

EBRP   Estrategia Boliviana de Reducción de la Pobreza (Bolivian poverty reduction strategy)

EBRP-PSE   Programa de Seguimiento y Evaluación de la EBRP (EBRP Monitoring and Evaluation Program)

INE   Instituto Nacional de Estadística (National Institute of Statistics)

MCS   mecanismo de control social (social control mechanism)

Proserpci   Programa para el Seguimiento y Evaluación de la Estrategia de Reducción de la Pobreza y Cumbres Internacionales (Program for the Monitoring and Evaluation of the Poverty Reduction Strategy and International Summits)

UDAPE   Unidad de Análisis de Políticas Económicas y Sociales (unit for the analysis of economic and social policies)

This chapter is based on a background country report by Elizabeth Jimenez (2004) and inputs by Carlos Mollinedo-Trujillo. The study was undertaken in the second half of 2004 and has been partially updated to reflect conditions in the summer of 2005. Substantial changes may have occurred that are not reflected in this chapter, and readers are encouraged to seek additional information if they wish to focus on the system of this particular country.

History and Context

I n March 2001, the government of Bolivia presented the Estrategia Boliviana de Reducción de la Pobreza (EBRP), its poverty reduction strategy (PRS). The strategy was adopted as a national framework for the implementation of development and poverty reduction policies. The EBRP action plan became the reference point for internally and externally financed government programs and projects.

The Law on National Dialogue, promulgated in December 2000, was conceived as the "instrumental and legal means to make the [poverty reduction] strategy work." The law focused largely on two main issues: (1) the national compensatory policy aimed at the distribution of Heavily Indebted Poor Countries (HIPC) Initiative resources according to distributive parameters and (2) the institutionalization of the participation of civil society organizations (CSOs) in the process of the identification, monitoring, and evaluation of poverty reduction policies.

In 2003, the government prepared a revised EBRP to be launched later that year. This launch did not occur. The draft EBRP proposal for 2004–7 represents an attempt to reshape the objectives and procedures of the poverty reduction action plan and seeks to accomplish the following:

- align the EBRP objectives with the MDGs and thereby accommodate the overall objectives of poverty reduction in the nine MDGs
- narrow poverty reduction policies into three strategic objectives: (1) develop micro-, small- and medium-size enterprises so as to boost job creation; (2) develop access to and improve the quality of a minimum set of services in education, health care, and basic sanitation; and (3) eliminate social exclusion based on gender, ethnicity, or age
- reform the EBRP monitoring and evaluation (M&E) system

An outbreak of civil unrest led to a change in the government administration in October 2003. This severely affected the actions and programs of the PRS, as well as the poverty M&E system. The effort to establish this system was suspended. The National Board for Economic and Social Policies has now reviewed the main PRS documents, but there has been no follow-up.

Description of the PRS Monitoring system

Origins of the system

The National Board for Economic and Social Policies is responsible for the overall assessment of economic and social policies. The Unidad de

Análisis de Políticas Económicas y Sociales (unit for the analysis of economic and social policies, UDAPE), which was in the Office of the Presidency, but now sits within the Ministry of Economic Development, is the technical secretariat for the board. UDAPE led in the drafting of the EBRP, which provided an initial description of the EBRP M&E system. The need to organize the system soon became a priority. UDAPE was therefore charged with identifying appropriate institutional arrangements to support the development of the EBRP M&E system.

In October 2001, the Programa de Seguimiento y Evaluación de la EBRP (EBRP Monitoring and Evaluation Program, EBRP-PSE) was launched through government decree. The institutional arrangements for the implementation of the EBRP-PSE were first discussed in a meeting of the National Committee for Social Policies and were later approved by Congress.

The system

The EBRP-PSE includes four main areas of activity:

- M&E at the national level, which encompasses four elements:
  1. monitoring specific actions identified in the EBRP action plan at the national level and monitoring the implementation of medium-term policies identified in the EBRP
  2. monitoring intermediate, outcome, and impact indicators at the national level
  3. monitoring the allocation and application of public resources
  4. conducting an overall reassessment and definition of impact evaluation methodologies

- M&E at the municipal level, which covers, among other activities, the identification of institutional channels so as to ensure a two-way flow of information between the central and the local levels; this includes three components:
  1. conducting assessments of the institutional capacity of the agencies responsible for this flow
  2. identifying intermediate, outcome, and impact indicators at the municipal level
  3. monitoring allocations to and levels of application of public resources at the municipal level

* integration of information channels, which comprises two elements:

  1. the integration of existing information systems to ensure timely access to and exchange of information between central and local authorities
  2. assessing the possibilities of developing and applying quick-survey instruments to measure progress in EBRP implementation at the municipal level

* activities that would lead to the design and implementation of a mechanism to disseminate the results of M&E and encourage feedback. Dissemination activities are meant to target CSOs, the National Committee for Social Policies, the National Committee for Economic Policies, and Congress. This set of activities was also to include the organization of a national dialogue event every three years

Main institutional actors

The structure of the EBRP-PSE was initially organized around two key interinstitutional bodies. One was the Comitado Interinstitucional para el Seguimiento y la Evaluación (Interinstitutional Committee for Monitoring and Evaluation, CISE), which is led by UDAPE and involved the Instituto Nacional de Estadística (National Institute of Statistics, INE) and the Vice Ministry of Strategic Planning and Popular Participation.

The other body was the Interinstitutional Board for Monitoring and Evaluation, which included four working groups made up of deputy ministers or directors of governmental executing agencies and organized around institutions and decentralization; production issues; social issues; and sustainability. This board and its working groups were, however, later dissolved.

In addition, the technical secretary for national dialogue organizes a participatory process for reassessing poverty policies.

The UDAPE plays a pivotal role in the management and administration of the EBRP-PSE. The EBRP-PSE is intended as a second-tier system. This means that, through it, UDAPE acts as a clearinghouse for the data and information collected and processed by other institutions.

Thus, the four working groups of the interinstitutional board provide UDAPE with sectoral information, particularly on input, process (including policy actions), and output indicators.

The INE supplies information derived from population censuses and household surveys.

The Vice Ministry of Strategic Planning and Popular Participation coordinates the EBRP M&E process at the departmental and municipal levels. Its role is to ensure an adequate flow of information from the municipalities so that the UDAPE could track the progress of EBRP implementation at the local level, especially with regards to input, process, and output indicators.

The Vice Ministry of Public Investment and External Financing furnishes administrative and financial information on the execution of the public investment program at the national level and at the municipal level, though this latter function could be realized only in a few instances given the systemic weaknesses of local governments in maintaining administrative records.

The EBRP-PSE governmental decree recognizes the normative role played by the INE over the national statistical system. INE is expected to provide methodological and technical assistance to UDAPE and other stakeholders (the working groups) for the calculation of EBRP indicators.

Finally, the Vice Ministry of Strategic Planning and Popular Participation is in charge of disseminating EBRP-PSE information to the municipalities and providing adequate feedback.

Problems recognized by the government

The system faced a number of limitations (discussed below), and, as a result, CISE was planning to launch a new proposal for the EBRP-PSE in October 2003 as part of a revised version of the overall EBRP (EBRP 2004–7). This revised system never materialized due to the civil unrest and subsequent change in government.

Overall Status

The initial institutional framework for the EBRP-PSE was restricted by a series of limitations and weaknesses relating to both institutions and processes. Most of these problems have not yet been addressed. The most important of these are the following:

- the limited ownership by agents outside the center of government and the frequent turnovers in key political appointments

- the lack of a description of detailed interinstitutional agreements within a legal framework
- the unreliable data flow because of the nature of the system as a second-tier system
- the limited capacities of public sector agencies, particularly at the local level

A proposal for a revised EBRP M&E system was drafted in response to these and other limitations in the original EBRP-PSE. According to the proposal, the new system was to be founded on two subsystems: an M&E system for results-based public management and a system for impact evaluation that was to be overseen by CISE and would help assess the impact of policy actions on employment creation, income, and access to basic services.

The revised proposal did not, however, explain the purpose of this reform or present the specificities of each of the two subsystems. It suggested that all producers of primary information would be embedded in the system, while CISE would retain its main function as the body in charge of the analysis of primary information.

Key Topics

Leadership of the system

The National Board for Economic and Social Policies oversees the system. It is important to note, however, that, while ownership is strong at the center of government, it is weak at the ministerial level. Changes in top management positions due to political realignments also affected the functioning of the system. In particular, revisions in the allotment of responsibilities and in earlier commitments affected the Interinstitutional Board for Monitoring and Evaluation and CISE, though to a lesser extent. The turnover in key ministerial positions during political shifts in government administration contributed to a reduction in the board's ownership of the process.

Legal framework

Although a general legal framework is in place (that is, the Law on National Dialogue), it does not cover the detailed interinstitutional agreements and the creation of the manuals necessary to support the smooth flow of information between the various institutions. This would greatly reduce institutional accountability within the overall M&E system.

Roles and processes

The nature of the M&E system as a second-tier system implies that its technical viability, quality, and timeliness would depend on the reliability of the data flows from the first-tier data production systems administered by central and local public agencies. Overall, the M&E capacity of central public sector agencies is weak.

The division of tasks between UDAPE and INE has also been a matter of contention, as it seems that INE has not been able to fulfill its system function. In addition to its role in the coordination of the EBRP progress reports, UDAPE processes survey and census data for the preparation of the first EBRP progress report, although this is the formal responsibility of the INE. This confusion might partly reflect the limited capacity of INE to analyze the data it produces, but could also be a sign of institutional rivalry in a resource-constrained environment. The events surrounding the preparation by INE of the Programa para el Seguimiento y Evaluación de la Estrategia de Reducción de la Pobreza y Cumbres Internacionales (Program for the Monitoring and Evaluation of the Poverty Reduction Strategy and International Summits, Proserpci) might be yet another sign of this rivalry.

After the interinstitutional board and its four working groups were dissolved, the roles and responsibilities of the remaining actors were altered, and the links between CISE and sectoral agencies changed drastically.

Finally, the interaction between UDAPE and the mecanismo de control social (social control mechanism, MCS), a formal mechanism for CSO participation in the EBRP, occurs without any definition of procedures or structured communication channels. As a result, information requests often reach UDAPE in a disorderly fashion and, in some cases, are not answered in a timely manner. This lack of fluid communication creates tension between the UDAPE and the MCS and generates a certain level of mistrust. The interaction is also affected by a perceived ambiguity about the concrete role of the mechanism in the EBRP-PSE.

Capacity

The original design of the EBRP-PSE ignored or underestimated the limited institutional and technical capacities of various public sector agencies. The coordination capacity within the four working groups of the interinstitutional board was largely overestimated. The working group members belonged to heterogeneous sectors and often did not share common interests or objectives. Agreement on the type of indicators, procedures, and information flows were difficult to achieve. In addition, the working regulations and procedures (for example, the rotating work-group leadership) proved a burden in terms of internal dynamics. Because of a lack of incentives, members were also typically not able or willing to provide the level of effort and time required. Finally, the inherent weaknesses were exacerbated by the turnover in top management positions that resulted in many institutions from changes in ruling parties.

After only a year, the groups were no longer meeting regularly and were eventually dissolved. This left a substantial gap in the coordination of the agencies in charge of the execution of the EBRP and the CISE. UDAPE filled this void by establishing a one-on-one working relationship with and gathering information directly from key sectoral agencies and line ministries. Surprisingly, the new EBRP-PSE proposal prepared in 2003, but never officially presented, called for the reestablishment of the interinstitutional board.

The inability of UDAPE to perform its functions stems primarily from its lack of permanent staff (the director is still an interim position) and the confusion surrounding its role in government. In addition, financial and human resources were never raised to match the needs created by the expanded mandate of UDAPE in the coordination of M&E. This is exacerbated by the dissolution of the working groups and the growing demands of the MCS.

Finally, the institutional capacity of local governments represents a more serious obstacle than the shortcomings in central government capacity. The flow of information from the municipalities to the Vice Ministry of Strategic Planning and Popular Participation has been extremely limited. Only in a few cases and as a result of specific requests put forward by the MCS did some municipalities produce and disseminate socioeconomic and financial information. A full assessment by municipalities of their role in applying the HIPC resources assigned to them has still not been carried out because the Vice Ministry of Public Investment and External Financing does not possess the human and financial resources necessary to supervise and carry out annual audits of the financial accounts of all 314 municipalities.

Moreover, most municipalities, but especially the poorest ones, do not have the capacity to handle the accounting and reporting procedures required by the Directorio Único de Fondos (Board of National Funds), a national body that manages social and regional development funds.

Participation

The Law on National Dialogue institutionalized CSO participation in the identification, monitoring, and evaluation of EBRP policies and programs. The National Forum 2002, which was organized by the Catholic Church as part of the Jubilee 2000 campaign, and the National Dialogue 2000, which was organized by the government, were important precursors to the Law on National Dialogue. The law established that national dialogues must be undertaken every third year to assess EBRP implementation progress.

The participation of CSOs in the M&E system also occurs through the MCS, the national board of which was elected in 2002 by means of a constitutive assembly of 53 organizations. It encompasses national, departmental, and municipal structures. The municipal-level structures are called vigilance committees. The MCS has an official role in:

- providing general social supervisory control at the national level
- collaborating with government agencies in identifying a set of indicators to be used in monitoring the EBRP at the national, departmental, and municipal levels
- participating in tracking the results of EBRP programs and projects
- appointing representatives to the Board of National Funds
- receiving timely and accurate information on the management of the Board of National Funds through which HIPC resources are assigned to municipalities
- reporting possible cases of the mishandling of public resources
- providing support for and promoting social supervisory control mechanisms at the local level

Despite the substantial contribution of the 2002 Law on National Dialogue to the institutionalization of the MCS, a concept not discussed in the political arena until then, the situation has changed drastically over the past few years. There is still confusion as to what, how, where (for example, at the central or local levels), and by whom social supervisory control should be exercised. The challenge resides in the definition of the significance of participatory M&E in practice and the way M&E should be carried out. Recently, MCS activities have included monitoring the transfer of HIPC resources to municipalities, supervising the estimation of figures on poverty at the municipal level, and monitoring the implementation of specific EBRP programs.

The draft 2004–7 EBRP proposal called for the institutionalization of participatory planning activities through the stipulation of agreements between the three *government* levels (central, departmental, and municipal) and the *stakeholders* active in the social and productive sectors. While this programmatic statement signaled a determination to reform the MCS, the document did not identify specific measures to make the proposal operational, nor did it hint at the changes required in the MCS institutional framework.

The National Dialogue II proposal has now been completed, and the results will soon be published. It is important to note that there is little policy relevance in the outcomes expected besides the general confirmation that more emphasis should be given to productive activities.

The legitimacy of the national- and departmental-level MCS bodies has been questioned by various sectors in Bolivian civil society. This is largely due to the lack of transparency that, some claim, characterized the election of the members of these bodies.

The legitimacy of the vigilance committees has been recognized among communities. They have existed for almost a decade now and have developed close links with CSOs and local authorities. Recently, a national confederation of vigilance committees has been created. This underlines the need for mechanisms for internal coordination and articulation and reveals the detachment of the vigilance committees from the MCS departmental bodies that were supposed to represent them.

Outside the MCS framework, CSOs have also mobilized so as to ensure their own participation. For example, the Program of Participation for Social Control set up by the Social Commission of the Bolivian Episcopal Conference of Caritas, the Catholic Charities of Bolivia, is now undertaking M&E for health and education policies. Joint training of CSOs and UDAPE staff has also enhanced the ownership of participatory monitoring tools, such as citizen report cards, within the government.

Products

The direct outputs produced by CISE during about three years of M&E activities included the publication of four EBRP progress reports, a set of booklets covering sociodemographic information and poverty-related indicators at the departmental level, and a series of booklets on poverty-related issues that was produced by the Pastoral Commission of the Catholic Church.

Although the four progress reports represent the most important outcomes of the M&E activities, they are tangible proof that, after almost three years, the process of determining what should be monitored and the best monitoring methods is ongoing. The second EBRP progress report, of July 2002, presented an important set of municipal-level indicators that the EBRP was expected to track, though it never did. This list was the result of a major participatory exercise carried out within three regional workshops and organized by the Vice Ministry of Strategic Planning and Popular Participation, in coordination with UDAPE and the MCS and with the involvement of local authorities and members of the vigilance committees. However, in the third EBRP progress report, which came out in February 2003, this list was not included, and values for the indicators were not estimated.

Dissemination

The UDAPE was largely responsible for the content and analysis underlying the EBRP progress reports. The extent of the distribution of these reports was less than had been originally planned by the UDAPE. When distribution did take place, such as, for example, through the members of the MCS (who are considered the primary audience for these reports), UDAPE did not receive much feedback. On the other hand, the less technical publications were widely disseminated.

Finance and donor support

CISE institutions never estimated the cost involved in M&E. Nor did the internal resources increase as a result of the new responsibilities related to the EBRP M&E activities. Donor contributions were mainly in kind in the form of training, consultant time, workshops, seminars, and publications, making it difficult to assess the total value of these contributions. To a certain extent, the lack of significant planning and coordination and the degree of informality that have characterized the donor support for EBRP M&E may have generated inefficiencies in the use of the available resources. A clearly established, transparent strategy for economic support might have reduced unnecessary tensions and led to more efficient outcomes.

The INE is the only institution that put forward, through Proserpci, estimates of funding requirements. However, the INE proposal addresses not merely the institutional needs linked to EBRP M&E activities, but also the larger objective of complete institutional reform. In the latest version, the INE proposal calls for $15.8 million over three years.

Lack of funding is also a constant complaint of MCS members. Until now, the MCS national body has received $81,000 from Caritas, the Catholic Charities of Bolivia, to cover operational expenses. Members of the MCS departmental committees work part time on a voluntary basis and use facilities provided by the regional offices of Caritas. The vigilance committee members are assigned a monthly allowance from the administrative budgets of municipalities to cover expenses. These committees are therefore the only MCS body that can rely on a relatively steady flow of funding for operations. The amount is established by law as a percentage of a municipality's overall budget, although this is not always strictly enforced. In addition, the MCS has access to funds provided by various donors to carry out specific activities or earmarked for specific projects. The amount and origin of these funds have, however, never been publicized, which has led to speculation and tensions within and outside the MCS.

Lessons

The new government is currently preparing a consultation process for the formulation of a fresh EBRP. In terms of monitoring, INE has been preparing an M&E plan (Proserpci) since October 2003. The initial Proserpci proposal did not receive the required political support within the government because it was deemed too ambitious and expensive even before it was officially presented. The INE is currently working on a revised proposal. The plan stresses the importance of strengthening the institutions responsible for the collection of primary information.

The new proposal for the EBRP-PSE recognizes that the implementation of an M&E system requires specific actions to enhance the collection and quality of primary information, namely, censuses, surveys, and administrative data. Moreover, the proposal highlights the need to encourage participatory budgetary planning at the municipal level, as well as assessments of the results. The proposal fails, however, to address existing institutional weaknesses.

3

Guyana

History and Context

The formulation of the poverty reduction strategy (PRS) in Guyana built on the national development strategy. It outlined national goals in economic growth, wealth creation, and the reduction of poverty. The national PRS steering committee, which is coordinated by the head of the Presidential Secretariat, developed the Poverty Reduction Strategy Paper, which was finalized in November 2001 and supplemented in April 2002. The first PRS progress report (PRS-PR) was delivered in June 2004. The second report was completed in August 2005.

This chapter is based on a background country report by Aline Coudouel and Ferdinando Regalia (2004) and on inputs by Homa-Zahra Fotouhi and Lucia Hanmer. The study was undertaken in the second half of 2004 and has been partially updated to reflect conditions in the summer of 2005. Substantial changes may have occurred that are not reflected in this chapter, and readers are encouraged to seek additional information if they wish to focus on the system of this particular country.

Description of the PRS Monitoring System

Origins of the system

The design and implementation of the PRS monitoring and evaluation (M&E) system was undertaken in October 2003. The system is designed as a two-tier system, that is, a high-level central unit collects information from sectoral ministries and regional committees. The detailed building blocks for the institutional framework of the M&E system are currently being put in place. The progress on M&E has been much slower than desired. This is partly because of delays in establishing an M&E structure, the lack of ownership, limited human resource capacity, and hesitancy in tracking budget allocations and expenditures at a disaggregated level.

The government is leading in the implementation of the PRS coordination and M&E framework. Originally, this was to be achieved through five separate activities: (1) monitoring inputs: tracking the resources allocated to sectors and programs for the achievement of PRS goals and ensuring that, once allocated, these resources are actually used; (2) monitoring outputs: ensuring that, once resources are spent, outputs are actually delivered; (3) monitoring outcomes: assessing whether the desired outcomes are achieved; (4) communicating and evaluating progress: ensuring that all interested stakeholders are aware of the progress and the plans, are conscious of bottlenecks and their causes, and are participating in the identification of solutions; and (5) enabling actions: when shortcomings and bottlenecks have been identified, monitoring whether appropriate action has been undertaken.

Most of these activities have not been fully implemented. This reflects the fact that the PRS monitoring system is not yet functional. Monitoring inputs can only be provided at the most aggregate level. Priority programs have only recently been identified, and the application of resources cannot be effectively tracked through the current system. The monitoring of outputs and outcomes has not begun. Communications are not yet as effective as expected. Finally, enabling actions cannot be defined because shortcomings and bottlenecks have not been identified.

The second PRS-PR, issued in August 2005, correctly recognizes the serious limitations that remain in carrying out M&E activities. These include (1) lack of an M&E system database to track poverty allocation and expenditures; (2) lack of appropriate data so that regional M&E coordinators and committees may undertake public consultations in communities; (3) lack of analysis of allocations and expenditures for pro-poor spending at the regional or national level; and (4) great difficulty in the measurement of the outputs and outcomes of poverty programs owing to weaknesses in the institutional framework for developing social statistics.

Main institutional actors

As part of the original design of the system, the government established the *PRS M&E unit* in the policy coordination and program management unit (PCPMU) of the Office of the President. The PRS M&E unit is expected to play a pivotal role in the institutional framework and is responsible for progress reporting, public communication, coordinating and guiding the work of the four other structures, liaising with line ministries and other agencies, and coordinating with the Ministry of Finance to generate budget data disaggregated by region. In addition, it is mandated to manage and provide technical support for M&E capacity-building activities among key ministries and other agencies. It is also in charge of the annual PRS-PR and the quarterly reports to the national PRS steering committee. In practice, there have been significant delays in carrying out the intended activities, and the PRS-PR highlights the lack of a functioning PRS monitoring system.

Outside the core system, the M&E unit facilitates interaction with the following subnational government bodies: (1) PRS regional committees (PRS-RCs), which are regional government bodies; (2) regional democratic councils, which are regional government bodies with responsibilities in education, health, and public infrastructure, among other areas; the resources administered by the councils are allocated by the central government; and (3) neighborhood democratic committees, which are local institutional bodies that represent groups of villages or small towns; the committees play a more limited role as municipal councils, and some of the 65 committees are not in operation. However, given the lack of statistical data and resource tracking information, these subnational government bodies are not yet able to perform systematic and appropriate M&E activities.

PRS focal points were established in seven ministries and five agencies to take the lead in monitoring the sectoral progress of the PRS and to liaise with the PRS M&E unit and the thematic groups (discussed below). The PRS ministerial focal points are in charge of determining indicators and targets, as well as monitoring and evaluating the progress toward and compliance with sectoral targets. The outputs of these activities are provided to the PRS M&E unit as part of PRS monitoring and for the PRS-PR. PRS ministerial focal points are also responsible for ensuring consistency among sectoral budget allocations, program formulation, and PRS goals. These focal points are only now starting to operate in a few key ministries.

The work of the *national PRS steering committee* is supposed to be based on information provided by the PCPMU, the ministerial focal points, and the regional and local committees. The steering committee consists of four government officials (two from the focal points) and 11 representatives of civil society organizations (CSOs), such as trade unions, religious bodies, the private sector, and nongovernmental organizations. During a CSO workshop in November 2003, over 80 CSOs selected representatives to the committee.

The committee was created to strengthen information sharing between government and CSOs, as well as to guide the PRS M&E unit in ensuring that a participatory and inclusive approach is adopted. It is also charged with assisting in communicating PRS plans to the public and keeping stakeholders informed of the processes.

The PRS M&E unit submits activity reports to the committee, which, in turn, assists the unit with the communication of PRS plans and relevant information to the general public and key stakeholders. Committee members coordinate and participate in regional and national consultations on the PRS-PR with CSOs, and they also gather feedback. In the medium term, the committee is expected to generate greater CSO involvement in the preparation of the PRS-PR. To achieve this goal, the committee identifies and promotes capacity-building activities to enable CSOs to participate more effectively. Given the lack of statistical data and because poverty-related programs have not been identified, the steering committee has not yet carried out its intended functions.

The *PRS regional committees* do not receive data on the resources budgeted or expended on priority poverty-related projects in their areas. Therefore, it is not possible for them to contribute substantively at this time. This problem has been recognized by the PCPMU, which is looking into ways to address the issue. The committees will play an important role in the monitoring of PRS implementation at the regional level. The first five PRS-RCs were established with the objective of engaging individuals, CSOs, and local governments in PRS M&E activities. The number of PRS-RCs will gradually be increased to cover all regions. Each PRS-RC consists of up to 10 members, including two regional coordinators selected through a public application process, one representative of the regional democratic councils, two people elected during regional consultations carried out in early 2004, and up to five people selected through a public application process. The PRS M&E unit provides technical support to the PRS-RCs and sets up training programs in M&E methodologies and community consultation management for the members of the PRS-RCs.

The PRS-RCs are meant to assist communities in accessing information and participating in local PRS activities, as well as building local capacity for monitoring and evaluating PRS implementation. The PRS-RCs will carry out quarterly monitoring exercises, the nature and scope of which will depend on regional priorities. Findings will be shared with the PRS M&E unit and relevant line ministries and will be used for the PRS-PR. In addition, each PRS-RC will review the budget assigned by the central government to the region, as well as the initiatives in the poverty reduction program to be executed by the regional democratic councils. For this reason, each PRS-RC is expected to consult with local stakeholders to determine which initiatives should be monitored. Each PRS-RC will also carry out quarterly field visits and mini-consultations to ensure ongoing community participation. Finally, each PRS-RC will manage a PRS information center, which will consist of a display area in a public building.

Five *thematic groups* have been established at the central level, but they meet only infrequently. They are focusing on governance, education, health, housing and water, and infrastructure. The groups consist of technical personnel from line ministries and donor agency representatives. Their objective is to improve coordination, planning, implementation, and the monitoring of programs and projects. Their functions include reviewing sectoral strategies to achieve PRS goals, addressing resource gaps in sectoral programs, monitoring performance relative to sectoral targets, and increasing the efficiency of donor interventions through better donor coordination.

General Evaluation

The PRS M&E implementation efforts in Guyana were only undertaken at the end of 2003; the first PRS-PR was produced in June 2004, and the second in August 2005. The last part of this section highlights a number of the preliminary findings.

Key Topics

Leadership of the system

The government of Guyana's ownership of and commitment to the PRS M&E implementation plan is illustrated by the fact that the coordination of the national PRS steering committee resides with the head of the Presidential Secretariat, the most senior civil servant in the country. In addition, both the PRS secretariat and the PRS M&E unit are housed in the executive implementation unit in the Office of the President. Notwithstanding this high level of support and responsibility for the PRS M&E, the system has not yet produced the desired output, and there is broad agreement within the international community, the PCPMU, and the public at large (illustrated by the PRS-PR consultations) that M&E needs to be strengthened substantially in terms of both statistical data and systems so as to achieve the intended outcome.

Legal framework

No proposal has been made to develop a legal framework to strengthen the PRS M&E system. No interinstitutional agreements specifying the roles and obligations of various actors, including the type and frequency of the information to be collected and shared, have been formally stipulated.

Roles and processes

The roles and responsibilities of the various actors specified in the implementation plan of the PRS M&E system are well defined. No important actors appear to have been omitted from the original design, and no explicit overlap of functions seems to exist.

There is, however, early evidence suggesting that institutional links need to be strengthened. A high turnover among staff in the PRS M&E unit has negatively influenced the flow of information between the PRS M&E unit and the line ministries. The focal points in the line ministries provide inputs for the PRS-PRs. However, as a result of staff turnovers and the lack of a fully functioning system, the PRS-PRs have not always accurately reflected the progress being made in PRS implementation at the sectoral level.

Capacity

Significant staff turnover is undermining the unit's ability to operate and initiate viable working relationships with other actors in the system. There are also systemic capacity issues in the financial and administrative systems administered by line ministries. (The systems have nevertheless been able to produce data on outputs for the PRS-PRs, for example, the number of bridges built, house lots allocated, pregnant women tested for HIV, and so on.)

In addition, the two major donors involved in this area, the Inter-American Development Bank and the World Bank, have started to reach beyond the PRS M&E unit and engage staff at the technical level to help define solutions for shortcomings in the system.

Participation

The preparation of the PRS involved extensive civil society consultation, and several civil society members were included in the original national PRS steering committee. The committee was then reconstituted at the end of 2003, and a wide range of CSOs were invited to nominate representatives from various constituencies (for instance, religious, labor, gender, and youth leaders). Committee members were selected by the Office of the President from the names put forward by the CSOs.

In addition, the consultations with civil society on the first PRS-PR were extensive and robust. The draft report was widely disseminated via a posting on the Web, and abridged versions were made available through well-attended public meetings.

The consultations on the second PRS-PR were also extensive. The main concern of participants in the consultations both in the capital, Georgetown, and in the regions was the lack of a functioning M&E system.

Products

The PRS M&E unit compiles the annual PRS-PR for the national PRS steering committee. These reports are widely circulated in draft form to generate feedback.

Dissemination

The government has been relatively active in terms of the dissemination of information. This has included the broadcast of five television programs on the PRS and M&E PRS activities; flyers, posters, and other written materials distributed in the five regions initially selected; briefings of the regional democratic councils and most neighborhood democratic committee members; and the Web posting and dissemination of PRS-PRs. Partly as a result of the lack of capacity, these activities have not been carried out as regularly and as broadly as was desired.

Donor alignment

Originally, the proliferation of other M&E subsystems and reporting practices by various donors within the same institutions that are members of the PRS system contributed to delays in the adoption of a much-needed unified strategy to tackle systemic institutional weaknesses in M&E at the ministerial level. However, more recently, the main institutions active in this area, namely, the Inter-American Development Bank and the World Bank, have been working together through a coherent and comprehensive approach to assist the government in upgrading M&E.

In addition, the recent effort by the PRS M&E unit, line ministries, and M&E RCs to identify poverty-related programs may help achieve progress in this area. Once these programs have been agreed to by all stakeholders, it is intended that donors will align their programs with these poverty-related priorities.

Finance and donor support

There is no new budgetary allocation by the government to fund PRS M&E activities. In terms of funding, various programs are under way. The United Nations Development Program is supporting community-based monitoring and capacity-building activities. The Inter-American Development Bank and the World Bank are providing funding for the institutional strengthening of the Bureau of Statistics, statistical units in sectoral ministries, and the PCPMU.

Early Lessons

It is still too early to assess the performance of the PRS M&E system in Guyana. A number of preliminary findings have, however, been identified, as follows.

Roles and processes

Despite the relatively effective design of the system, there has been only limited efforts to provide resource tracking either from the budget side or from the expenditure side, particularly at the regional level. The government has identified priority poverty-related programs and intends to track allocations and expenditures within these programs regularly. This information will then be provided to the PRS-RCs to enhance their ability to monitor PRS implementation at the regional level.

Stronger buy-in among senior civil servants in the line ministries is required. This might be fostered by a clearer description by the PRS M&E unit of its expectations in terms of the contribution of the line ministries to the system and a more regular dialogue with all stakeholders, including line ministries and M&E RCs.

Greater alignment between donor reporting requirements and PRS monitoring would help strengthen the system by facilitating joint reporting to donors and the PRS M&E unit by line ministries. This has already been initiated given that the World Bank and the Inter-American Development ment Bank are working closely together on M&E issues and in supporting the Bureau of Statistics.

Finally, the government has not revised its framework since the Poverty Reduction Strategy Paper in 2001, and an updated program would encourage greater buy-in by line agencies.

Capacity

The government is currently receiving assistance in its endeavor to improve the capacity of the PRS M&E unit and enhance its relatively weak capacity for data collection. Improvements will, however, require substantial and dedicated efforts. A new household income and expenditure survey was launched in September 2005; this will be important in updating poverty analysis. It is expected to be completed in 2006. In addition, a map of the access to basic services and a data and analysis drilldown in a prototype line ministry are being carried out; both of these initiatives are intended to link with budgeting and M&E exercises.

The PRS M&E unit plans to provide technical support and capacity-building programs to key ministries and PRS-RCs. In addition, the implementation plan includes measures to strengthen the capacity of the Bureau of Statistics in key areas of survey design, collection, processing, and analysis, as well as measures to provide information technology equipment for data management and dissemination. Given that the Bureau of Statistics presides over the national statistics system, it should play a leading role in capacity-building activities in coordination with the PRS M&E unit.

Participation

While there has been an open, participatory process with civil society, the outcome has been a weaker role for the national PRS steering committee. The committee is currently preparing a work program to guide its operations, and it hopes to assume a much more active role in promoting the participation of CSOs in future PRS-PRs. It is recommended that the work program include greater national and regional consultations on the PRS-PRs and on the capacity-building activities to enable CSOs to participate more effectively in M&E tasks, for example, through the PRS-RCs. Useful budget and expenditure tracking information should be made available to such bodies for priority programs. There is also a need for clearer relationships among committees.

Dissemination

The government, through the PRS M&E unit, is planning to enhance communications and strengthen its outreach program. It is important that communications be regular, open, and candid and be perceived as such and that they provide a basis for addressing and correcting weaknesses in the system. At the moment, communications and discussions seem to be restricted to the yearly PRS PR exercise.

4

Honduras

ACRONYMS AND ABBREVIATIONS

CCERP   Consejo Consultivo de la ERP (ERP consultative council)

ERP   Estrategia de Reducción de la Pobreza (poverty reduction strategy)

GTI   Grupo Técnico Inter-Institucional (interinstitutional technical group)

INE   Instituto Nacional de Estadística (National Institute of Statistics)

SEDP   Secretaría de Estado del Despacho Presidencial (State Secretariat of the Office of the Presidency)

SIAFI   Sistema Integrado de Administracion Financiera (integrated financial and administrative system)

SIERP   Sistema de Indicadores de la Estrategia de Reducción de la Pobreza (system of indicators for the poverty reduction strategy)

SISPU   Sistema de Inversiones del Sector Público (public sector investment system)

UNAT   Unidad de Apoyo Tecnico (technical support unit)

UPEG   Unidad de Planificación y Evaluación de la Gestión (unit of management planning and evaluation)

This chapter is based on a background country report by Margarita Diaz (2004) and inputs by Dante Mossi and Florencia Castro-Leal. The study was undertaken in the second half of 2004 and has been partially updated to reflect conditions in the summer of 2005. Substantial changes may have occurred that are not reflected in this chapter, and readers are encouraged to seek additional information if they wish to focus on the system of this particular country.

History and Context

The Estrategia de Reducción de la Pobreza (ERP), the Honduran poverty reduction strategy (PRS), emerged in response to the need for a long-term planning framework that would make it possible to reduce, in a sustainable fashion, the social vulnerability affecting Honduras throughout its history and compounded by Hurricane Mitch in October 1998. The National Reconstruction and Transformation Master Plan, which was presented by the government and Honduran civil society at the meeting of the Advisory Group for the Reconstruction of Central America, proposed the development of such a strategy.

Two milestones marked the preparation of the ERP: the declaration of eligibility by the Board of the International Monetary Fund and the Board of Executive Directors of the World Bank inviting Hondurans to partake in the benefits of the Heavily Indebted Poor Countries (HIPC) Initiative in December 1999 and the country's signature of the United Nations Millennium Declaration in February 2000. The ERP emerges not only as evidence of an awareness of the problems generated by poverty, but also as a means to comply with agreements reached with international development agencies.

The ERP was approved by the government in August 2001 and endorsed by the executive boards of the International Monetary Fund and the World Bank two months later. Implementation of the EPR coincided with the formation of a new government, which revised the strategy in January 2002.

The first ERP progress report was presented in February 2004. The report incorporated a recalibration of the ERP goals to ensure their consistency with medium-term forecasts of the macroeconomic and fiscal situation.

The PRS Law was modified in 2004 (through decree 76-2004); one important advance was the inclusion of more civil society representatives and the Consejo Consultivo de la ERP (ERP consultative council, CCERP).

In March 2005, Honduras reached its HIPC completion point, resulting in an influx of relief funds that was greater than the influx of interim relief funds provided until then.

Description of the PRS Monitoring System

Origins of the system

The ERP established the need for a viable and efficient scheme to facilitate adequate follow-up and monitoring of ERP implementation and of global and intermediate indicators. Accordingly, the Secretaría de Estado del Despacho Presidencial (State Secretariat of the Office of the Presidency, SEDP), which is in charge of the coordination of the ERP, defined the institutional framework for monitoring and evaluation (M&E). This was accomplished in consultation with the CCERP.

Main institutional actors

The *Secretaría de Estado del Despacho Presidencial* is directly involved in the development of the Sistema de Indicadores de la Estrategia de Reducción de la Pobreza (system of indicators for the poverty reduction strategy, SIERP), the information system for tracking ERP progress. Among other functions, the SEDP is also responsible for coordination of the Council of Ministers and for leading the working sessions of the Economic Cabinet and other sectoral and multisectoral cabinets on behalf of the president of the Republic in the president's absence.

In addition to the SEDP, three intergovernmental institutional structures are in charge of coordinating and guiding sectoral agencies in the implementation and monitoring of ERP activities, as follows.

1. The *Gabinete Social* (Social Cabinet) provides institutional leadership for the ERP process. It is the decision-making body for all matters regarding the ERP and is presided over and coordinated by the president of the Republic. Members of the Social Cabinet include the Secretariats of Education; Health; Labor and Social Security; Agriculture and Livestock; and Culture, Arts, and Sports; the Directorates of the Honduran Social Investment Fund; the National Agrarian Institute; and the Technical Secretariat of International Cooperation. When necessary, the cabinet includes representatives from other agencies that play a role in the monitoring of ERP implementation, especially the Secretariat of Finance. The Instituto Nacional de Estadística (National Institute of Statistics, INE) and the Central Bank of Honduras may be requested to join meetings that deal with M&E for the ERP. The Social Cabinet is responsible for establishing guidelines and setting priorities for ERP

actions, coordinating the initiatives of the institutions responsible for ERP implementation, defining the eligibility criteria for HIPC projects, and discussing relevant M&E.

2. The *Consejo Consultivo de la ERP* was created by decree in 2002; it is presided over by the president of the Republic. The council supports the Social Cabinet, acting as an advisory body. Its members include the coordinator of the Social Cabinet, the Secretariats of Finance, Education, Health, Natural Resources and the Environment, and Interior and Justice, as well as a representative of the Association of Municipalities of Honduras. The CCERP includes representatives of key civil society organizations (CSOs), including manufacturing and agricultural worker unions, women's organizations, local community organizations, indigenous group organizations, entrepreneur organizations, and nongovernmental organizations. Two representatives of the donor community participate as observers. The CCERP is mainly responsible for advising the Social Cabinet on the eligibility and prioritization of ERP interventions, discussing M&E issues and ERP progress reports, and supporting the implementation and monitoring of the ERP at the local level. Two important recent activities of the CCERP are an assessment of the progress of the implementation of a tracking mechanism for HIPC resources and the design and implementation (together with the SEDP) of the SIERP.

3. The *Instituto Nacional de Estadística* is a small, highly efficient entity that is mandated by law to carry out surveys. In order to maintain control of its size, the INE contracts out most of its survey work. It is also important to note that line ministries, such as health and education, can and should contract the INE to carry out these surveys since the INE is well positioned to incorporate these requests into its own survey work. Thus, resources to finance the surveys necessary for identifying new indicators could come from the same relief funds.

The *Grupo Técnico Inter-Institucional* (interinstitutional technical group, GTI) provides technical support to the Social Cabinet. Members include deputy ministers and the management planning and evaluation directors of the Secretariats of the Office of the Presidency; Finance; Interior and Justice; Education; Health; Public Works, Transport and Housing; and Agriculture and Livestock. Representatives of the Honduran Social Investment Fund, the Program of Family Allowances, the Women's National Institute, and the INE are also members. The GTI plays a key role in articulating programs and interventions across sectors within the ERP framework.

The system of indicators

The initial 2002 design proposal for the SIERP was comprehensive, but ambitious in terms of financial, technological, and human resource requirements. It did not explicitly include a set of indicators to track financial and physical advances in ERP projects and programs, since this was delegated to the national system of management, another monitoring system designed at the time. The national system of management was never implemented, however, and a new proposal was elaborated for the SIERP that involved easier requirements in terms of technology and human resources. The implementation of the new proposal is to be supported by a five-year master plan.

The SIERP is a second-tier monitoring system; it builds on existing management information systems and monitoring systems in line ministries (secretariats) and program implementation units. SIERP objectives include the following:

- coordinating the collection of information regarding physical and financial indicators of the progress achieved in ERP projects and programs and intermediate and impact indicators; hence, the SIERP is conceived as a management tool to inform decision making and the allocation of resources that works in coordination with the Sistema Integrado de Administracion Financiera (integrated financial and administrative system, SIAFI) and the Sistema de Inversiones del Sector Público (public sector investment system, SISPU)
- improving the operational and institutional capacity of the agencies involved in ERP implementation
- strengthening the capacity of institutions to manage their monitoring subsystems
- providing a consultation and dissemination mechanism for the results of ERP implementation

In the original SIERP design, the day-to-day operation of the SIERP was the responsibility of the SIERP central unit within the Unidad de Apoyo Tecnico (technical support unit, UNAT) of the SEDP. In practice, however, this central unit relies on the work carried out by the UNAT sectoral specialists, and the UNAT as a whole is, in fact, in charge of the

SIERP operation. Its mandate includes the coordination of the system; updating the database and maintaining the reliability of information; the provision of technical support to sectoral agencies in the production of primary information in coordination with and following the standards determined by the INE; the analysis and preparation of ERP progress reports; the provision of technical support to the Economic, Social, and Sectoral Cabinets in the formulation, monitoring, and analysis of economic and social policies; and the dissemination of SIERP data, including the administration of the SIERP Web page.

The SIERP obtains its information from three sources: (1) information relating to macroeconomic variables, internal and external financing, public revenues and expenditures, and financial and physical indicators of progress in programs financed though the Poverty Reduction Fund is collected through the SIAFI and is delivered by the Central Bank, the Secretariat of Finance, and the Technical Secretariat of Cooperation; (2) sectoral information on the outputs and outcomes of the implementation of ERP activities is provided by line secretariats, as well as deconcentrated and decentralized structures; and (3) information derived from household surveys and population censuses is provided by the INE.

The SIERP design calls for a liaison person in each member agency. In the sectoral ministries, these are usually the directors of each of the Unidad de Planificación y Evaluación de la Gestión (unit of management planning and evaluation, UPEG). The SIERP design also includes plans to sign interinstitutional agreements between the SEDP and secretariats and other deconcentrated or decentralized agencies that implement ERP programs.

Overall Status

In March 2004, the SIERP was presented on the official Web site of the system (www.sierp.hn). An intensive review of the current prototype and the consolidation of links with the national information network is under way to establish a solid foundation for the SIERP. The main result of this process is the design of the master plan for SIERP implementation, which is conceived as a tool for determining the strategic guidelines, main theories, and specific activities required for SIERP implementation.

It might be said that the SIERP is in a pilot implementation stage. There are already clear indications of a need to strengthen information flows, however. Improving interinstitutional coordination will, in turn, lead to enhanced information flows.

Key Topics

Leadership of the system

The government's ownership of the process and its commitment to the full implementation of the SIERP were reaffirmed during the consultative group meeting held in June 2004. The government commitment is the result of the stance taken by the institutional structure in charge of coordinating ERP implementation (the Social Cabinet, the CCERP, and the GTI) and monitoring (the UNAT). This structure favors cross-sectoral work and interinstitutional coordination and supports a technical approach to the design, implementation, and evaluation of ERP programs and projects.

Despite the strength of the ownership of the system at the center, the ownership is weak among intermediate-level technical personnel in the line ministries and sectoral agencies in charge of the execution of the ERP. This represents a threat to the full implementation of the SIERP.

Legal framework and procedures

The legal framework for the implementation of the SIERP is not firmly established. The implementation plan calls for the stipulation of interinstitutional agreements between the SEDP and the line ministries and other governmental institutions in charge of ERP implementation. These agreements are expected to include a binding definition of the type of information that should be provided to the SIERP, along with the frequency of provision. Moreover, they should also specify the responsibilities of the UNAT in feeding information back to sectoral agencies. While the agreements have not yet been stipulated, they are under discussion.

The INE, the Central Bank, the Secretariat of Finance, and other members of the GTI are in the process of discussing issues related to the content, format, and frequency of the periodic information exchanges required by the SIERP. This will be the first step toward the establishment of a more institutionalized link among the SIERP, the SIAFI, and the SISPU and will strengthen the link between the monitoring of results and the feedback into the budgetary process.

Coordination

The definition of the roles and functions of the central government agencies participating in the SIERP is relatively clear. There are no indications that key institutions have been excluded from the SIERP institutional arrangements, with the important exception of local governments. Discussions regarding the role of local governments as a source of primary information for the SIERP are still at an initial stage. Addressing this issue will be important given the interest of donors in disaggregating ERP indicators at departmental and municipal levels.

In practice, the fulfillment of stated roles and functions has not been completely satisfactory. Although the UNAT, the INE, and the Secretariat of Finance have been most successful in fulfilling their functions, there is room for improvement. The UNAT and the Secretariat of Finance, in particular, are working on the full integration of the SIERP with the SIAFI and the SISPU based on a common technological platform.

The statistical departments of the line ministries have not demonstrated a full understanding of the overall purpose and function of the SIERP. The work plans developed by line ministries do not include the interinstitutional coordination activities required by the SIERP as priority tasks. Moreover, ministries have not budgeted for their SIERP responsibilities. Improvements in the quality and use of administrative data at sectoral levels are critical for ensuring the monitoring of intermediate indicators.

In terms of processes, the UNAT is preparing a five-year master plan for the SIERP, with technical assistance from the U.K. Department for International Development. The objective of the master plan is to define the steps required to achieve the technical and institutional consolidation of the SIERP. The plan should contain a better definition of procedures and data collection and processing methodologies by the INE and an estimation of resource requirements.

Capacity

Given the second-tier nature of the system, the SIERP relies on information and data produced by other agencies. The success of the system therefore depends on the capacity within agencies. The weak M&E capacity within line ministries and sectoral institutions is a critical problem that threatens the viability of the overall system.

The recent history of the implementation of sectoral M&E systems helps elucidate the challenges being faced in the full implementation of the SIERP. After the elimination of the Secretariat of Planning, the UPEGs were created in each secretariat to plan and evaluate programs and activities. It is widely recognized that most UPEGs never fulfilled their mandate. Although the situation is slowly changing in some secretariats, the UPEGs generally rely on low-paid, long-tenured staff with insufficient technical qualifications, few training opportunities, and limited or no technological support. Quality control processes on information and data are rare. The supervision of local data collection by the central level is usually very weak. Even within secretariats, some project- or program-implementation units manage their own information systems, with no or weak links to the systems administered by the UPEGs. As a result, multiple monitoring systems often exist within a single institution.

Similarly, the reliability of the information produced by the SIAFI and the SISPU depends on the quality of information input by public sector agencies. Quality control mechanisms are currently weak, and most administrative registers follow protocols that have never been submitted to rigorous evaluation. Another important issue relates to the poor analytical capacity of public sector agencies in using the information produced by their M&E systems. This is reflected in the lack or sporadic production of periodic reports based on the information produced by the M&E subsystems of the secretariats.

The recently created INE is gradually assuming a leadership role in the national statistical system. It is responsible for providing technical assistance to sectoral agencies so as to improve the quality of administrative records, promote methodological standardization, and, in data collection activities, avoid the duplication of efforts and the wasting of resources.

Participation

The majority of the population and civil society representative bodies are unaware of the existence of the system. A key problem is the lack of technical capabilities among CSOs. The efforts to be made by the government and by development partners to increase the potential of civil society in the development of the SIERP will be laid out in the master plan currently under development.

The government is taking steps to institutionalize six existing sectoral working groups to ensure civil society participation in the M&E of PRS implementation. Each working group is a tripartite structure composed of representatives of the donor community, the government, and CSOs. The main function of these groups is to ensure a participatory approach in the design, implementation, and monitoring of sectoral programs. They should guarantee the institutionalization, on a permanent basis, of the national dialogue that is currently taking place in the context of the consultative group.

The vice-ministry in charge of the relevant sector will coordinate the work of each sectoral working group. Representatives of other governmental agencies will be appointed by the GTI. The UNAT will support the six working groups. CSO members will be selected and supported by the CCERP and a national civil society forum.

In addition, CSOs have independently mobilized to ensure their own participation. For instance, as a result of the increased capacity of CSOs, participatory M&E in four projects in education and health was due to start in late 2004. This will involve CSOs and the government and will use citizen report cards.

Decentralization

One of the commitments assumed by the government with respect to development partners is the disaggregation of information at the departmental and regional levels. Although compliance with this commitment seems rather complex, the authorities have expressed their interest in achieving it using available technical instruments. To this end, the INE and the SIERP central unit are conducting an exhaustive review of the Living Standards Measurement Survey, which will make it possible to disaggregate indicators at the departmental level.

Obtaining disaggregated information at the municipal level is, for the time being, not viable because of limitations in the instruments currently used to measure living conditions in municipalities.

Products and dissemination

The dissemination plan for information on ERP progress includes a Web page, ERP progress reports, analysis produced by the UNAT based on the information contained in the SIERP, and pamphlets or straightforward publications distributed to a wider audience.

The SIERP Web page has been a recent achievement and has the potential to become an important element of dissemination for SIERP information. The content of the Web page is not yet complete, and information about progress in ERP implementation at the departmental and municipal levels is limited. This is not surprising given the outstanding issues regarding the production of primary information at both the central and local government levels that will need to be tackled in order to achieve a fully functioning SIERP. In the medium term, the SIERP Web page is expected to include quarterly information on the financial and physical implementation of ERP programs and projects.

To date, progress reports have been carried out on an ad hoc basis and entirely by the UNAT. They are therefore not, strictly speaking, the outcome of the SIERP system, which is not yet fully functional. Until now, the government has considered the consultative group meetings the most appropriate forum for the dissemination and discussion of ERP progress reports with the donor community and CSOs.

Finance and donor support

The Poverty Reduction Fund mandates the allocation of resources for M&E activities and pro-poor public expenditure tracking. In practice, however, no funds have yet been allocated to the SIERP from this fund.

The government has preliminarily estimated that the full operation of the SIERP would require an additional $800,000 over the next four years. The World Bank, the Swedish government, and the U.K. Department for International Development are important cofinanciers of the recently approved PRS technical assistance credit. Through this credit, the World Bank and the U.K. Department for International Development are providing technical assistance to the UNAT and the UPEGs to improve coordination and the production of sectorwide data and to strengthen the monitoring of PRS implementation. This credit has also involved the allocation of resources to strengthen the responsibilities of the INE, in particular to ensure the quality of administrative records. The Inter-American Development Bank financed the preparation of the first SIERP proposal. The early stages of the implementation of the revised SIERP proposal prepared by the UNAT have been financed through internal resources.

Lessons

The government, civil society, and partner agencies have identified a number of shortcomings in the implementation of the SIERP. Although the system appears coherent on paper, the actual system fails to address severe capacity constraints and the issue of the weak ownership among line ministries. Planning and evaluation units in the ministries have limited capacity. Moreover, there is a problem of fragmentation across agencies. Monitoring is generally not seen as a priority within the administrative culture.

The development of a national M&E system implies an interinstitutional pooling process through which there are clearly defined roles and responsibilities, agreement on technical and computer requirements, and a will to participate and collaborate. Partnerships and institutional agreements strengthen institutional capacities and lead to the identification of shared purposes and the achievement of specific goals. Currently, there are no information flows throughout government. There is a strong need for M&E activities to become a priority and for clear channels to be established for information to flow, particularly between the UNAT and the other agencies.

The complex structure for monitoring and evaluating multisectoral programs and projects relying on different financing sources and responding to the diverse requirements of development partners presents a fundamental challenge. Although there is familiarity with the implementation aspects of projects and the various monitoring formats of the development partners, the country lacks experience in the execution of a portfolio of projects involving a sectoral approach and a national monitoring system.

The lack of an institutionalized culture of continuous M&E makes it necessary for the coordination unit of the SIERP to redefine indicators, identify reliable sources of information, and verify the periodicity of information flows so as to improve the quality and the relevance of institutional records and national statistics. This means there must be an expanded vision of the importance of up-to-date and good-quality data for decision making.

Moreover, agencies lack the analytical ability to use information, though the INE is now starting to assist sectoral agencies in improving the quality of their records. Given that the INE is a relatively new institution, its capacity will need to be strengthened in order for it to fulfill this role. The development and implementation of a national statistical plan, in coordination with all the agencies of the national statistical system, but first and foremost the secretariats, should be a medium-term objective of the institution.

There are major human resource constraints and no real quality control. Tackling the weaknesses of the sectoral subsystems and taking steps to integrate and rationalize these subsystems are of paramount importance for the success of the SIERP. Such consolidation is required before subsystem outputs can be fed into the SIERP.

5

The Kyrgyz Republic

ACRONYMS AND ABBREVIATIONS

CDF   Comprehensive Development Framework
MLSP Ministry of Labor and Social Protection
NSC   National Statistics Committee
PMS   poverty monitoring system

History and Context

In Soviet times, living standards were measured according to the supply of food and basic consumer goods, as well as household budgets. The relevant indicators were maintained following independence, but failed to result in purposeful action aimed at poverty reduction. It was only in 1996 that the National Statistics Committee (NSC), supported by the World Bank, conducted the first poverty status survey that allowed the rigorous analysis of poverty and its determinants.

This chapter is based on a background country report by Elvira Ilibeozova (2004) and on inputs by Ekaterine Vashakmadze. The study was undertaken in the second half of 2004 and has been partially updated to reflect conditions in the summer of 2005. Substantial changes may have occurred that are not reflected in this chapter, and readers are encouraged to seek additional information if they wish to focus on the system of this particular country. The study is the first step in a broader assessment of the poverty reduction strategy monitoring system undertaken by the government.

The national Poverty Reduction Strategy Paper was adopted in September 2002, together with the Comprehensive Development Framework (CDF) for the country until 2010. Prior to the adoption of the CDF and the poverty reduction strategy (PRS), there was participation by a broad audience, including government structures, civil society, nongovernmental organizations (NGOs), and international organizations.

Description of the PRS Monitoring System

Origins of the system

The Poverty Reduction Strategy Paper is a component of the first stage of the CDF. They are nonetheless separate documents and involve different monitoring frameworks, neither of which is operational. Following the approval of the CDF, a matrix of activities was developed to bring the efforts of all stakeholders in the poverty reduction process together to form the foundation of the poverty monitoring system (PMS).

Main institutional actors

The CDF monitoring and evaluation (M&E) system includes the following institutions and basic elements.

The *national CDF council* is chaired by the president, who determines membership. It includes leaders and individual members of Parliament. While Parliament is not directly involved in developing the PRS, it participates in strategy formulation and implementation by reviewing government reports, approving or rejecting government programs, and adopting the relevant legislation. The CDF council formulates strategies and policies; it relies on data provided by the NSC that are summarized and prepared by the CDF secretariat.

The *CDF secretariat* is part of the Economic Policy Department in the Office of the President. The department is responsible for providing data and analytical support to the president, ensuring presidential supervision over economic activities, and carrying out human resource policies within the executive branch. Moreover, the department is required to monitor, analyze, and evaluate the CDF and the PRS with respect to coordinating the implementation of the resolutions of the national CDF council; formulating policy proposals; coordinating the activities of CDF and PRS stakeholders;

developing CDF and PRS action plans; integrating national, regional, and sectoral CDF and PRS programs; developing information systems; assisting in the development of regional and sectoral programs; analyzing the implementation process; developing indicators; ensuring information dissemination; and encouraging open dialogue with civil society.

In addition, the department is to coordinate the implementation of the CDF through the CDF secretariat, the functions of which are to include providing information to the council, preparing annual progress reports, disseminating information, coordinating all CDF processes and the actions of stakeholders, evaluating progress and resource capacity, recommending changes in the PRS, and forecasting development prospects.

Overall Status

Overall, the system is weak. It is highly centralized within the presidency, and very few resources have been allocated for implementation and operations. In spite of its extensive power, the secretariat does not exercise sufficient coordination and control of the PMS. The secretariat is also subject to time constraints because of its other commitments to the president. In principle, very few data are collected by the secretariat; collection is limited to data provided by the NSC and line agencies. However, in practice, only 25 percent of the required data are routinely provided, and there are signs that NSC figures are not considered entirely credible, and there are fears that internal political influence might lead the NSC to underestimate the incidence of poverty.

Key Topics

Leadership

Oversight of the system is the responsibility of the national CDF council, which is led by the president. The president determines the membership of the council, which includes members of Parliament.

Coordination

Institutionalization is important for the successful operation of the PMS. Institutionalization will require clearly defined responsibilities among all participants and a clear distribution of roles in the implementation of the matrix of action within the CDF and the PRS. Currently, institutionalization is extremely weak, and the PMS is highly fragmented. The responsibilities of the individual actors are not clearly defined. The most successful work is being done at the NSC, the Ministry of Health, and the Ministry of Labor and Social Protection (MLSP).

There are a number of parallel schemes involved in the PMS, but there is poor interaction among them. Line ministries are not well informed about available methodologies, indicators, and the roles and responsibilities of other stakeholders. The only exception is the NSC; NSC indicators are used by all participants in the PMS.

There is no established system of coordination, hierarchy of relationships, or horizontal interactions for data exchanges. Also, the administrative leverage is inadequate for improving executive discipline among managers in individual ministries, agencies, and territorial structures. This has resulted in nonexecution or low quality in the execution of M&E responsibilities.

One of the main problems is the lack of a properly structured legal and regulatory framework for the PMS. Even at the top level, contradictions result in poor-quality, unsustainable management. Another vital issue is the lack of a permanent institution within the government that is responsible for system implementation and coordination. Despite the fact that the CDF secretariat is located in the Economic Policy Department of the Office of the President, it does not have adequate status and lacks the competence and capacity to provide effective M&E so as to meet information needs within the government.

Capacity

No resources have been specifically assigned for the M&E system. Although some technical capacity has already been built at the central and regional levels, it requires updating. Local structures need technical PMS capacity. The most important problem relates to creating and strengthening human capacity. Currently, there are large turnovers and transfers among staff, and new staff require extensive training. The problem is particularly acute in the local structures of the MLSP and NSC. At all levels, however, specialist knowledge on M&E should be increased.

Participation

Parliament holds open hearings on the implementation of projects and the national budget, and representatives of civil society and the media attend these hearings. Although public expenditure is discussed at the hearings, poverty reduction indicators are not, and monitoring information is not used.

Similarly, there is no institutionalized involvement among NGOs. Although some NGOs have become specialized in social research, they only become involved in the formal PMS system if donors and private sources bring them in. There are also problems in poverty measurement in the NGO sector. These include a lack of professional skills among NGOs, unsystematic research, and the use of small samples only. NGOs generally produce poverty indicators that are much less favorable than the official indicators and are therefore not used by government agencies in decision making. There is a need to build capacity, support activities, and promote transparency in order for NGOs to play a more significant role in poverty monitoring.

Civil society is fairly passive, and the PMS has no public profile. Civil society involvement is mainly limited to participation in donor projects. There was no meaningful dialogue with government bodies during the definition of the system for monitoring the implementation of the PRS. In fact, the involvement of civil society has diminished from the levels attained during the development of the CDF.

There is no civil society involvement in the publication of PMS information for the general public. Despite public hearings, the public is unable to influence or change the documents being presented. Nor do the media fully report on the implementation, outcomes, or specific activities of the PRS.

Decentralization

There is no involvement of subnational government entities in the CDF and PRS monitoring system and no reliable regional disaggregation of statistics. Regional data depend on "social passports" prepared by the MLSP for the purposes of distributing benefits locally.

Indicators and data sources

In practice, the NSC is the main source of data. The NSC receives quarterly tables from the secretariat that contain lists of the indicators to be supplied. The secretariat compiles these data into reports to the national council, as well as a periodical CDF bulletin. Some general information is also placed on a Web site. The central NSC office does not conduct research, but compiles statistics from its regional offices. In practice, NSC figures are not of much use among line agencies.

In addition, there is a lack of trust in the figures provided by the NSC, which are considered underestimates. This mistrust generally stems from the fact that, although the NSC makes use of international methodologies, it is a government agency and is under the influence of some political actors.

The role of the line agencies is not clearly defined, and there is no effective supervision or horizontal communication. The capacity of the line agencies in M&E is low, and they usually provide only general statistics. For example, the Ministry of Health provides information on the number of beds in the public health services system; the Ministry of Education supplies data on the number of students; the Social Fund provides information on pensions; and the Ministry of Labor and Social Protection furnishes data on benefits. These entities do not, however, offer information on indicators such as access to education and public health services or poverty-related indicators that require additional calculations, research, and data from other sectors. Moreover, they are only able to supply data on 25 percent of the required indicators (although they are slightly more successful in health and social protection), and some data, for instance, the incidence of poverty among children, are neglected altogether.

The scope of the activities implemented through the PMS is not adequate. This is mainly caused by the fact that the matrix lacks clear indicators on resources, productivity, the efficiency and impact of activities, and the intermediate results of activities. Consequently, stakeholders do not understand their responsibilities, and the CDF and PRS secretariat is unable to coordinate and monitor poverty reduction activities.

Dissemination

No single agency coordinates the distribution of PMS information. There is no complete or systematic strategy for the distribution and use of information and no targeted information flows from the sources of information to specific groups of users.

Link to the policy process

There is no particular link to the budget process or the policy-making process.

Donor alignment

International organizations and donors play an important role in the development, operations, and sustainability of the PMS, which has been created largely as a result of their technical and methodological assistance. There is, however, no coordination of donor efforts in poverty monitoring.

The Ministry of Finance tried to coordinate donor assistance through the creation of a database, but this was rendered meaningless because of irregular technical support. The United Nations Development Program also tried to create a map of donor assistance through the establishment of a Web-portal listing all its projects. Unfortunately, since termination of the project, the map has not been updated.

The donor community, together with the government, has undertaken the next step by creating a database on donor assistance and by improving coordination. A new structure has been established that includes the vice prime minister, a representative of the Ministry of Finance, and the heads of all donor organizations. The new structure highlights strategic issues in the development of uniform approaches to coordination. In addition, a working group on coordination has been created that includes representatives of donor organizations and the government. The working group meets once a month.

Finance and donor support

There is no dedicated funding of the PMS in the budget except for the methodology of the NSC. No budget allocations are provided for the introduction and computerization of the MLSP data system. This adversely affects the quality of the data collected.

In October 2002, a consultative meeting of donors and international organizations (for which the PRS became a priority document in the development of projects) approved a draft strategy stating that $700 million would be provided for the implementation of the CDF and PRS.

Lessons

A number of positive features indicate the potential of the CDF and PRS. There has been a clear demonstration of political will by the government. Financing for the CDF and PRS is being provided by international organizations, and there is a willingness among these organizations, as well as the donor community, to harmonize and coordinate actions and resources. Moreover, international organizations and donors are already providing technical assistance. Some measurement of poverty indicators at the regional and national levels is being carried out by the NSC. There are also indications of positive experiences in the measurement of poverty and the development of parameters at the local level using techniques of the United Nations Development Program, the MLSP, and NGOs.

In terms of system weakness and the lessons learned, there are significant signs of a need for a comprehensive system of controls to support M&E among all government programs and projects. Overall, there is a need to instill a culture of M&E at all levels, as well as to improve technical skills and offer ongoing M&E training programs. In order to develop a system of indicators for the PMS, a dialogue among all stakeholders is required. Additional options have been highlighted, as follows:

- developing qualitative indicators, backed by analysis, on the efficiency and impact of poverty reduction programs
- shifting away from the manual processing of the social passport database (MLSP) to computer processing in order to satisfy the need for reliable data at the grassroots
- developing a matrix of actions for the implementation of the CDF and PRS that provides indicators of productivity and the efficiency of impact for each ministry and participant
- developing a set of measures directed at strengthening the coordination of assistance by donors and international organizations with a view to avoiding overlap at the local and sectoral levels
- clarifying the institutionalization of the PMS through the establishment of a center of analysis
- strengthening the capacity for poverty data collection, the development of schemes, evaluation, and analysis.

- increasing NGO and civil society participation
- developing a mechanism to provide government agencies and other stakeholders with convenient and timely databases for analysis
- raising the status of the secretariat of the CDF and PRS
- strengthening the technical capacity of PMS participants, particularly at the grassroots
- improving the reliability of the PMS in covering many aspects of poverty at all levels by developing methodologies and indicators for the grassroots and for line ministries and focusing on the collection of qualitative indicators that measure productivity, efficiency, and causality
- disseminating materials in the Kyrgyz and Uzbek languages in order to increase public participation
- expanding the list of poverty monitoring information that is freely accessible and increasing the distribution and use of this information among civil society and the general public
- uploading information on the Web

6

Malawi

History and Context

Serious efforts to address poverty in Malawi began in the mid-1990s and culminated in the Poverty Reduction Strategy Paper (PRSP) that was produced in 2002. The PRSP articulated policies likely to reduce poverty and emphasized the need to monitor and evaluate the implementation and achievement of the goals of the poverty reduction strategy (PRS). The existing plan for a coordinated PRS monitoring and evaluation (M&E) system has not been implemented, and many stakeholders are not aware of their roles.

This chapter is based on a background country report by Ephraim Chirwa (2004) and inputs by Antonio Nucifora. The study was undertaken in the second half of 2004 and has been partially updated to reflect conditions in the summer of 2005. Substantial changes may have occurred that are not reflected in this chapter, and readers are encouraged to seek additional information if they wish to focus on the system of this particular country.

Description of the PRS Monitoring System

Origins of the system

Although poverty strategies go back to 1994, there is no tradition of M&E in Malawi. Since that time, the government has produced three policy documents. It is apparent from these that M&E is still not accorded a high priority. Monitoring systems in the Policy Framework for Poverty Alleviation Program and Vision 2020 are poorly defined; this has resulted in disjointed systems that focus primarily on donor-funded projects.

While the third of these policy documents, the PRSP, considers M&E a key to the achievement of poverty reduction, the related M&E system has not been fully implemented. The PRSP contains a broad framework for M&E, including a set of indicators (focusing mainly on inputs). Although it highlights the need for an integrated system at the national, district, and local levels, the roles of the various institutions are not clearly laid out. An M&E master plan (MEMP) that elaborates on the M&E strategies of the PRS was completed in January 2004. However, the master plan has also not yet been implemented.

Main institutional actors

The institutional structure proposed in the MEMP contains layers of institutions through which monitoring data will flow. It envisages that data will flow down to local governments and civil society organizations. Although the MEMP defines the responsibilities of the various institutions, many are not yet aware of their roles.

The *Monitoring and Evaluation Division* (MED) of the Ministry of Economic Planning and Development is responsible for the implementation and overall coordination of the PRS M&E system. In 2003, it surveyed line ministries and regional governments on the existence of planning units and M&E facilities and developed the MEMP.

The *technical working committee* is supposed to consider technical reports by the MED and advise the committee of principal secretaries (chaired by the secretary to the president) and the cabinet. However, due to the lack of data, neither the technical working committee nor the committee of principal secretaries has been constituted. Consequently, the link to the policy process has not yet been established. Moreover, the activities of the PRS monitoring committee have also been negatively affected in that the committee is supposed to take recommendations from the technical working committee.

The *National Statistical Office* (NSO) is expected, through periodic surveys, to be the main provider of data on outcomes and impacts. The surveys include an annual Core Welfare Indicator Questionnaire Survey, as well as the Integrated Household Survey and the Demographic and Health Survey, which are to be conducted every five years. However, due to funding problems, it has not been possible for the NSO to conduct these surveys within the planned time intervals. For example, the second Integrated Household Survey was carried out seven years after the first one.

In terms of outcome and impact monitoring, the *district assemblies* are expected to manage a database on poverty.

Existing poverty monitoring systems

Existing M&E activities are disjointed, and there are limited information flows between the various actors. The following M&E activities that are under way are ad hoc and are mainly linked to donor projects:

Monitoring activities in selected line ministries. The institutional framework of M&E activities in most line ministries is weak, and only a few ministries have officially created operational M&E units. Furthermore, some of the ministries with M&E units lack a legal and administrative foundation for an M&E system and have failed to define the role of the units. The Ministry of Finance is the only example of a ministry that links its monitoring specifically to the PRS.

There is no systematic production of monitoring reports. Although some ministries indicate that they do produce reports, these are ad hoc and are mainly produced when specifically required by donors.

There is little or no exchange of information between ministries, and most M&E units do not send their reports to other ministries. MED fails to coordinate monitoring and lacks the political power and effective leadership to influence the ministries. Ministries are unaware of MED's formal leadership role, and there has been no flow of information from the line ministries to the MED. Consequently, some of the line ministries (the Department of Local Government, the Ministry of Agriculture, and the Ministry of Health) are developing M&E systems independently of the national framework.

In addition, there are substantial capacity constraints in the line ministries, and no staff have been assigned to monitoring activities. In some instances, these tasks are undertaken by planning officers as secondary functions. There are also no work plans for M&E units, and no separate budget has been allocated for monitoring activities. Finally, most units are poorly equipped with computers and vehicles.

Local authorities. Because of the financial constraints being experienced by district assemblies, similar and perhaps even greater problems exist among local authorities. Most district assemblies define monitoring as field visits funded by donors to donor-funded projects. Most district assemblies do not collect data to monitor key indicators of the PRS, and there is no information on pro-poor expenditures. In a few cases where data on PRS indicators have been collected, the process has been ad hoc, and the roles of the various stakeholders have been vaguely defined.

Many of the line ministries have not decentralized their activities and still operate through the central government system. Consequently, they may not feel obliged to comply with data requests from district assemblies. Moreover, data in the sectoral ministries may not be available; monitoring activities are seldom undertaken, and, even where monitoring does take place, it focuses on donor-funded programs. Few district assemblies have operational databanks.

However, the MED, in collaboration with the Ministry of Local Government, is now in the process of establishing M&E units in district assemblies. With funding from the United Nations Development Program, 40 M&E officers are being recruited to start work on the first of January 2006.

The *National Statistical Office.* The NSO is charged with collecting national data under the Statistics Act. Since the launch of the PRS, one Core Welfare Indicator Questionnaire Survey and two Integrated Household Surveys have been carried out. The NSO is, however, unable to provide district-level disaggregation. Moreover, due to resource problems, the survey program is behind schedule, and plans to develop a statistical master plan are in the pipeline.

Progress in M&E made by the NSO is restricted to a needs assessment funded by the U.K. Department for International Development. This has underlined that the process tends to be donor driven and largely dependent on the willingness of donors to fund the statistical master plan.

In addition, the NSO is responsible for the Malawi Socio-Economic Database, which is established at the level of the district assemblies; the NSO is therefore supposed to capture output indicators at the district level. The district assemblies are expected to send updated information to the NSO, which, in turn, should integrate the information from the districts and the line ministries into one database to be provided to the MED. Although members of district assemblies have been trained, they do not all have computers, and the system has not been institutionalized.

Research institutions and universities do not play any significant role in poverty monitoring.

The role of *civil society organizations* in the PRS M&E system is vague. Some of these organizations are carrying out monitoring activities (for instance, service delivery satisfaction surveys), but the coordination of activities is limited. Moreover, the results are typically not being communicated to local governments.

The role of *communities* in existing monitoring systems is not defined, and there is no indication that M&E activities are being undertaken. There is a meager flow of information between the village development committees and the area development committees, and no evidence that these committees meet. The committees do not have the capacity to produce monitoring reports, and most lack the financial resources even to purchase stationary. Finally, most of the committees are not aware of their roles in monitoring activities.

Overall Status

There is currently no systematic information collection on PRS implementation. Moreover, there are a number of problems with establishing the MEMP, including the following:

The MED is central to the system, but has been unable to offer help in establishing functional M&E units in line ministries because of a lack of resources.

There are serious questions regarding the ownership of the system or the PRS by the government. The entire PRS is largely donor dependent and donor driven.

There is also heavy donor dependency in the funding of M&E activities because such activities are seldom provided for in ministry budgets.

There are major capacity constraints within the central government and local governments, as well as within the institutions responsible for data collection.

Key Topics

Leadership of the system

Although policy documents assign the leadership role to the MED, more specifically the committee of principal secretaries, supported by a technical working committee (neither of which have been established), these committees are not operational. However, the MED has recently agreed with the United Nations Development Program, the European Union, the government of Norway, and the U.K. Department for International Development on the terms for a three-year program of support for the implementation of the PRS M&E master plan (for an initial $3.6 million), based on a basket funding arrangement. These funds will be used to strengthen sectoral and district M&E capacities and to enhance the ability of the Ministry of Economic Planning and Development to manage evaluations, reviews, and impact assessments and coordinate M&E activities nationwide. The M&E division of the Ministry of Economic Planning and Development will organize quarterly meetings of government officials, donors, and nonstate stakeholders to review progress and identify emerging issues and additional activities for funding.

The PRS and the PRS M&E system are subject to strong external influences. This results largely from the link between the access to Highly Indebted Poor Countries funds and the endorsement of the PRSP by international financial institutions and Parliament.

Coordination

In the improved political climate, the MED has become more proactive in its coordination role. In collaboration with the Ministry of Finance and the NSO, the MED M&E unit led in the development of a PRS M&E master plan through a process of consultation involving other government institutions, civil society, the donor community, the parliamentary budget and finance committee, and the principal secretaries. Whereas the development of an M&E master plan was initially suggested by donors, the government took full ownership of the process, wrote the final report, and has shown strong commitment to the achievement of the objectives. However, the MED is currently understaffed: there are several vacant positions that need to be filled urgently to ensure that the unit can effectively carry out its coordination and advisory role. Like other government agencies, the Ministry of Economic Planning and Development faces a challenge in attracting and retaining qualified, experienced staff because of the poor and deteriorating conditions of government service.

Capacity

Most institutions involved in poverty monitoring are short in capacity. This relates to a lack of quantity and quality in human resources, as well as leadership, management, and organizational skills. Most ministries and district assemblies do not have active, operational M&E units.

Participation

Participation has not been institutionalized. The few scattered activities are uncoordinated and have not been used by the government. Parliament has, however, made greater use of its budgetary powers since 2001 in connection with the PRS process in order to debate on and influence the content and have integrated the know-how of civil society actors in the process.

Decentralization

Substantial progress has been made in devolving funding and activity programming and planning to the districts. This is a major step toward decentralization.

Indicators

Data from district assemblies and sectoral ministries show that there is a lack of understanding of poverty monitoring indicators. Most institutions are unaware of the indicators falling within their jurisdiction and of the pro-poor expenditures and activities that should be monitored.

Links to the budget and the policy process

The most elaborate mechanism of the PRS M&E system relates to the monitoring of expenditure inputs and outputs, but particularly inputs. Monthly subventions to ministries are dependent on the provision of information on actual expenditures from the previous month. Although the compliance of most line ministries is good in terms of providing financial reports, these are not complete, and sanctions are usually waived because of political pressure. Moreover, there is no evidence that this information is used for budget formulation. There has also been no annual public expenditure review since the PRS was launched. The challenge lies in generating demand for information in a country where information and analysis are rarely used in decision making.

Finance and donor support and alignment

Donors indicate a willingness to support monitoring activities as part of the PRS implementation process. The United Nations Development Program and the United Nations Children's Fund actively fund the Malawi Socio-Economic Database with a view to developing a system to monitor the progress toward achievement of the Millennium Development Goals. Likewise, the Norwegian Agency for Development Cooperation is funding the Integrated Household Surveys for monitoring poverty outcomes. However, donors select the activities or districts for funding, and their varying agendas and financial packages result in a fragmented PRS M&E system and no pooling of resources. Some donors have agreed in principle to support the implementation of the PRS M&E system jointly.

Lessons

Two years after the launch of the PRS, the PRS M&E system in Malawi remains ad hoc and fragmented. While the institutional framework for poverty monitoring involves the identification of various actors, many institutions are unaware of the system. While the MED has been trying to coordinate the M&E agenda, it has not received the needed attention at higher levels so as to be able to make progress.

The PRS is not accorded a high priority and is viewed by many as donor driven. The options and updates being discussed include the following:

- Greater appreciation of the importance of M&E is needed in the cabinet. A new unit on policy design and monitoring was created in the Office of the President in early 2005 with somewhat overlapping responsibilities with the MED, but it has not been able to change the status quo.
- It is important to introduce a culture of results-based decision making. So long as decisions in the highest offices of government continue to be made in the traditional way, monitoring activities will remain a low political priority. In order for the PRS M&E system to be effective, data must be seen to be used by decision makers.
- A basket approach to the funding of poverty monitoring is critical to ensuring the development of a more integrated system. This has been undertaken recently, under United Nations Development Program leadership, in an attempt to coordinate donor support more effectively.

7

Mali

ACRONYMS AND ABBREVIATIONS

Afristat   Economic and Statistical Observatory for Sub-Saharan Africa
DNPD   National Development Planning Department
DNSI   National Statistics Department
ODHD   Observatory for Sustainable Human Development

History and Context

The government of Mali adopted its first national poverty reduction strategy (PRS) in 1998. The document provides a policy framework for guiding antipoverty measures in the country and links with sectoral policies and programs. The PRS process had to be revised when the Highly Indebted Poor Countries (HIPC) Initiative was launched, a prerequisite of which was the development of a Poverty Reduction Strategy Paper

This chapter is based on a background country report by Francesca Bastagli (2004b) and inputs by Virginie Briand and Quentin Wodon. The study was undertaken in the second half of 2004 and has been partially updated to reflect conditions in the summer of 2005. Substantial changes may have occurred that are not reflected in this chapter, and readers are encouraged to seek additional information if they wish to focus on the system of this particular country.

(PRSP). Consequently, an interim PRSP was proposed in July 2000, and a complete PRSP was finalized in May 2002.

The crossover between the PRS and the PRSP initially posed problems and caused confusion, particularly in the definition of the respective roles. Despite the overlap with the existing strategy, it is now generally agreed that the PRS falls within the PRSP, which therefore provides the overall framework.

Description of the PRS Monitoring System

Origins of the system

A monitoring and evaluation (M&E) system was developed by the PRSP coordination unit in the Ministry of Economy and Finance in March 2003. The document is a good attempt at taking stock of existing M&E activities and building them into a system. It identifies three components of government monitoring flows: the vertical dynamics (the flow of information between actors within a sector); the horizontal dynamics (information flows between sectoral administrations), and the role of civil society. Moreover, it distinguishes financial resource monitoring, program implementation monitoring, and impact monitoring.

Main institutional actors

The *PRSP coordination unit* is responsible for coordinating the PRS process, including M&E efforts and information dissemination. It is a "light" structure located in the Ministry of Economy and Finance. Its activities are supported by the technical secretariat in the National Planning Department. A reform is under way to increase the human capacities of the structure. A decree was expected by the end of 2005. The team was then to be constituted of a coordinator, an information and communications assistant, four senior analysts, and eight assistant analysts divided into four units: budget and macroeconomic policies, institutional development and the improvement of governance and participation, sustainable human development and reinforcement of basic social services, and basic infrastructure development and support for productive sectors.

The *policy committee* is also responsible for oversight and coordination of the process. It is presided over by the prime minister and includes nine ministers, seven civil society representatives, the Joint Committee of

Mali–Development Partners (presided over by the minister of economy and finance), and the steering committee (headed by the secretary general of the Ministry of Economy and Finance). Members of the steering committee include representatives of thematic groups (see below), the ministries, and the PRSP coordination unit. The committee represents the meeting point of all the various actors who receive and review the annual PRSP progress reports and helps to ensure the representation and participation of all stakeholders in the oversight and coordination process.

The *national technical committee*, headed by the secretary general of the Ministry of Economy and Finance, is organized into 13 PRSP *thematic groups* and nine *regional committees*. The thematic groups meet regularly, maintain attendance sheets, and help bring ministry officials and civil society together. They take stock of the progress of action plans for their respective thematic areas. They are supposed to prepare annual reports to help in drafting the annual PRSP progress reports. For various reasons, including lack of capacity, these reports have not been prepared annually. Since 2002, two annual reports have been prepared. The first one covers the year 2002, and the second one, which was delivered in August 2005, assesses the progress made between 2003 and 2004.

During the elaboration phase of the PRSP, 11 thematic groups were set up, and two were added at a later stage (mines, energy, and water, and gender and poverty). The gender and poverty thematic group grew out of an existing group on poverty, gender analysis, and monitoring and is now the thematic group on poverty, solidarity, and social protection. It is headed by the technical counselor of the Ministry of Social Development, Solidarity, and the Aged and prepared its first report on "Social Protection, Solidarity and Related Aspects" in July 2003.

According to the M&E plan, monitoring at the regional and local levels will be carried out by the nine regional committees of the national technical committee. However, due to human resource constraints in terms of both recruitment and qualifications, the regional committees are not yet operational.

The *National Development Planning Department* (DNPD) is housed in the Ministry of Planning and National Development and is responsible for publishing the annual PRSP progress report. The report is compiled from annual sectoral reports submitted by the thematic groups and dealing with progress in PRS implementation in each sector. More broadly, the DNPD is responsible for monitoring government projects, macroeconomic development, and donor coordination.

The *National Statistics Department* (DNSI) is also housed within the Ministry of Planning and National Development. It is the central body responsible for data production. In terms of poverty monitoring, it collects data through surveys and centralizes the information collected by line ministries. It also provides technical support to the statistical departments of the ministries.

A new statistical law approved by the government and submitted to the National Assembly redefines and strengthens the responsibilities of the DNSI, particularly the decentralized responsibilities. The law does not, however, address the issue of increased autonomy, even though the possibility of increasing the independence of the DNSI (in terms of financial autonomy) has been discussed. The DNSI therefore continues to operate as a department in the Ministry of Planning and National Development. A workshop was held in November 2005 to validate the DNSI master plan, which will be used to plan statistics production for the next five years and provides a diagnosis of the difficulties faced by the national statistical system.

PRS assessment is primarily the responsibility of the newly reinstated *Observatory for Sustainable Human Development* (ODHD). Drawing on information produced by the DNSI and the planning and statistics units in the line ministries, the observatory is responsible for the analysis of PRSP impact indicators. Moreover, it publishes and disseminates annual reports on national human development and progress in achieving the Millennium Development Goals.

The ODHD was first established in 1996 and operated until 2000, when its activities were suspended during the elaboration of the PRSP. It was reconstituted in September 2003, and its statute is currently being modified. The ODHD suffers from a lack of clear legal status. Its continued activity is not ensured partly because of a lack of external funding. The ODHD is currently situated in the Ministry of Social Development, Solidarity, and the Aged.

Planning and statistics units in each line ministry prepare data on the execution of projects and report on the implementation of programs.

Other institutions involved in monitoring activities and producing information that feeds into the PRSP M&E process include the *National Budget Department*, which monitors the implementation of the medium-term expenditure framework and the program budget; the *National Public Debt Department*, which monitors HIPC funds; and the *Finance and Audit Office*, which monitors the anticorruption program.

Overall Status

Mali's first PRSP progress report was completed in April 2004. It provides insight into the performance of the PRS monitoring system, including specific comments on the institutional challenges encountered. It highlights that the agencies in charge of monitoring and evaluating the implementation of the PRS had experienced delays in carrying out their responsibilities and had not fully embraced their roles.

Moreover, the PRSP progress report notes the following problems in respect of methods, tools, and indicators: the lack of clear baselines and targets, an inadequate national information system, a weak culture of results-based management, a strong focus on budget monitoring at the program level and a consequent lack of attention to process and intermediate indicators, and a lack of reliability of various information sources.

According to the second PRSP progress report, several institutional M&E mechanisms (orientation groups, thematic groups, regional committees, technical secretariat) are still not operational or functional. The report underlines the lack of capacity among various national, sectoral, and regional structures in charge of the M&E process. Though some progress has been made, the second report acknowledges that the difficulties in methods, tools, and indicators recorded in the first progress report are still apparent.

The analysis of Mali's monitoring system highlights the need for greater clarity in the allocation of roles among the various institutions and for a clearer separation between PRS implementation and monitoring responsibilities to ensure that there is no conflict of interest or institutional confusion.

Key Topics

Leadership of the system

Overall, the government focus on poverty reduction is high; this is borne out by the first poverty reduction plan in 1998, as well as the 2002 PRS. There are, however, indications that ownership is, at times, undermined by donor intervention. The elaboration of a PRSP in the context of an existing poverty reduction strategy is viewed by some as an external imposition contributing to institutional confusion and weakened ownership.

Furthermore, the demand for information derived from monitoring is weak. The first PRSP progress report was only completed in 2004 and was largely written by a consultant funded by the United Nations Development Program. This suggests that the process has not yet become institutionalized.

Coordination

The institutions with the key monitoring responsibilities are housed in three different ministries. The Ministry of Planning and National Development currently hosts the DNSI and the DNPD. The PRSP coordination unit operates out of the Ministry of Economy and Finance, even though its responsibilities (PRSP coordination and medium-term strategic planning) require close coordination with the DNPD and the DNSI. The ODHD is located in a third ministry, the Ministry of Social Development, Solidarity, and the Aged.

This institutional dispersion of actors is said to encourage participation by different bodies. This argument is used to justify the housing of the ODHD in the Ministry of Social Development, Solidarity, and the Aged, a ministry that is smaller and has weaker capacity than others. Supporters of this arrangement argue that the mandate of the ODHD covers topics (such as human and social development) addressed directly by the ministry. On the other hand, the location of the ODHD in the ministry implies it has weaker resources to draw upon and adds an additional actor to an already complex system.

The number of actors involved in the PRSP and M&E system is high, but this does not appear to be of particular concern to coordinators of the system; witness, for example, the recent increase in the number of thematic groups from 11 to 13.

Recent institutional developments also point toward institutional instability. The transformation of the Ministry of Planning and National Development and the transfer of the DNPD and the DNSI from one ministry to another, while not greatly affecting staff composition or day-to-day operations, does contribute to interinstitutional tension and confusion concerning the allocation of responsibilities.

There is uncertainty as to who is ultimately responsible for PRSP monitoring. While coordination formally lies with the PRSP coordination unit in the Ministry of Economy and Finance, staff at the Ministry of Planning and National Development argue that their ministry is the main body responsible for PRSP monitoring.

Participation

The poverty monitoring system is participatory and involves a number of institutions composed of different stakeholders. Participation is institutionalized through the thematic groups. The thematic group on poverty, solidarity, and social protection is particularly popular. It currently has approximately 30 participants per meeting and is divided into two working groups: poverty monitoring and analysis and social protection and solidarity monitoring (activities of the Ministry of Social Development, Solidarity, and the Aged).

There is a framework agreement between the state and civil society regarding the involvement of nongovernmental organizations (NGOs) in project implementation and monitoring. Although the framework is strong, direct NGO involvement in monitoring is fairly recent, and its role still unclear.

The frequency of and high attendance at thematic group meetings offer good examples of participation. However there are indications that these meetings could be reinforced by practices that ensure more representative participation and a greater focus on more substantial issues. Moreover, participation during the data collection and reporting phases could be strengthened by establishing a more detailed plan on NGO involvement in carrying out these activities and reporting information to central players.

The rural development sector participation process provides an illustration. Several groups worked on the preparation of the first rural development strategy component of the PRSP. Discussions within commissions and groups (agriculture, rural development, infrastructure, irrigation, fisheries, and cattle breeding) were followed by a plenary commission that approved the contributions of the subgroups. Various structures participated in the discussions: technical services of the departments, donors via the Joint Commission, and civil society (NGOs, the private sector, consumer groups, and artisans). Regions were integrated in the process as well, and all the structures participated at varying levels and degrees in the preparation of the report. There was a strong commitment to base the PRSP on a participatory process, which led to the creation of a consultation framework aimed at taking into account the different points of view. Nevertheless, the experience demonstrates the difficulties associated with such a process: (1) because of a lack of time to build ownership of the process, as well as insufficient technical knowledge, some civil society participants and regional advisors considered their interactions with national authorities limited; (2) because of insufficient human resources, there was significant turnover within some working groups; and (3) the participation of department technicians was not sufficient to ensure a process of ownership at more senior levels and throughout the department.

Decentralization

In 1992, the Malian government launched a decentralization process that contributed to the reshaping of the administrative landscape of the country into 703 communes, 49 cercles, 8 regions, and 1 district (Bamako). The transfer of responsibilities and resources from the central government to local communities has been slow, however.

The design of the PRSP monitoring system reflects this trend of decentralization and assigns PRSP monitoring responsibilities to decentralized bodies, more specifically, the nine regional committees of the PRSP technical committee.

The M&E plan sets out the desirable information flow between the local and central levels. However, the plan is hampered by local capacity constraints, and the decentralization process is therefore not yet functional. Moreover, the nine projected regional committees have not yet been established.

In the process of extending the M&E system to local institutions, it is advisable to build on existing decentralized bodies (as opposed to adding additional ones to the system) and to undertake a realistic assessment of capacity, which could be strengthened through targeted training and capacity building.

The decentralization process is not recent, but most of the progress has occurred during the last 15 years. Today, the process faces two main challenges: the decentralization of financial resources and the reinforcement of local capacity to use and manage these resources. From the point of view of the M&E system, decentralization highlights a third difficulty: the insufficient level of information at the regional and local levels. To assess and monitor the impact of the PRS, information on poverty and other indicators is needed at all levels of government. This knowledge would reinforce the decentralization process through a better understanding by local authorities of their population in terms of basic needs. In other words, there is a need for spatially disaggregated data as part of a broader geographic information system. Yet, in Mali today, as in many other countries, while different types of disaggregated data exist, they are scattered among departments, institutes, donors, NGOs, and so on. An integrated geographic information system would serve as a better monitoring and decision-making tool. Steps have been taken to contribute to such a geographic information system, including through the preparation of a poverty map for the country.

Indicators and data sources

There is no agreed single set of the indicators that need to be monitored, and this lack of clarity is exacerbated by the fact that donors sometimes put pressure for follow-up on additional indicators (see below).

Dissemination

The PRSP M&E plan assigns key responsibility for the dissemination of information to the PRSP coordination unit. This includes organizing the publication of monitoring documents and the dissemination of these documents to technical departments, the regions, development partners, and NGOs. Moreover, the coordination unit will design a strategy for information dissemination to the public (including radio, television, municipal meetings, and so on).

Despite ambitions in the M&E plan, reporting, dissemination and feedback remain weak. This is borne out by the low awareness about the annual PRSP progress report among key stakeholders in the monitoring system. Moreover, the limited degree of dissemination is out of proportion with the amount of data collection under way. Important survey information exists, but reporting is slow and incomplete. Monitoring activities undertaken regularly by line ministries and the DNSI yield relevant information on living conditions; yet, official reporting is delayed, and reports often do not build on existing information. Furthermore, notwithstanding the high quantity and frequency of meetings and workshops, information does not appear to be circulating.

The institutional framework does not facilitate the feedback of poverty monitoring information into policy-making and budgetary processes, which are not integrated. For example, the existing institutional rivalry and overlaps in responsibilities between the Ministry of Planning and National Development (responsible for the PRSP progress report) and the Ministry of Economy and Finance (housing the PRSP coordination unit and responsible for budget formulation) negatively affect the feedback of PRSP monitoring information.

Donor alignment

The M&E plan notes the influence of donors over the monitoring system. Although the prioritization of indicator selection is recognized in principle, there is pressure for the monitoring of a large number of indicators in order to ensure the completeness of monitoring information and satisfy donor requests for information. In particular, the plan proposes that a rather long list of indicators be maintained because certain donors, including the European Union, tie their budget aid to the performance of selected indicators. The argument is that selecting many indicators will limit the risk of losing large amounts of aid if a specific indicator does not meet the agreed target.

Each donor has its own procedures and preoccupations. In the context of M&E, this means expectations are not the same, for example, in terms of the indicators to be monitored. The resulting pressure on the PRSP unit can be strong, and donor requirements may also affect the evaluation process since, in some sectors, each donor is in charge of its own projects. For instance, in the rural sector, there are more than 70 projects, which makes it difficult for the authorities to have an effective global rural development strategy. The transaction costs of dealing with multiple donors are also high for the authorities. Work to increase the effectiveness of aid has started through efforts aimed at harmonization through consultative meetings on budget support.

Finance and donor support

Donors fund a great deal of the data collection and analysis and influence the shape of institutions. The United Nations Development Program, in particular, plays an active role in PRS monitoring through its support for the ODHD. The World Bank has supported the 1994 *Enquête malienne de conjoncture économique et sociale* (Malian survey of economic and social conditions), the 2001 *Enquête malienne pour l'évaluation de la pauvreté* (Malian poverty assessment survey), and the 1-2-3 survey on employment, informal sector, and household consumption and poverty. In addition, a participatory poverty assessment is expected to be launched in 2006 by the DNSI in collaboration with the World Bank. The Economic and Statistical Observatory for Sub-Saharan Africa (Afristat) has supported DNSI activities on request, working with the DNSI on the 1-2-3 survey, the rural census, and the development of methodologies for data analysis. It also initiated the Common Minimum Statistical Program, launched in 2000 in all member countries of Afristat, and aims to improve and harmonize the statistical information required for decision making and to reinforce regional integration.

The above efforts have been coordinated to some extent. Afristat, the World Bank, and the United Nations Development Program have collaborated on the design of a database to be housed in the DNSI. However, much remains to be done to improve donor coordination so as to ensure the development of a sustainable monitoring system.

Lessons

The PRSP M&E plan has made a serious attempt to systematize information on existing monitoring activities and to assign broad monitoring responsibilities clearly. In addition, there have been efforts to address institutional instability. For example, the new statute of the ODHD awards it permanent status and was formulated in reaction to the gaps in its operations (because of its temporary status) and its complete reliance on donor funding.

However, a number of weaknesses are evident in the system; these relate in part to the institutional framework. There are too many actors in a highly dispersed, loosely coordinated system, and it is not entirely clear where the overall leadership is located. Consequently, there is an increased risk of duplication and overlap in monitoring efforts. The reporting duties of the ODHD, for example, may cover indicators monitored by the thematic groups. Similar duplications are evident in the reporting of the line ministries and the respective thematic groups.

While the allocation of broad monitoring responsibilities is clear on paper, there are also a number of inter- and intrainstitutional tensions. The Ministry of Planning and National Development and the Ministry of Economy and Finance are both keen to maintain strong monitoring responsibilities. This type of institutional framework with a high number of actors, who are distributed among a variety of institutions, requires particularly strong information communication, dissemination, and feedback. Experience so far indicates that, despite the frequent meetings and workshops, existing information and reports are not disseminated widely to all actors. Also, on the budget side, the lack of coordination and interaction among institutions means that the link between the budget and the PRSP remains weak, as it is in many other countries.

The large number of actors involved in poverty monitoring creates a need for strong coordination and oversight. As the main PRSP monitoring coordinator, the PRSP coordination unit needs to be reinforced. The PRSP coordination unit's mandate covers PRSP monitoring, but not all poverty monitoring activities; and, in this respect, the exact roles of the DNSI and the ODHD (as both PRSP and non-PRSP monitoring actors) need to be spelled out. Likewise, the responsibility of supervision over these two institutions requires clarification. Finally, the continued implementation and functioning of the system hinge on the identification of a clear, single set of indicators.

8

Mauritania

ACRONYM AND ABBREVIATION

PRLP Programme Regional de Lutte contre la Pauvreté (Regional Program for Poverty Reduction)

History and Context

Mauritania's Poverty Reduction Strategy Paper (PRSP) was adopted in January 2001 following a participatory preparation process. The main operational approach of the poverty reduction strategy (PRS) comprises four-year action plans. These are supported by multi-year public investment plans, which are reviewed annually and are subject to detailed mid-term evaluations. There are also Programmes Regionaux de Lutte contre la Pauvreté (Regional Programs for Poverty Reduction, PRLPs), which are evidence of the operation of the PRS at the regional level and set priority actions for each region. The PRLPs are being implemented

This chapter is based on a background country report by Christian Bonifas (2004) and inputs by Nicola Pontara and Hawa Wague-Cisse. The study was undertaken in the second half of 2004 and has been partially updated to reflect conditions in the summer of 2005. Substantial changes may have occurred that are not reflected in this chapter, and readers are encouraged to seek additional information if they wish to focus on the system of this particular country.

gradually. Monitoring and evaluation (M&E) of the PRLPs are carried out according to the same framework as the M&E for the national plans of action. The allocation and impact of priority public expenditures are reviewed in quarterly Heavily Indebted Poor Countries (HIPC) Initiative reports, which are produced by the government and focus on the use of HIPC resources, and in public expenditure reviews, which are elaborated jointly by the World Bank and government authorities (issued in 2004, 2005, and ongoing). The government is currently preparing a new PRS.

Description of the Monitoring System

Origins of the system

Between 2001 and 2004, there was no single reference document or legal regulation defining the M&E system. Rather, the system consisted of a set of uncoordinated and dispersed activities. During this period, many different activities were carried out in many locations with no common outlook or central coordination concerning the objectives, responsibilities, and priority procedures. These included monitoring the Millennium Development Goals (MDGs), preparation of the first PRLP, implementation of the components of the master plan for statistics, development of various M&E schemes among public agencies or important programs, and programs to modernize public administration. This recently changed through the adoption of the 2005 decree on the organization of the M&E system for the PRS (see below).

Institutional framework and main institutional actors

The M&E system constitutes a critical component of any PRS. Its main objectives include poverty monitoring, the monitoring of PRS implementation, and evaluation of the PRS.

In Mauritania, the system has separate institutional mechanisms for each of these objectives. The system consists of oversight functions and technical functions.

Oversight and discussion bodies

The *interministerial committee for poverty reduction* is chaired by the prime minister and includes members from all large ministries and agencies. Originally, the committee supervised the elaboration and validation of the PRSP and was meant to play the same supervisory role in implementation. However, the committee did not meet regularly. Since 2005, the committee has been in charge of the overall coordination of the PRS process, the review of reports on PRS implementation, the approval of annual action plans and multiyear programs of implementation, and the review of MDG reports.

The *dialogue committee* is chaired by the minister of economic affairs and development. It includes senior executives in the main ministries and other agencies, together with representatives of municipalities and civil society. Originally, the committee was responsible for the technical preparation of the PRSP, as well as the promotion of a participatory approach. It has now been reconstituted as a forum for discussing results, organizing consultations, ensuring communications on progress, and strengthening the capacity of nongovernmental agents. In practice, until the 2005 decree, the committee only met twice a year to discuss the annual progress report.

The *donors committee* is composed of all development partners and the government. Its mandate is to review the implementation of the PRS and the progress toward the MDGs, evaluate the issues faced in the implementation of priority programs supported by donors, and ensure greater alignment and coordination among donor activities.

Technical bodies

The *technical committee for poverty reduction* is chaired by the adviser in charge of development policy in the Ministry of Economic Affairs and Development. It comprises a coordination secretariat, a representative of the technical ministries, and the presidents of the thematic groups. Originally, the committee was in charge of PRSP coordination and activities related to the monitoring of PRSP implementation. In practice, however, the committee mainly met to validate the annual progress report. In 2005, its mandates were broadened to include the preparation of a quarterly synthesis note on PRS implementation, a biannual report, and an annual report on the basis of inputs from ministries and government agencies.

The *technical sector committees* exist at the departmental level and include department executives (planning and monitoring and financial and statistical services) and resource persons, as well as representatives of technical departments, civil society, and development partners. The committees are required to centralize information, elaborate and monitor programs, and assist in decision making in the ministerial departments. There are currently 38 committees.

The *technical thematic groups* include representatives of the ministries, civil society, and development partners, as well as resource persons. There were originally 13 groups, but their number was reduced to five in 2005. The groups focus on cross-cutting issues, including the delivery of basic services (health care, education, water, sanitation, electricity, and telecommunications), the promotion of economic activity among microenterprises and cooperatives, growth and competitiveness, governance and capacity strengthening, and M&E.

The *public expenditure technical committee*, created in 2005, is responsible for the overall monitoring of public spending through the review of priority expenditures identified in the PRS.

In order to reinforce the participatory approach, the following mechanisms were introduced:

- *Interregional workshops* were held annually after the PRS initiative was launched. They were attended by elected regional leaders and representatives of nongovernmental organizations, civil society organizations, and development partners. Originally, representatives of the 12 regions would gather at these workshops at four sites. In 2005, the interregional workshops were replaced by workshops for each region.
- The *national poverty reduction conference* is presented in the PRSP as a general assembly for poverty reduction. The conferences are held at the same time as the publication of the year-end balance sheet. They bring together numerous resource persons and representatives of the government, Parliament, mayoral administrations, nongovernmental organizations, unions, and development partners.
- In addition to the submission of the PRSP to *Parliament* at the end of the preparation process, the deputies discuss the results of each four-year plan. However, no monitoring procedure is planned in between the preparation process and the discussions.

Overall Status

Originally, the system did not assign specific responsibilities to the various participating institutions. The lack of terms of reference and procedural modalities, in particular for the committees and working groups, weakened the management of the system. Given the collegial structure, this was compounded by the absence of a permanent secretariat. This limited the value of the products of the monitoring system. In particular, the structure within which the working groups operated was largely ad hoc, and there was no systematic process to establish priority indicators, focal programs, data collection, or the format and content of reports. Attendance was limited, and the working groups were mostly isolated from monitoring bodies in the sectoral ministries. Finally, the resources of the coordination secretariat of the technical committee for poverty reduction were inadequate.

Nonetheless, even during the initial phase, there was some progress in rehabilitating the statistical system, though the capacity of the National Statistical Bureau remains limited, the flow of information among actors in statistics is still deficient, and the quality of data needs improvement (see below).

The recent alterations to the system reflect the limitations revealed earlier in the process. In particular, the rationalization of the working groups, the clear definition of the roles and responsibilities of various actors, and the significant increase in the capacity of the coordination secretariat (six permanent experts) are likely to remove some of the major constraints observed early on.

Key Topics

Coordination

The coordination secretariat facilitates collaboration among the main institutions, supervises the preparation of the annual report, and organizes dialogue within this framework. Initially, the system involved a multiplicity of actors with varying interests and capacities and did not assign specific responsibilities to institutions. Consequently, it was difficult for the coordination secretariat to distribute tasks and organize the flow of information. The recent simplification and rationalization of the system has already allowed for improvements in the process of coordination among actors.

Capacity

The system still suffers from limited capacity in terms of both level and competency in the collection of the information required for M&E of the PRSP. Specifically, there is a lack of analytical capacity; and low wages have led to the loss of skilled staff, which affects the sustainability of administrative activities, the implementation of work plans, and the efficiency of working groups.

Participation

Until the adoption of the PRSP, reviews of economic policy were predominantly confidential. The participatory approach that has been followed since the PRSP represents an important step in improving the governance of public policies, although it has not been extended to policy evaluation. The technical thematic groups have facilitated discussion on the main themes relating to the implementation of the PRSP and have contributed to an easier flow of information for monitoring the different domains of the national PRS.

The participation of civil society, development partners, and the private sector has recently been institutionalized. The inadequate capacity of civil society to participate effectively is also a constraint.

Indicators and data sources

Despite much technical assistance, as well as seminars and forums dealing with the selection of indicators, a number of problems still exist. These relate to the appropriateness of the selected indicators with respect to the objectives of the PRS, the integration of the MDGs, the adoption of clear definitions that conform with international norms, the selection of the most appropriate source in the case of multiple sources that may be used for calculations, the subsequent implementation of reference documentation on the indicators (metadata), and the capacity of the national statistical system to produce the necessary data based on reliability requirements and deadlines.

There is a clear need to review existing indicators, as well as establish a second group of indicators that serve as a basis for the monitoring of poverty and the implementation of priority programs under the PRSP. Simultaneously, there is a need for the harmonization, standardization, and documentation of indicators. These challenges have been recognized and are guiding the preparation of the new PRS, which will ensure that progress is made in these areas.

The statistical system, analysis, and evaluation

The efforts involved in the PRS have resulted in important progress in rehabilitating the *statistical system*. These improvements have been achieved in line with the master plan for statistics adopted in July 2000 by the interministerial committee on statistics. Statistical surveys carried out between 2000 and 2004 considerably enriched the demographic and socioeconomic database. Some sectoral statistical systems were set up, which decentralized the collection, processing, and analysis of questionnaires. For example, the health information system produced a health map and a hospital information system; economic statistics and an employment information system were established; and a social database was initiated in 1999.

Despite the improvements, a number of challenges remained. For instance, the master plan for statistics needed to be based on demand and reflect the priorities of the PRS; a review mechanism was needed; and the specialized commissions were running out of steam.

This led to the adoption of a new law on statistics and a new national strategy for the development of statistics, with support from the Economic and Statistical Observatory for Sub-Saharan Africa and Paris21. The new framework addresses some of the limitations of the previous system and anchors the activities of the statistical system within the data needs for PRS elaboration, implementation, and M&E.

Overall, the capacity for *analysis* remains relatively weak. However, Mauritania established the Centre Mauritanien d'Analyse de Politiques (Mauritanian Center for Policy Analysis), a research center that focuses on key topics raised in PRS design and implementation. This has filled some of the gaps, although analytical services in the line ministries remain weak, and there is limited demand by decision makers.

Although there have been 11 *evaluations* of sector strategies, these have not been systematic. Furthermore, the commitments laid out in the PRS have not materialized. For instance, the "exhaustive mid-term evaluation" of the PRS as a whole, which was scheduled for 2003, has not taken place. The weaknesses of the evaluation component relate primarily to the fact that there are no legal requirements for evaluation and no autonomous institution has been assigned this responsibility. As a result, evaluations are often led by the institutions that implement them. However, the preparation of the new PRS involves planning for an evaluation of the first PRS that should address some of these weaknesses.

Products

Annual thematic reports, as well as an annual implementation report on the M&E of the PRSP, have been produced. These reports have provided the opportunity for discussion during interregional workshops and national conferences and contribute, at least formally, to the participatory approach considered for the PRSP.

There have been quarterly synthesis reports on actions taken through HIPC resources. These reports are produced by the technical committee in charge of the programming and monitoring of actions financed through HIPC resources, which is chaired by the minister of finance. The committee reviews budget implementation data for each action and feed back on outstanding issues (absorption capacity and the distribution of spending across sectors). Other current initiatives include a first tracking survey in the health sector, a public expenditure analysis, and the development of functional classifications of expenditures.

There are medium-term expenditure frameworks (MTEFs) in eight sectors (rural development, transport infrastructure, health, education, energy, water and sanitation, fisheries, and urban sectors) that specify the planning of priority actions. The preparation of these provides the opportunity to review sector policies and identify performance indicators for every program. The validity of the sectoral MTEF exercise has been partially undermined, however, because of the absence of a global MTEF setting the overall budget envelope. To remedy this situation, a first global MTEF was developed in 2003 (for 2004–6) and used for the preparation of the 2004 budget law. Despite significant progress, problems persist in the system; for instance, the development of the MTEF for 2005–7 has been delayed, and there has been a lack of full integration with the budget process.

Dissemination

There are periodic publications of administrative statistics on education and health. The national statistical system has published a compact disc of all surveys, plus 108 studies and reports conducted on poverty between 1980 and 2000. There are several Web sites, and a substantial amount of data is now available on line.

Despite this, information dissemination channels are not well organized and do not encourage the establishment of documentation centers that are regularly supplied with new products. There are indications of a need for a database that might serve as a reference for all national multisectoral monitoring processes (the PRSP, MDG reports, the Human Development Report) and regional monitoring (the PRLPs).

Lessons

One of the main lessons of the Mauritanian experience is the need for well-defined roles and responsibilities among the various actors in the system and a unified, regulated framework. Until these are established, activities will remain scattered or focused only on the preparation of the annual reports. The experience also underlines the importance of institutional coordination and of a strategy for the dissemination of M&E information (the reporting system, information access among stakeholders, the organization of data exchanges, and so on). In addition, the experience also underlines the need to improve indicators for monitoring the PRS and MDGs, as well as adjustments in the statistical information system so as to meet the demand for information.

The consolidation of the M&E system will face challenges in the future, including the implementation of a national strategy for the development of statistics that effectively plans and coordinates the activities of various agencies and focuses on demand, strengthened analytical capacity, more effective dissemination of information with formats adapted to the needs of various actors, as well as the strengthening of the capacities of civil society, greater use of monitoring information in the design of public actions, and greater alignment of planning tools (such as the MTEF) with the budget process.

More generally, the experience shows that a PRS monitoring system should be based on the reinforcement and rationalization of existing structures and not the creation of new ones. It should integrate and simplify existing monitoring systems. In the same spirit of rationalization, the system should coordinate assistance from development partners.

9

Nicaragua

ACRONYMS AND ABBREVIATIONS

CONPES	Consejo Nacional de Planificación Económica y Social (National Council for Social and Economic Planning)
ERCERP	Estrategia Reforzada de Crecimiento y Reducción de la Pobreza (Strengthened Growth and Poverty Reduction Strategy)
INEC	Instituto Nacional de Estadística y Censo (National Institute of Statistics and Census)
PND	Plan Nacional de Desarrollo (National Development Plan)
SECEP	Secretaria de Coordinación y Estrategia de la Presidencia (Secretariat for Coordination and Strategy of the Presidency)
SIGFA	Sistema de Información Gerencial Financiera y Administrativa (integrated financial and administrative management system)
Sinasid	Sistema Nacional de Seguimiento a Indicadores de Desarrollo (national system to monitor development indicators)
Sinasip	Sistema Nacional de Seguimiento de Indicadores de Pobreza (national system to monitor poverty indicators)
SNIP	Sistema Nacional de Inversión Publica (national system of public investment)
UCTE	Unidad de Coordinación Técnica Estadística (unit of statistical and technical coordination)

History and Context

N icaragua launched the Estrategia Reforzada de Crecimiento y Reducción de la Pobreza (Strengthened Growth and Poverty Reduction Strategy, ERCERP) in July 2001 and has since prepared two progress reports, in November 2002 and 2003. The ERCERP preparation efforts were coordinated by the Secretaria de Coordinación y Estrategia de la Presidencia (Secretariat for Coordination and Strategy of the Presidency, SECEP), which is in the process of updating the strategy.

In January 2002, there was a change in government, and, during 2003, the current government prepared the Plan Nacional de Desarrollo (National Development Plan, PND), which was presented in a preliminary version during the Consultative Group meeting in October 2003. The PND elaborates on the poverty reduction strategy (PRS); indeed, it constitutes the updated strategy (PRS-II), which was presented to the Board of the International Monetary Fund and the Board of Executive Directors of the World Bank in early 2006. The PND has been prepared through a broad consultation process at the national and regional levels; it emphasizes the strengthening of the economic growth pillar of the PRS.

Description of the Monitoring System

Origins of the system

The design of the monitoring system, the Sistema Nacional de Seguimiento de Indicadores de Pobreza (national system to monitor poverty indicators, Sinasip), was undertaken in late 2002 under the leadership of the SECEP. The first Sinasip proposal was never implemented. In the context of the preparation of the PND and despite the delay in the implementation of the original Sinasip plans, the SECEP presented a revised monitoring and evaluation (M&E) system proposal in December 2003: the PND M&E system, known as the Sistema Nacional de Seguimiento a Indicadores de Desarrollo (national system to monitor development indicators, Sinasid).

This chapter is based on a background country report by Aline Coudouel and Ferdinando Regalia (2004) and on intensive inputs by Florencia Castro-Leal. The study was undertaken in the second half of 2004 and has been partially updated to reflect conditions in the summer of 2005. Substantial changes may have occurred that are not reflected in this chapter, and readers are encouraged to seek additional information if they wish to focus on the system of this particular country.

Sinasid introduced the following proposed changes to the original Sinasip design:

- The list of indicators and actions the system was expected to track was expanded to include ERCERP and PND indicators and policy actions, the Millennium Development Goals, and the policy actions involved in the Poverty Reduction Support Credit.
- The establishment of territorial units within the departmental technical units. These decentralized structures will be charged with formulating and monitoring the implementation of public investment programs and projects at the departmental level. The proposal does not, however, specify the role of the territorial units relative to other institutions or their contribution to the system.
- The Unidad de Coordinación Técnica Estadística (unit of statistical and technical coordination, UCTE) assumes direct responsibility for quality control over the primary information provided. This mandate could cause conflict with the mandate of the Instituto Nacional de Estadística y Censo (National Institute of Statistics and Census, INEC), which, by law, is responsible for supervising the application of quality standards by all primary information providers in the national statistical system.

Sinasid is designed to coordinate interinstitutional information and data collection processes for monitoring PND indicators and ensure their overall quality; provide timely data to inform the formulation, planning, and assessment of public expenditures and the investment program in line with PND objectives; strengthen the tracking mechanisms for pro-poor public expenditures, and complement the information produced by the two existing information systems: (1) the Sistema Nacional de Inversión Publica (national system of public investment, SNIP), which tracks progress and result indicators on all the programs and projects in the national program of public investment; the public investment unit in the SECEP administers SNIP, and (2) the Sistema de Información Gerencial Financiera y Administrativa (integrated financial and administrative management system, SIGFA), which is administered by the Ministry of Finance and Public Credit and is responsible for providing the UCTE with quarterly information on disbursement by sector, subsector, program, projects, and geographical area.

The Sinasid system is a second-tier monitoring system, which means that it uses secondary data produced by the M&E systems of existing institutions and agencies, including the National Statistics Office, line ministries, and the Central Bank. These institutions are responsible for the production and validation of primary data at the national, departmental, and municipal level.

Main institutional actors

The system comprises the SECEP, the technical statistical committee, line ministries, and other agencies providing primary data, as well as civil society organizations (CSOs).

The *Secretaria de Coordinación y Estrategia de la Presidencia* is in charge of the coordination of the system. Within the SECEP, two units play key roles: (1) the UCTE, which went into operation at the beginning of 2003 and is in charge of interinstitutional coordination activities, including information and data gathering; the monitoring, analysis, and dissemination of PND indicators; and the dissemination of results on PND implementation progress; and (2) the Unidad de Análisis de la Pobreza (poverty analysis unit), which includes four SECEP sectoral specialists (education, health, water and sanitation, and economic growth) and is in charge of the analysis of the information contained in the system, the preparation of ERCERP progress reports, and the preparation of reports relating to the implementation of the PND.

The UCTE also presides over the *technical statistical committee*. This committee is responsible for the technical coordination of data providers, including the INEC, the Central Bank, and line ministries. Its function is to address methodological issues relating to the calculation of PND indicators and to ensure consensus.

Primary institutions. Each institution providing primary data is expected to select a liaison officer from among its personnel. It is envisaged that this liaison person will be responsible for the interinstitutional coordination with the SECEP and will provide data and information to the UCTE to keep the system updated. The type and periodicity of the information to be provided to the UCTE will be set out in interinstitutional agreements on the basis of technical standards established by the technical statistical committee and the INEC methodology.

The new proposal suggests the inclusion of *departmental technical units* that are decentralized regional structures for formulating and implementing public investment plans and projects. Although the proposal envisages territorial M&E units within these technical units, it is vague regarding their exact role.

In terms of the participation of CSOs, the system relies on the *Consejo Nacional de Planificación Económica y Social* (National Council for Social and Economic Planning, CONPES), a structure created during the preparation of the ERCERP. Set up in early 1998 in the context of Hurricane Mitch, the CONPES is the primary channel of communication between the government and civil society on social and economic strategies. In March 2002, a presidential decree changed the CONPES by eliminating government representation and adding representatives of women's organizations, youth groups, autonomous regions, and the media. This was done to strengthen the independence and autonomy of the council's deliberations and recommendations. Another decree later that year reformed the selection process for the CONPES members. The CONPES has multiple roles in the system. It is a user of the system. It implements a consultation strategy on the ERCERP progress reports and the PND at the central and local levels (in coordination with the UCTE). It leads an outreach program to strengthen the capacity of CSOs in M&E activities. Finally, it compiles CSO feedback on the progress reports.

Overall Status

The implementation of Sinasid and its predecessor, Sinasip, has been relatively limited. This is due to both the complexity of the design and the fact that the proposed structure for carrying out the information flows has not yet been implemented. Despite the lack of the institutionalization of the basic flows of information, the ERCERP, the two ERCERP progress reports, and the PND (which contains a progress report for 2003 and 2004) have been prepared, albeit through ad hoc efforts. Because the system is yet to be fully implemented, it is too early to conduct an evaluation.

Key Topics

Legal framework and procedures

Sinasid has been launched. However, to achieve full implementation, it must be officially established, which could be achieved by means of a presidential decree; it also requires a work plan. In July 2001, SNIP operations were strengthened through a presidential decree establishing SNIP administrative guidelines. Full implementation of Sinasid would benefit from a similar decree establishing the roles and responsibilities of the SECEP, line ministries, and other agencies, as well as defining Sinasid administrative guidelines. To date, no interinstitutional agreements between the SECEP and other agencies have been signed that define the roles and responsibilities of each party within Sinasid. Such agreements would enhance the flow of information.

Leadership of the system

The government of Nicaragua is committed to the full implementation of Sinasid. The system is in the early stages, however, and a work plan for full implementation has not yet been developed.

In terms of ownership by line ministries, the line ministries have repeatedly expressed their interest in the full implementation of Sinasid and in the establishment of a Web-based dissemination strategy. This commitment arises from the hope that the system will reduce the number of sectoral indicator queries that the ministries receive from various stakeholders.

Coordination

Sinasid is comprehensive and extremely ambitious. The net interinstitutional arrangements are relatively complex. Moreover, the system is dependent on the development of an Intranet network so that public sector institutions may input data and information into the system, which would require substantial investment in information technology. Slow progress has been a result of the lack of both technical investment and leadership.

Overall, the SECEP has not been able to implement the system fully. This is so despite the importance of the SECEP operations as outlined in the ERCERP, the PND, the ERCERP progress reports, and the joint staff assessments in the ERCERP progress reports, despite fairly strong progress in selected line ministries and the related information systems, and despite the availability of financial resources.

Capacity

In terms of capacity, the starting point is relatively good. Both the line ministries and the INEC have been developing their capacity, and there are no apparent bottlenecks in the implementation of Sinasid. The INEC has improved its technical capacity over the past decade through support provided by the Program for Improvement of the Surveys of Living

Conditions and is now focusing on client orientation and its ability to react swiftly to demands from data users, including public sector agencies.

A substantial amount of work has already been done on information systems at the ministerial level, together with improved coordination through SIGFA and SNIP. The Ministry of Health, for example, stands out because of its existing M&E system, which is used to support investment and resource allocation decisions. The ministry and its decentralized units, in coordination with the SECEP, are guiding programming activities, the allocation of resources, and investment planning by closely tracking PRS intermediate, output, and outcome indicators produced through administrative records at the local level and information produced by SIGFA and SNIP.

SIGFA and SNIP have been strengthened and represent the backbone of these ministerial systems in terms of financial and administrative information and physical input and output data.

Donors have been supporting the development of the capacity of departmental technical units to participate in the monitoring system. Efforts are also under way, in coordination with the donor community, to take steps to unify M&E and reporting practices.

Participation

Extensive consultations took place with civil society during the preparation of the ERCERP and the PND. The ERCERP, the ERCERP progress reports, and the PND have been presented to the CONPES. Feedback has been gathered through a series of regional workshops and over the Internet.

Under the coordination of the CONPES, a series of initiatives are currently under way at the municipal level to strengthen participatory M&E; some of these initiatives fall within the program to support the implementation of the ERCERP. Additional efforts to develop capacity in social accountability at the local, departmental, and national levels are being supported by the World Bank, the U.K. Department for International Development, and other partners, including training in budget monitoring, participatory M&E, and community feedback mechanisms through pilot user scorecards. Given the delays in the implementation of Sinasid, these initiatives have not, however, been fully integrated in the system.

In addition to the formal channel provided by the CONPES, civil society has mobilized independently to ensure its own participation. Examples of such unofficial initiatives include the organization, by the civil coordinator for emergencies and reconstruction, of two social audits with 16,000 households in 150 communities across the country. Similarly, a network of more than 300 CSOs created a program of citizen control over public policies, 2003–6, that was implemented in 20 municipalities.

Products and dissemination

The SECEP has prepared the ERCEPR, a first ERCERP progress report in November 2002, and a second progress report in November 2003. The ERCERP, the ERCERP progress reports, and the PND were presented to the CONPES. Feedback was gathered through a series of regional workshops, but also over the Internet. The ERCERP, the ERCERP progress reports, and the PND are also posted on the SECEP Web site.

Finance and donor support

Overall, the system appears to be well resourced. Neither the weaknesses in the line ministry systems, which have begun to be successfully addressed, nor the shortages in the availability of resources, are delaying the implementation of a first stage of the PND M&E system. In fact, the SECEP has recently received financial support from the Inter-American Development Bank and the World Bank through the Poverty Reduction Strategy Technical Assistance Credit and the Emergency Social Investment Fund Credit to cover some of the fixed and operational costs, which are estimated at around $1.5 million for a period of four years.

Lessons

A key lesson derived from the experience of Sinasid and its predecessor, Sinasip, is that a modular approach should be adopted for the first stage of implementation. This would build on existing systems and might be more manageable, promote consistency and ownership, and prevent duplication. Whereas the current PND M&E system proposal extends to areas already covered by other systems, it may be better for other countries attempting to build similar systems to monitor a less ambitious set of indicators, which could then be expanded during a second phase.

In addition, the proposed network of institutional coordination arrangements is complex, and network implementation has been limited.

No interinstitutional agreements have been established between the SECEP and sectoral agencies to define the type, frequency, and format of information flows. As a result, during the preparation of the first ERCERP progress report, focal points in the line ministries provided inputs and contributed to the analysis only on the basis of existing communication channels between them and sectoral specialists in the poverty analysis unit team of the SECEP. This occasionally resulted in a duplication of effort, because the focal points were required to provide similar information to the poverty analysis unit and the UCTE (both of which are units of the SECEP). In addition to the need for clear channels, this highlights the need for a clarification of the roles of the UCTE and the poverty analysis unit so as to avoid duplication.

The technical statistical committee has not been able to perform its function and has only met once so far. As a result, the INEC has had to respond to the requests of line ministries relating to methodological issues through bilateral meetings outside the committee. Moreover, the fact that the proposal charges the UCTE with responsibility for quality control could lead to tensions, since this function has already been ascribed to the INEC. These two institutions might instead coordinate inputs and recommend changes in the methodology used to calculate indicators, as well as changes in data gathering and data processing.

The two-tier design of Sinasid should emphasize the importance of the production of high-quality primary information, given that Sinasid uses existing information supplied through the systems of the INEC and the line ministries. Some ministries, including health, education, agriculture, infrastructure, and transport, are already making efforts to tackle weaknesses in the measurement of outcome and impact indicators and to strengthen analytical capacity. This could provide a strong foundation for a simplified, incremental system.

Despite extensive CSO participation and recent changes in the CONPES, particularly the withdrawal of the government, may have reduced the opportunities for direct dialogue between CSOs and the government and, as a result, reduced the influence on policy making. Overall, although the reforms signal the endorsement of the CONPES by the authorities and allow broader participation, the government uses this forum only occasionally.

10

Niger

ACRONYMS AND ABBREVIATIONS

DGEPP   Directorate General of Evaluation of Development Programs
NSO   National Statistics Office

History and Context

Niger's first national poverty reduction plan was adopted in 1998. Subsequently, in January 2002, the country launched its poverty reduction strategy (PRS) and the associated Poverty Reduction Strategy Paper (PRSP). The national plan and the strategy led to an increased focus on the design of a poverty monitoring and evaluation (M&E) system. During the elaboration phase of the PRS and following PRS implementation, a number of initiatives, workshops, documents, and studies were prepared with the goal of establishing a system to track progress in PRS implementation and assess the impact of policies on poverty and living conditions.

This chapter is based on a background country report by Francesca Bastagli (2004a) and inputs by Saloua Sehili and Quentin Wodon. The study was undertaken in the second half of 2004 and has been partially updated to reflect conditions in the summer of 2005. Substantial changes may have occurred that are not reflected in this chapter, and readers are encouraged to seek additional information if they wish to focus on the system of this particular country.

Unfortunately, the actual monitoring of progress toward improvements in indicators has been weakened by the absence of good survey data and by weak capacity in processing the existing information base.

Description of the PRS Monitoring System

Origins of the system

As part of PRS preparations, an initial diagnosis of existing M&E capacity was undertaken in 2001. This involved examination of the strengths and weaknesses of monitoring activities at the planning, sectoral ministry, regional, and project levels. The PRS noted a variety of data sources, but underlined that duplication, lack of coordination, and lack of harmonization among methodologies limit the comparability of different sources. While the PRS makes reference to data collection, analysis, and the selection of indicators, it contains few details on institutional arrangements and policy feedback. It concluded that there was a need to develop a harmonized system for M&E of government programs, strengthen technical skills at all levels, strengthen existing training programs to support M&E and ensure the sustainability of interventions and the adequacy of content, strengthen the M&E culture, and build a dialogue with donors so as to harmonize initiatives in M&E.

Despite the limited emphasis on the structure of the system, the PRS helped focus attention, foster debate, and encourage the initiation of a number of studies related to poverty monitoring. Moreover, it called for the establishment of a poverty reduction information system to gather data from existing sources. Although the PRSP secretariat (see below) produced an M&E strategy, this is short on details regarding the roles of the various actors in the system. The first PRSP progress report (July 2003) criticizes the system for its continuing lack of coordination and the overlap with other systems. Although there has been subsequent development, there is still no comprehensive plan.

Main institutional actors

The *PRSP permanent secretariat* was created during the formulation of the PRS. It is located in the cabinet of the prime minister and therefore exercises both a political and strategic role. The unit is responsible for the overall coordination of the implementation and M&E of the PRS. It consists of nine people; one staff member is responsible for PRS M&E, and the others coordinate PRS implementation in various sectors.

The permanent secretariat publishes the annual PRSP progress report, which consolidates information from annual sectoral reports submitted by individual ministries. Although ministries currently send their reports directly to the permanent secretariat, it is likely that, in future, they will be sent to the Directorate General of Evaluation of Development Programs (DGEPP; see below) in the Ministry of Finance and channeled from there to the permanent secretariat.

Niger's new statistical law, approved in April 2004, created the *National Statistics Office* (NSO) out of the old Direction de la Statistique et des Comptes Nationaux (Directorate of Statistics and National Accounts) situated in the Ministry of Finance. The NSO has recently been taken out of the ministry and made fully autonomous. The main rationale behind the increased autonomy is the NSO's need for greater financial and human resources. Access to such resources was restricted under the previous structure due to the statistics directorate's dependence on the budget of the Ministry of Finance and the fact that recruitment procedures limited hiring.

Although the NSO has been formally created, its actual operation in accordance with the new law awaits the drafting and implementation of two decrees. Until then, the NSO will continue to function as the statistics directorate did. In reality, the NSO is therefore still under development, but its managers have been appointed, which should help in the preparation of a statistics strategy. Both the World Bank and the European Union have provided support to the NSO.

The *poverty observatory* will be a permanent structure situated within the NSO. Its regulations are still being drafted, and it has therefore not yet been officially established. There is agreement that it should have a limited structure, with few permanent staff, and that experts should be brought in for particular tasks. The observatory will be the principal analytical body of the system. It will define data needs, develop surveys, and supervise NSO poverty-related activities. Moreover, it will publish the annual Millennium Development Goal report and the Human Development Report.

The *national statistical council* will oversee the entire statistical system and provide a meeting point for all actors in the monitoring system. Its members will include all stakeholders, including representation of civil society. The minister of finance will be in charge, and the position of vice chair will be held by a member of the PRSP secretariat. The council's main responsibility will be to provide broad guidance to and oversight of NSO activities. It will convene once or twice a year. Additional details on its operations have not yet been determined.

The newly established *Directorate General of Evaluation of Development Programs* in the Ministry of Finance is responsible for the M&E of all government programs and projects. Its responsibilities include the provision of technical support for M&E work in line ministries and the maintenance of a database containing monitoring information of all government programs and projects.

The *directorate of studies and planning* in each line ministry monitors indicators in the respective sector, compiles administrative data collected at the local level, and publishes the annual report on ministry activities. These reports are sent to the NSO and the DGEPP. Moreover, the directorates prepare annual sectoral reports that are submitted to the PRSP secretariat for the annual PRSP progress report. The directorates also complete reports at the request of institutions and donors.

Overall Status

The institutional arrangements of the system represent a relatively compact architecture, particularly in comparison to the complex systems of other countries. The system is two tier, meaning that poverty monitoring (outcomes and impacts) and PRS monitoring (inputs and outputs) are distinct activities and that they feed into a single monitoring system. As in many other countries, there is evidence that coordination functions have been assigned to several bodies. While responsibility for the coordination of PRS monitoring resides with the PRSP secretariat, the relationship of this function and the coordination of poverty monitoring efforts allocated to the poverty observatory and to the national statistical council are not entirely clear.

In addition, there is potential for reporting responsibilities to become burdensome. Monitoring directorates in line ministries may be overwhelmed in that they are currently reporting to the DGEPP in the Ministry of Finance, the NSO, and the PRSP secretariat and have separate obligations to donors and other international agencies requesting information. As a result, better role definition is required to address the risks of overlap and overburdening in responsibilities, as well as to mitigate against possible tensions and rivalries.

On the other hand, substantial progress has been made in data collection. PRSP progress reports have repeatedly stressed weaknesses in household surveys, but progress has been achieved recently. A survey on employment and living conditions was completed in Niamey in 2004. A new national survey was completed in the summer of 2005, with modules on employment, education, health, income sources, household consumption, agriculture, microcredit, the perceptions and priorities of the poor, and the evaluation of projects and investments carried out in communities. The government has budgeted funds for a follow-up budget and consumption surveys, which will be useful in revising the national account and in measuring inflation, among other tasks. A general census of agriculture and livestock (RGAC 2004/5) is under way and will allow for a better understanding and modernization of the agropastoral sector. Finally, the United Nations Development Program is funding work to assess basic needs requirements in the country, and a new Demographic and Health Survey (EDSN/MICS III) is being implemented to enhance the monitoring of progress particularly toward the MDGs.

Progress has also been achieved in terms of the information base for the implementation and revision of the PRS. For example, the authorities have funded an independent technical and financial audit of the special program of the president of the country. This audit will be complemented by a qualitative analysis of the factors that enable households to emerge from poverty that is to be launched, with Bank support, by the PRSP secretariat. In addition, the coordination unit for the rural development strategy has requested a separate study on ways to maximize the impact of the rural investments funded by the president's program. Together, these initiatives should provide a stronger information base for revising the PRS early in 2006, but close follow-up will be needed to avoid delays and ensure that all these initiatives are part of a coherent strategy to establish more effective M&E.

Key Topics

Leadership of the system

Government commitment to the creation of a PRS monitoring system is high as evidenced by the number of documents and workshops being issued relating to monitoring. It is difficult to determine the extent to which there is internal demand for information, however. While, according to the government, there is a demand for monitoring information during the policy process, this demand is not being met. This is a result of resource constraints. The lack of resources is shaping the degree of ownership of the poverty monitoring process. The historical reliance on donors and other external funding is considered to have weakened country initiative and ownership.

Capacity

Delays in data production and analysis, as well as poor data administration (see below), are being attributed to understaffing. At the DGEPP, for example, one individual is responsible for the administration of the entire database. The responsibilities of this individual include data insertion and analysis on the basis of requests made by other DGEPP staff. The DGEPP M&E plan itself observes that such situations increase the risk of mistakes and limit the analysis of data.

Participation

While communication and coordination among national stakeholders and international agencies could be improved, Niger presents an interesting case because of the Nigerien Network of Monitoring and Evaluation (see ReNSE, at http://www.pnud.ne/rense/). In 1999, a staff member of the United Nations Children's Fund launched the network, an informal group of M&E professionals. It provides a lively, ongoing forum for discussion and information dissemination on issues of M&E.

During the formulation phase of the PRS, participation was guaranteed through the thematic groups. Although they no longer meet regularly and have not been assigned specific monitoring responsibilities, the groups are consulted for comments on the annual PRSP progress report and were to be reconstituted for the PRS review in 2005.

Various participatory workshops have been held, such as an April 2003 workshop organized by the Central Office of the Census on priority themes and indicators to be elaborated. Furthermore, a workshop conducted in June 2003 made progress in the selection of indicators (and there is now a consensus on about 60 core indicators).

Although the national statistical council will be the main consultative body, it has not yet been established. The details of participation still require clarification, particularly regarding the representation of all stakeholders. While plans for participation are in place, they have not yet been implemented.

Decentralization

A slow process of general decentralization is underway, and this process is difficult to advance due to low capacity at the local level. Currently, line ministries report administrative data to the central offices. However, there are capacity constraints in the ministry regional offices. Furthermore, although regional services of the NSO have been planned, they have not yet been established.

Indicators and data sources

There have been some lags in the dissemination of monitoring results as evidenced by the fact that the 2001 census has still not been made entirely public. The delays in data dissemination are being exacerbated by capacity and financial resource constraints. Moreover, the awareness of the various sources of data across government is weak. Nonetheless, the main constraint in Niger has been the shortage of data rather than the obstacles in processing data. A workshop conducted in June 2003 made some progress in the selection of indicators. The PRSP synthesis document lists 42 indicators and, for each, the frequency of production, the level of disaggregation, the source, and the institution responsible; there has been a subsequent agreement on monitoring approximately 60 core indicators. With the implementation in 2005 of the first comprehensive national household income and expenditure survey, many of the outcomes will now be easier to monitor.

It is also worth noting that there is consensus on the importance of analyzing the spatial dimensions of poverty in Niger (the construction of a poverty map) and assessing the feasibility of creating a geographically disaggregated information system to inform budget allocations at the local level and to help local authorities during the process of decentralization. This geographic information system could integrate existing sources of data (the 2001 census, the school map at the Ministry of Education, the national health information system at the Ministry of Health, the geographic information system at the Ministry of Hydraulics) into a more coherent, flexible, and unique overall system. If such a system were to be created, much of the work involved would consist in ensuring consistency in data formats

and geographic code identification and in building a user-friendly methodology for accessing these data. Support will need to be provided to the
country in implementing this geographic information system.

Separately, establishing a code in the budget nomenclature that will
facilitate the monitoring of poverty-related expenditures is also a priority. In
this nomenclature, the categories of spending deemed to be directly related
to poverty reduction are likely to be different from the list of priority expenditures to be protected under the country's budget regulation and cash management process, as some of these expenditures (for example, part of the
wages to be paid to public servants) are not necessarily related to poverty-
related activities, and some poverty-related activities, while important,
may not need to be protected to the same extent as other types of spending in the short run. Overall, better identification and classification of those
expenditures considered directly linked to the fight against poverty will also
help strengthen the coherence between budget laws and the objectives and
targets of the poverty reduction strategy.

Products

Besides the annual PRSP progress report, poverty monitoring outputs
include the Millennium Development Goals Report and the Human
Development Report currently drafted by academic researchers and the
United Nations Development Program. The latter two reports will be prepared by the poverty observatory once it becomes operational.

Dissemination

Several concrete steps have been taken to encourage information feedback
into the policy process. These include the strategic coordination and timeliness of reporting and the dissemination of information, such as, the publication of the annual PRSP progress report to influence the budget. Yet,
in reality, there is no evidence that this has been provided for. Information
dissemination has also been achieved through workshops, such as the April
2003 workshop held in Niamey on 2001 census data.

Finance and donor support

Because of a shortage of national resources, the role of donors in shaping
the M&E system is significant. In terms of data collection, a number of

individual surveys and databases, as well as the analysis of information, emerge from and are financed by donor projects. Survey and data analyses carried out by the NSO and other government and academic bodies rely heavily on external funding. Even administrative or routine data systems that operate more independently rely on donor funding, and the line ministries operating such systems address specific data inquiries by external agencies.

Donors have also contributed to the institutional profile of the poverty monitoring system. The establishment of a poverty observatory was strongly backed and funded by the European Union and the United Nations Development Program. However, more coordination among donors would result in reducing the duplication of effort and the over-burdening of the NSO and line ministries.

Lessons

As in many other countries, one of the key weaknesses of the M&E system in Niger is the lack of a comprehensive, integrated monitoring plan. The introduction of a poverty observatory and the reporting flows that have been created between the directorates of studies and planning in the ministries and the PRSP secretariat are examples of efforts to strengthen monitoring activities. However, because Niger is such a poor country, there is often a lack of capacity for systematic M&E.

There is an agreed list of indicators to be followed by the PRSP, and participation has been implemented and encouraged throughout the PRSP process. There have also been gains in data collection; the first national income and expenditure survey in 10 years was implemented in 2005.

However, stronger coordination and oversight functions are required. While the location of the PRSP secretariat in the Office of the Prime Minister and the clear allocation of PRSP coordination responsibilities to this unit ensure continuity and political weight, the responsibilities in co-ordination to be carried out by other institutions are less clear, as illustrated, for example, by the incompatibility within the geographic information systems and databases. The creation of a new structure for the NSO, which will include a poverty observatory, is a sign that progress should be achieved in the M&E system in coming years.

11

Tanzania

History and Context

Poverty monitoring arrangements in Tanzania are significantly affected by
the country's poverty reduction strategy (PRS) process, as well as by the
systems and traditions of the government. The following background
features have greatly influenced the country's poverty reduction efforts:

This chapter is based on a background country report by David Booth (2004) and inputs
by Johannes Hoogeveen and Louise Fox. The country report was completed in 2004.
Tanzania adopted a second poverty reduction strategy (PRS II) within the National
Strategy for Growth and the Reduction of Poverty (MKUKUTA) in June 2005. This
led to significant changes in the poverty monitoring system. Some points in this chapter may therefore no longer apply; however, the authors have made an effort to indicate
specific instances within the text. The historical situation is nonetheless instructive in
terms of the problems faced early on in the poverty reduction strategy process.

The PRS builds on a long tradition of planning to achieve economic and social goals. Poverty eradication strategies predate the PRS initiative; they stretch as far back as 1964. These strategies were, however, mostly technocratic exercises, often donor driven, and not well linked to political processes.

The national policy process showed a tendency toward fragmentation. There are no central institutions capable of guaranteeing overall policy coherence, with the result that policy formulation tended to be disconnected from implementation. At the end of the 1990s, reform plans were formulated without reference to resource constraints and without feedback from the ground. There was no real cabinet function, and funding for government departments was unpredictable. Monitoring was therefore a low-stakes activity.

Fragmentation increased over the 1990s and was exacerbated by uncoordinated donor activity. This reduced the chances of translating formally agreed public policies into action. The Poverty Reduction Strategy Paper (PRSP) initiative reflected these tendencies.

The cabinet agreed on Tanzania's full PRSP in mid-2000. The PRSP was not, however, coordinated with the medium-term plan for economic growth and poverty reduction, and this resulted in both obstacles and opportunities in the development of the poverty monitoring system (PMS). Most of these points have been addressed through Mkakati wa Kukuza Uchumi na Kuondoa Umaskini Tanzania (the National Strategy for Growth and the Reduction of Poverty, MKUKUTA).

Description of the PRS Monitoring System

Origins of the system

When the cabinet agreed on Tanzania's full PRSP in mid-2000, the PRSP contained little detail regarding the appropriate framework for *monitoring* the strategy's implementation. Later that year, agreement on the institutional framework was reached. The framework envisaged the establishment of a national poverty monitoring steering committee that would report to a PRSP technical committee that was already functioning. Moreover, the need for smaller specialized technical working groups was identified and agreed upon. Following additional elaboration, the structure of the PMS was defined in the poverty monitoring master plan issued in November 2001. This coincided more or less with Tanzania's completion of the

Heavily Indebted Poor Countries Initiative, which had been made conditional on one year of successful PRSP implementation.

While the *monitoring of the PRS I* appears to have gotten off to a slow start, it was, in another sense, already in place. Various monitoring activities were under way, and the monitoring of the national poverty eradication strategy of 1998 had already been included among the duties assigned to the Poverty Eradication Division (PED) in the Office of the Vice-President.

Main institutional actors

The institutional framework agreed at the October 2000 workshop comprised the following institutions.

The *national poverty monitoring steering committee* is supported by the PRSP technical committee. It is a broad-based committee; the members represent key ministries involved in the PRSP, civil society, academic institutions, the private sector, religious groups, and international development agencies. Its key responsibilities include overseeing the monitoring process and guiding the preparation of the annual report.

The *poverty monitoring secretariat* supports the steering committee. It consists of key staff members in the Office of the Vice-President, the Ministry of Finance, and the Office of the President (Planning and Privatization). It organizes committee meetings, liaises with the working groups, and prepares working papers. In addition, it serves as a central clearinghouse for documentation, provides information to stakeholders, prepares financial reports, and coordinates the consultation process.

The *technical working groups* became operational in May 2001. Their first task was to produce inputs for the poverty monitoring master plan. In addition, the working groups were required to oversee the implementation of this plan, as well as the major outputs of the PMS. To facilitate cooperation, there is overlapping membership among the groups. The four technical working groups include the following:

- The *survey and census group*, chaired by the director general of the National Bureau of Statistics, coordinates the production of poverty-relevant data sets through household surveys and the population census. This group includes representatives of the National Bureau of Statistics, the Eastern Africa Statistical Training Center, the Bank of Tanzania, the Planning Commission, academic institutions, the Macro-Policy Group on Gender, and international development agencies.

- The *routine data group* is coordinated by the Office of the President (Regional Administration and Local Government, RALG). Because most data sources are linked to service delivery and services are increasingly becoming decentralized, this group works mainly at the local level. It reviews current systems, develops indicators, suggests system improvements, determines baselines, and assists in capacity building. The group consists of representatives of the RALG, the local government reform program, ministries responsible for major sectoral data systems, the National Bureau of Statistics, and international development agencies.
- The *research and analysis group* is chaired by the director for macro-economic planning in the Office of the President (Planning and Privatization). It sets priorities in research and analysis and proposes funding mechanisms. Research on Poverty Alleviation, a research institute, provides a secretariat. Membership includes representation from the government (Office of the Vice-President), the Central Bank, the National Bureau of Statistics, academic and research institutions, civil society, gender groups, and international development agencies.
- The *dissemination, sensitization, and advocacy group* is chaired by the director for poverty eradication in the Office of the Vice-President. It is responsible for ensuring that PMS data and information are presented to stakeholders in a user-friendly format. The group includes representation from the Office of the Vice-President, the RALG, the Office of the President (Planning and Privatization), the Ministry of Finance, the Ministry of Education, the National Bureau of Statistics, civil society organizations, international development agencies, and the private sector.

Changes in the pipeline: problems already identified

Although the system is new, it has integrated many existing elements and inherited problems from existing poverty monitoring activities. A number of technical working groups are facing difficulties in maintaining their overlapping memberships, particularly in retaining links with key users on the policy side. This is partly because demands on people's time, especially within the government, are so substantial.

The location of the secretariat (and the principal entity receiving donor-funded technical support) in the Office of the Vice-President was already fixed. The monitoring of budget execution was formally defined as one of the activities encompassed in PRS monitoring. Together with the limitations on the budget process at that time, the institutional division of labor tended to engender a situation in which results monitoring occurred in parallel with arrangements for strengthening the financial accountability of ministries, departments, and agencies. However, the problem is now being addressed.

There is also a duplication in planning processes. The Office of the President includes a division for planning and privatization, which runs a medium-term plan for economic growth and poverty reduction that overlaps with the PRS. There is no consultation between the two entities, and, while the medium-term plan was sent to Parliament, the PRS was not.

Several of these arrangements are set to change as a result of the alteration in the content of the PRS, the new structure that the government adopted after the elections, including the transfer of the PED to the new Ministry of Planning, Privatization, and Empowerment, the new poverty monitoring master plan, and the new budget guideline process. It may, however, be significant that the initiative to strengthen the link between the PRS and the budget arose through the external evaluation commissioned for the 2004 Public Expenditure Review.

Overall Status

Although the PRSP has resulted in a change of direction, substantial progress is heavily dependent on the improvement of other government systems, more particularly, public service reform and budget reform.

Due to the fact that the PMS competes with other monitoring and reporting requirements for budget support, the relationship between these two is a key issue for the future. The link to the budget is generally weak, but some progress is evident in the fact that the World Bank Public Expenditure Review has become an annual assessment process that is led by the Ministry of Finance and that is relatively participatory. There is a fully functional medium-term expenditure framework and a technically advanced financial information system that allows the monitoring of budget execution.

The PRS has succeeded in increasing the absolute level of resources going to priority sectors (for instance, primary health and education, water, rural roads, and agriculture). However, the increase in resources comes mainly from donor funding, while government resources are being applied elsewhere. According to the government, the priority sector concept is too rigid. The PRS II has abandoned priority sectors in favor of cluster strategies that articulate pro-poor policies across almost all sectors. Now, inputs into the budget formulation process will have to be justified with reference to these cluster strategies, that is, in effect, sector policy makers have a material incentive to develop outcome-oriented rationales for what they do with their allocations from public resources. For the first time, they are being given reasons to make use of data on results.

In a direct complement to this, the PMS has made impressive progress in the production of survey data, including a household budget survey, a Demographic and Health Survey, a census, and a labor force survey.

The working groups have proved too burdensome for some members, with the possible exception of development partner members who are over-represented in the system, and, as a result, attendance has become irregular. Moreover, agencies are often territorial about their own monitoring and evaluation activities, and this is a problem that cannot be solved simply by adding more committees.

Key Topics

Ownership

Ownership revolves around whether the PRS and monitoring system are institutionally mainstreamed. Based on policy traditions, the risk is that the monitoring system will track results for which no one is held specially responsible. In order for a substantial change to occur in the levels of commitment and accountability within the country, there is a need to link negotiations over budget allocations to results-oriented cluster strategies.

Leadership of the system

Key oversight rests with the national poverty monitoring steering committee, which includes ministries, broad civil society representation, and international development agencies.

Coordination

Coordination of the system is assigned to the PED. At the apex of the system, the PRS technical committee is nominally responsible for key outputs such as the annual progress report, but has lacked clear terms of reference. Initially, an official of the Ministry of Finance chaired the committee rather tentatively, although observers have noticed improvement in the last year or so. The poverty monitoring steering committee is thought by some to be too large for the chair (the permanent secretary, Office of the Vice-President) to manage effectively.

The overburdening and understaffing of the PED has been an issue for several years, and the option of restricting the mandate of the PED to monitoring and allowing another body to take over the coordination of the process may well be proposed. This may have political ramifications, however, and may address the problem in a merely administrative way.

Participation

Participation is institutionalized through the membership of civil society organizations on the steering committee and in the technical working groups.

Indicators and data sources

In practice, the PMS is restricted to impact and outcome indicators and neglects input and output (intermediate) indicators. As a result, it is not particularly useful for annual progress reports. Since the late 1990s, *survey data* have been relatively good. The research and analysis working group is backed by a number of respected research institutes, including Research on Poverty Alleviation, which acts as the secretariat. The Poverty and Human Development Report is the main output; it contains frank, serious analysis. However, the report points out that some of the data it uses are not suitable for annual reporting.

Tracking intermediate (input, process, and output) indicators is essential to fulfill the role of PRS monitoring arrangements in feeding useful information back to decision makers. This relies to a very important degree on routine data systems such as administrative and financial reporting and management information systems. Tanzania suffers from the usual problems encountered in many other countries, including a lack of skills and weak incentives at the local level, inconsistent indicators, and poor coordination (including within sectors), particularly between line ministries and local governments.

Data producers rarely have access to or use the analyzed data. While the local government reform program aims to make some local analysis possible, this is still part of a bigger plan. Moreover, there are indications that routine data gaps vary across sectors. For instance, statistics collected by the Ministry of Education and Culture are relatively reliable, which is in direct contrast to those collected by the Ministry of Health. In some sectors, for example, agriculture, almost no data are available.

An additional challenge relates to the functioning of the routine data group. Over the years, this group has failed to coordinate the routine data collection that is at the core of its mandate. The biggest issue relates to the fact that meetings, which are the responsibility of the RALG, are held irregularly and are poorly attended. According to some sources, the root of the problem lies in the fact that, for the RALG, the role of coordination is secondary to a major reform process the RALG is coordinating in local government.

Efforts are being made to tackle problems related to routine data, and, in the new PMS, the routine data group and the survey and census group have been combined under the joint leadership of the National Bureau of Statistics and the RALG.

Products

Annual progress reports constitute the main output of the PMS and are expected to provide useful annual feedback to both stakeholders and donors. However, because a PRS monitoring was originally skewed toward measuring impact and outcome indicators and lacked a strong focus on action, it was not particularly suitable for annual performance monitoring. There was therefore no formal logical framework setting out the chains of causation from policies and programs to final impacts. (This is expected to be addressed in PRS II.) In general, an absence of intermediate indicators, such as in this case, makes the measurement of accountability more difficult.

By contrast, budget-support performance assessment framework reviews are action focused in that they are specifically concerned with improving the functioning of public institutions and providing a broad indication of how each measure would contribute to PRS objectives.

It is necessary to consider more closely why the annual progress report lacks the features that would allow budget-support donors to rely on it to a greater extent and how this situation may be changed. Ultimately, aligning the annual progress report with minimum requirement donor reporting is a widely acknowledged challenge. (This has been addressed, to a large extent, in the new performance assessment framework and PRS II.)

Dissemination

Although the dedicated dissemination, sensitization, and advocacy group is a useful innovation, its results have been disappointing. There is a specific job to be done in linking up the potential data user and helping to generate a culture of evidence-based policy thinking. In practice, however, while this group seems to have done a fair amount of dissemination, it has not done much of the related sensitization or advocacy. Some of the other working groups see it as redundant and serving principally as a mailbox for the glossy reports they have produced.

Obstacles to greater data use arise predominantly from the incentive structures within the government. Although useful promotional activities could be undertaken, changes in the budget process are more likely to motivate the use of evidence-based results, and sensitization can accelerate this process.

The link to the policy process

It is a general finding that PRSPs are more effective if there is a means of translating the objectives of the strategy into priorities for public policy through the process of formulating and executing the national budget. Although Tanzania has not been in the forefront in this respect, there are a number of favorable features in the country's approach. There is a fully functional medium-term expenditure framework, program budgeting, and a good financial information system. On the negative side, however, there is limited accountability for policy results, and demand remains low.

A direct link to the PMS is now being established; key ministries are being required to provide outcome-oriented rationales for annual budget submissions. However, there is a danger that the delivery and monitoring systems for poverty reduction budgetary support will swamp the system of the national budget. The donor performance assessment framework integrates the World Bank's Poverty Reduction Support Credit monitoring framework. Strengthening the relationship between the performance assessment framework and the PRS monitoring system is therefore critical for aligning budget support with national policies, an issue that has been addressed in the new performance assessment framework.

Donor alignment

There has been a shift toward more budget support and improvement in the relations between the government and donors that predate the PRS and are symbolized by the commitment to produce a joint Tanzania assistance strategy. This has encouraged donors to assign a greater proportion of funds to budget support, which now accounts for close to 50 percent of official development assistance. Sectoral and cross-cutting common basket funds have also become more important. The government has not yet taken steps to include these in the medium-term expenditure framework sectoral ceilings, however, which would have the effect of equalizing the incentives facing ministries in terms of budget allocations and donor projects.

Lessons

Overall, the PMS in Tanzania appears coherent and well designed and includes some useful innovations. The system is quite complex, however, and faces a number of key challenges. A review of the structure and approach of the PMS is expected following the revision of the PRS. This will be a useful opportunity to revisit a number of organizational issues that have been pending since the elaboration of the poverty monitoring master plan.

In countries with PRSPs, monitoring activities have the potential to contribute to three principal dimensions of the PRS:

- greater commitment to and accountability for poverty reduction efforts within the country (country ownership)
- greater results orientation in national policy processes
- creation of the proper conditions so that poverty reduction efforts can take the form of a genuine partnership between national and international actors

The following options and lessons reflect these three dimensions.

Country ownership: Monitoring arrangements best serve in promoting country commitment to and accountability for poverty reduction policies if they are closely linked to a politically supported and maturing budget process. There has been difficulty linking the PMS (under the first PRS) to budget allocations. However, there are indications that, under PRS II, a more effective form of budget link is being introduced. This has already generated new demand for PRS-related information and confirms the proposition that poverty monitoring arrangements will always be affected by the surrounding institutions for policy making and public expenditure management.

Results- and evidence-based policy making: Routine data systems not only produce information of uneven quality, but are characterized by considerable duplication and waste. Although more significant efforts to tackle this issue have been placed on the agenda by the PMS review, the issue of incentives, which is often a key to enhancing the demand for monitoring data, also needs to be recognized on the supply side. While this does not represent a complete response to the problems in routine data collection, it should help reinforce the demand-supply relationship and the use of these statistics. In the end, however, the promotion of results-oriented policy will not be accomplished within the poverty monitoring sphere itself, but will occur as a result of the quality of the incentives generated in the wider system.

Enabling more effective partnerships: Tanzania's PRS matrix focuses mainly on outcomes, while, as a result of strong donor influence, policy actions are itemized separately in the performance assessment framework matrix. There needs to be a gradual convergence of the two instruments, and donors should align around the common instrument.

Finally, the role of poverty monitoring arrangements will always be greatly affected by the surrounding institutions involved in policy making and public expenditure management; these may be expected to change under the influence of political considerations and other factors. Indeed, recent changes have resulted in significant shifts in efforts to address many of the problems that plagued the first PMS.

Uganda

History and Context

U ganda developed its poverty reduction strategy (PRS)—the poverty eradication action plan (PEAP)—before the PRS initiative was launched in 1999. The first PEAP, in the mid-1990s, benefited from the strong domestic political impetus provided by Ugandan President

This chapter is based on a background country report by David Booth and Xavier Nsabagasani (2004) and inputs by Louise Fox. The study was undertaken in the second half of 2004 and has been partially updated to reflect conditions in the summer of 2005. Substantial changes may have occurred that are not reflected in this chapter, and readers are encouraged to seek additional information if they wish to focus on the system of this particular country.

Museveni's interest and focus on the need to reduce poverty. The second PEAP was adopted as the country's Poverty Reduction Strategy Paper (PRSP) and as the basis for Heavily Indebted Poor Countries Initiative completion in 2000. The PEAP was initially championed by officials in the combined Ministry of Finance, Planning, and Economic Development (MFPED) and strongly supported by both the president and donors. This combination gave it unusually significant prominence in domestic policy and created a solid basis for evidence-based policy making and implementation.

More broadly, in the late 1990s and early years of the new decade, a number of reforms created a more favorable environment for evidence-based policy making. This included a commitment to output-based budgeting, a medium-term expenditure framework that imposes hard budget constraints on sectors and local governments, and mechanisms to link the government budget and the PEAP and involve parliamentary scrutiny of the budget.

One of the features of the link between the PEAP and the budget is the poverty action fund (PAF), a virtual fund within the budget that ensures disbursements for selected priority subsectors. Despite its limitations, the PAF contributed to an important reorientation in spending during the first two PEAP periods.

In Uganda, the consultative budget process requires sectoral agencies to submit sectoral budget framework papers that provide a justification for their recurrent and capital funding requests. Despite limitations in the extent to which these budget framework papers are able to influence overall sectoral allocations, scrutiny of the consistency of these papers with the PEAP and reviews carried out by joint sectoral working groups (including government, donor, and other stakeholders) have shifted policy making somewhat to an orientation toward results.

The mechanisms that link the budget and the PEAP have encouraged donors to provide a greater share of their assistance through general budget support. This and the reduction in the number of donor-financed projects have, in turn, encouraged sectors to develop clear, comprehensive strategies and policies.

In June 2002, the Parliament created a new National Planning Authority, thereby possibly separating the planning and financing functions that were originally housed together in the MFPED. Although formally under the minister of finance, the new planning authority has its own board and reports directly to Parliament. It has a very broad mandate to produce medium- and long-term plans, guide other actors in decentralized planning processes, and monitor and evaluate development programs. The National Planning Authority is still being organized; it has few staff and, so far, has played a limited role in the PRSP process.

All these elements have shaped the context in which the PRS monitoring system has been designed and implemented. This context is generally conducive to the emergence of an effective PRS monitoring system, although some of the changes are recent and, to be sustained, will require steady commitment to evidence-based policy making.

Description of the PRS Monitoring System

The PRS monitoring system was established on a solid foundation, and the initial steps were promising for several reasons. First, reporting on poverty and the implementation of poverty reduction activities predates the requirements linked to the PRSP initiative, for instance, through the PEAP biannual poverty status reports and the background to the budget. A second factor is the development of a rational budget process, which has produced domestic pressure for evidence-based policy. Finally, Uganda has a relatively strong practice of collecting and analyzing data on poverty based on regular household surveys, public expenditure tracking surveys, the monitoring of the PAF by nongovernmental organizations (NGOs) at the local level, and participatory poverty assessments. A series of components was already in place when the PRS monitoring system was being designed to coordinate activities.

Main components of the system

The various monitoring agencies that existed prior to the PRS monitoring system include the following.

The *Uganda Bureau of Statistics* (UBoS) generates national accounts and carries out the census and major surveys. In theory, the bureau is also responsible for overseeing the quality of the data collected by other agencies (sectoral ministries, local-level agencies), although it has not played this role very actively. It has reasonably well-defined responsibilities, a corporate plan, and sufficient operational autonomy as an executive agency to carry out the plan. Its dependency on short-term donor funding, however, is an impediment to the regular implementation of the plan. A government-donor working group has been formed to address this issue (see below).

The *Economic Policy Research Center* is a government agency supported by the Africa Capacity Building Foundation and contracted by the MFPED to provide research services in support of the PRSP. It analyzes data produced by the UBoS, with assistance from donors and the guidance and cooperation of international researchers. The center is known for high-quality, independent research. With the World Bank, it has also developed the public expenditure tracking survey, an innovative instrument for estimating whether the inputs of the PEAP are being effectively delivered.

The *poverty action fund monitoring arrangements* at the local level are coordinated by the Uganda Debt Network, an NGO.

Ugandan participatory poverty assessments provide case studies of issues in policy implementation and reveal important sectoral and cross-sectoral issues. They have been influential and have triggered significant policy shifts.

The *poverty monitoring and analysis unit* (PMAU) was established in the MFPED in 1998 with support from the U.K. Department for International Development. (It was originally called the poverty monitoring unit.) Initially, it produced the poverty status reports every two years. Gradually, the unit focused more on analyzing progress under some pillars of the PEAP (and was then renamed the poverty monitoring and analysis unit). Although donor funded, it is relatively well integrated into the MFPED policy process. The unit's professional staff includes a poverty analyst, a policy analyst, and an Overseas Development Institute fellow. Attempts to coordinate a broader general poverty-related research initiative have not been successful.

Routine data systems are critical components of any PRS monitoring system for tracking changes in the composition of inputs and intermediate outcomes through administrative and financial reporting and management information systems. In Uganda, as in most other countries, routine data systems suffer from shortcomings. Thus, the data produced are typically facility based and need to be complemented by population-based information from surveys, censuses, or sentinel sites. Issues have arisen regarding the completeness and reliability of reporting. Indicators are not always consistent. Coordination is poor, including within sectors and between central and local agencies, leading to overlaps, gaps, and redundancies. The reporting burdens on administrators are excessive, and there is a lack of local analysis for local planning purposes.

Donor-supported *projects* house various systems for tracking single projects or clusters of projects supported by one donor. These systems formally remain outside the PRS monitoring system, potentially exacerbating pressures on national capacity. Efforts are under way to integrate these systems into the national system, thereby reducing duplications.

A first attempt at unifying the system

The monitoring elements described above have distinct origins. Efforts to provide overall coordination and direction began after the second PEAP was adopted as the country's PRSP.

A poverty monitoring and evaluation strategy was developed by the MFPED in June 2002, following broad discussions with relevant stakeholders. The strategy was intended to monitor PEAP policies and programs and meet the monitoring requirements of the World Bank's Poverty Reduction Support Credit. The strategy described activities, responsibilities, and a mechanism for increased coordination.

The poverty monitoring and evaluation strategy divided the leadership role among the principal organizations, as follows. The MFPED, through PMAU, monitored the intermediate and final outcomes (impacts) of the PEAP. The UBoS was charged with gathering national statistics on intermediate and final outcomes. Sectoral ministries, through their management information systems, provided assessments of sectoral performance in terms of inputs, activities, and outputs at the sectoral level, and district authorities undertook local PEAP implementation.

The strategy was also intended to engage various organizations in the validation of findings, including the Office of the Prime Minister, the Ministry of Public Service, the Inspectorate General of Government, the Uganda Evaluation Society, civil society organizations, and development partners. The UBoS was responsible for the standardization of concepts and measures. More specific responsibilities for analysis and research were allocated to the macro and budget departments of the MFPED, the Economic Policy Research Center, the Uganda AIDS Commission, and the Office for the Coordination of Humanitarian Assistance.

The strategy also created a poverty monitoring network to coordinate activities, exploit synergies among institutions, and minimize duplication. The network was to be chaired by the director of economic affairs at the MFPED and include representatives of all stakeholders at a high level.

The PMAU was to play the role of secretariat and convene meetings quarterly.

More specifically, the objectives and responsibilities of the strategy and the network included institutionalizing the functions of the PMAU, determining the frequency of household surveys to obtain district-level estimates, confirming that national service delivery surveys were undertaken by the UBoS and determining whether the national integrity survey should be transferred to the UBoS, mainstreaming qualitative research and the Uganda Participatory Poverty Assessment Project within the MFPED, streamlining reporting obligations between local governments and the central government, instituting incentives under the results-oriented management arrangements of the Ministry of Public Service to encourage the collection and use of monitoring information, and determining and institutionalizing civil society involvement.

A recent attempt at systemization

In August 2003, the cabinet approved a paper setting out a new system operating under the Office of the Prime Minister. This led to the development of the national integrated monitoring and evaluation strategy (NIMES). The NIMES coordinates all data collection, utilization, and dissemination relative to the PEAP and other national policy frameworks. It is not restricted to monitoring the PEAP and has a broader scope than the earlier poverty monitoring and evaluation strategy.

NIMES is not a new monitoring system, but rather a mechanism to coordinate existing monitoring and evaluation (M&E) activities more effectively through new committees and working groups. It followed an inventory of existing systems undertaken in January 2004. The inventory found a multitude of activities that were not linked into a system and therefore resulted in duplication, wasted resources, inefficient use of the limited capacity, and a number of unfilled information gaps.

The objectives of NIMES are to assist stakeholders in identifying their information needs, coordinate information systems to ensure these information needs can be met, provide information in a timely manner for national policy frameworks such as the PEAP, and build M&E capacity.

The idea behind NIMES is to create a series of forums where representatives of existing monitoring systems may address coordination issues. Two recent data-based initiatives under development are central to NIMES: (1) Uganda Info, which is to provide a platform for consolidating indicators

across sectors and geographical areas and (2) the local government information and communication system, which is a management information system for local governments that contains selected financial, administrative,
socioeconomic, and development indicators.

The system is still under development and will likely evolve, including
after the preparation of the third PEAP. Nonetheless, the following
arrangements are already in place:

- the Office of the Prime Minister: assigned the general mandate for coordinating policy implementation across government and strengthened
  to address this new function
- a cabinet subcommittee on policy coordination: attended by ministers
- an implementation coordination steering committee: attended by
  permanent secretaries
- a national M&E coordination committee: reporting to the implementation coordination steering committee
- three specialized working groups: reporting to the national M&E coordination committee and focusing on geographical information systems,
  district information systems, and research and evaluation
- a technical committee
- a full-time secretariat in the Office of the Prime Minister: responsible for
  the coordination of M&E on government policies and programs

In the fall of 2004, a separate government-donor sector working group
was formed to coordinate programs and funding for statistical development. The impetus for the formation of the group was the frustrating problem of shortages in short-term statistical funding. The initial goal of the
groups was to create a donor basket for UBoS funding. The goal was
expanded to include improvements in administrative and statistical data
planning and collection for the PRSP monitoring process, as well as reductions in the overlaps between these data sources. Initially, the group focused
on the UBoS. In January 2005, the government proposed that UBoS funding should be included in the PAF, thus giving it a protected status in the
budget. In June 2005, to facilitate this step and increase transparency, the
UBoS was granted a separate line in the overall budget. The UBoS is now
in the process of realigning its corporate plan with the M&E requirements
of the PRSP and working with the Office of the Prime Minister to cost out
the M&E proposed in the PRSP. These two exercises should result in a
UBoS plan that donors and the government would be committed to fund
and a partially completed PRSP M&E costing and budget.

Overall Status

The system is relatively advanced having been developed on a solid, high-level foundation. It is considered by many to be a leader in institutional innovation. While the system design is strong, system implementation continues to encounter problems because of rivalry, territoriality, and competition for access to donor resources.

Key Topics

Ownership

The PEAP has been more effectively mainstreamed institutionally than most PRSPs as a result of the strong political commitment to the strategy. As a result, the PEAP and key planning and budgeting arrangements have been relatively well linked, increasing the accountability for the PEAP. Since central elements of the PRS monitoring system have been tied in with this structure, the system is generally more strongly owned than are systems in most other countries.

The mainstreaming of the secretariat within the department of coordination and monitoring in the Office of the Prime Minister is likely to foster ownership, and the process of designing the NIMES also seems to have fostered ownership.

Another important development regarding country ownership is the strengthening of Parliament's role in reviewing budget allocations and disbursements in a results-oriented perspective. The MFPED has facilitated greater parliamentary interest in the results, including by providing Parliament with relevant information. There is scope for the NIMES secretariat and the MFPED to improve the quality of parliamentary briefings and, more generally, to increase the country ownership of the PEAP and the monitoring system.

Capacity

Additional resources have been devoted to the coordination of the NIMES in the Office of the Prime Minister. This is an important element for a successful system. However, the reporting requirements established by the NIMES for the various ministries, departments, and agencies are additional to the reporting already required by the MFPED and are likely to impose a strain on the capacity of these institutions.

Similarly, donors still support a very large number of projects in Uganda, most of which either set up their own monitoring mechanisms or impose additional burdens on the government's monitoring system (to meet each donor's internal reporting requirements). In both cases, a tax is imposed on the government's capacity for monitoring.

Overall, the quality of information supplied by the various actors in the NIMES is higher than the corresponding information in most PRS countries. However, important limitations remain, in particular on administrative data. These limitations are partly related to the capacity of sectoral agencies to collect good quality and timely information and are a central focus of the NIMES.

Besides the technical issues, there are also capacity constraints related to the incentives for the civil service. These incentives, whether at the institutional level or at the level of individual staff, may be partly responsible for duplication and poor coordination, which, in turn, strain technical capacity.

Participation

Participation in the PEAP is institutionalized through the poverty reduction working group. In terms of monitoring, NGOs have a wide range of independent M&E activities. Thus, there is extensive NGO involvement in the Ugandan Participatory Poverty Assessment Process, as well as in district PAF monitoring. In addition, the UBoS uses participatory processes to design some of its surveys.

Indicators

Until recently, PEAP monitoring tended to focus mostly on outcomes and impacts, and there was less concentration on inputs and outputs. This is reflected in the results and monitoring matrix. However, greater focus has now been placed on input and output indicators, as reflected in the PEAP policy matrix. This is critical in ensuring effective monitoring, since all levels are needed to track policies and programs and their effects and to promote accountability.

Products

Reporting on the PRS and on PRS implementation is carried out on the basis of two existing monitoring products: the poverty status reports prepared every two years (reporting on the PEAP) and the background to the budget paper prepared every year. References to the intended use of beneficiary assessments, client scorecards, and community-based monitoring in tracking PAF program implementation and service delivery have also been made. Finally, in an important innovation, sectoral joint review reports feature alongside the annual national budget framework paper during the budget elaboration process.

Link to the policy process

Overall, the PRSP process has altered the expenditure mix in Uganda toward programs and projects focused more on poverty. The share of these projects in the budget rose from 54 percent in 1998 to 76 percent in 2004. The share of education in the budget is now roughly 25 percent. The PRSP process also forces sectors to justify their policies more in terms of the poverty focus, and local government spending is being restricted to certain types of expenditures focused on poverty (for example, primary school books and so on).

The links between the PEAP and key planning and budgeting arrangements have been stronger in Uganda than in most PRSP countries. This has been enhanced in Uganda by the requirement to bring the sectoral budget framework papers in line with the PEAP during the budget process. Although compliance with the PEAP may not have influenced the indicative and final medium-term expenditure framework sectoral ceilings substantially, it has led to sectoral policy making that has become progressively more results oriented. Another factor reinforcing the link between the PEAP and the budget process is the transfer of responsibility for monitoring the Poverty Reduction Support Credit from the budget directorate in the Ministry of Finance to the Office of the Prime Minister.

The link between the budget and the PEAP has encouraged donors to focus their assistance through budget support. This form of support, which nests donor support within the budget, can play a fundamental role because it equalizes the incentives for ministries between donor and budget funding.

The inclusion of input, output, outcome, and impact indicators in the PEAP in the results and monitoring matrix and the policy matrix and, more generally, the effort to track the entire results chain are important changes that will help strengthen the link between the budget and outcomes.

A pending issue is the limited changes in civil service management. The system of results-based management operated by the Ministry of Public Service includes strategic plans and personal performance targets. However, this system is not yet fully linked to the budget planning process or integrated with human resource management.

Donor alignment and support

Donors have shifted part of their assistance to budget support, which both results from and strengthens the results focus of the PEAP and its link to the budget process. In addition, the development of the PEAP policy matrix is an important element in the establishment of more evidence-based policy and better alignment of donor monitoring arrangements with country systems.

On the other hand, donors continue to operate numerous projects, most of which establish their own monitoring systems or impose additional requirements on government institutions. The harmonization of reporting for donor-supported activities, which has improved in the context of budget support, is still in its infancy for projects.

Lessons

The efforts to build a coherent and effective PRS monitoring system started earlier in Uganda than in most other PRS countries because of the creation of the PEAP in the mid-1990s. Because Uganda's system is generally more advanced than others, important lessons learned in Uganda can help other countries.

Monitoring arrangements can better serve in the promotion of the commitment of a country to and accountability for poverty reduction policies if they are closely related to a maturing budget process. The PRS process in Uganda benefited at an early stage from high-level political commitment and close integration with the budget and budget execution.

The role of poverty monitoring arrangements is affected by changes in institutions charged with policy making and public expenditure management. Hence, developing a PRS monitoring system is a process. All the objectives cannot be achieved overnight, and there will typically be temporary setbacks and advances. This implies a need for flexible arrangements.

Increasing the capacity of stakeholders, particularly Parliament, and ensuring that data and analysis are disseminated in formats relevant to various stakeholders are important for the development of a successful system.

The coordination of data production and use can benefit from an effort to create venues for dialogue. However, incentives are the heart of efforts to enhance coordination. A PRS monitoring system can contribute to promoting results-oriented policy, but the main factor in such a shift remains the broader incentive structure in government systems.

Bibliography

Adam, Christopher S., and J. W. Gunning. 2002. "Redesigning the Aid Contract: Donors' Use of Performance Indicators in Uganda." *World Development* 30 (12): 2045–56.

Asche, Helmut. 2003. "Questions on the Social Monitoring of Poverty Reduction Strategies." Background paper, German Agency for Technical Cooperation, Eschborn, Germany.

Baker, Judy. 2000. "Evaluating the Poverty Impact of Projects: A Handbook for Practitioners." Directions in Development. World Bank, Washington, DC. Available in multiple languages at http://www.worldbank.org/poverty/library/impact.htm.

Bastagli, Francesca. 2004a, "Niger's Poverty Monitoring System: An Analysis of Institutional Arrangements." Unpublished working paper, World Bank, Washington, DC.

———. 2004b, "Mali's Poverty Monitoring System: An Analysis of Institutional Arrangements." Unpublished working paper, World Bank, Washington, DC.

Black, Richard, and Howard White. 2004. *Targeting Development: Critical Perspective on the Millennium Development Goals and International Development Targets*. London: Routledge.

Bonifas, Christian. 2004. "Setting Up an Integrated Framework for Monitoring and Evaluating the PRSP: Status Report and Proposals of Mauritania." Unpublished paper, Government of Mauritania, Nouakchott, Mauritania.

Booth, David. 2004. "Poverty Monitoring Systems: An Analysis of Institutional Arrangements in Tanzania." Unpublished paper, Department for International Development, London.

Booth, David, and Henry Lucas. 2002. "Good Practice in the Development of PRSP Indicators and Monitoring Systems." Working Paper 172 (July), Overseas Development Institute, London.

Booth, David, and Xavier Nsabagasani. 2004. "Poverty Monitoring Systems: An Analysis of Institutional Arrangements in Uganda." Unpublished paper, Department for International Development, London.

Brock, Karen, A. Cornwall, and J. Gaventa. 2001. "Power, Knowledge and Political Spaces in the Framing of Poverty Policy." IDS Working Paper 143, Institute of Development Studies, University of Sussex, Brighton, United Kingdom.

Brock, Karen, Rosemary McGee, and Richard Ssewakirjanga. 2002. "Poverty Knowledge and Policy Processes: A Case Study of Ugandan National Poverty Reduction Policy." IDS Research Report 53 (August), Institute of Development Studies, University of Sussex, Brighton, United Kingdom.

Catholic Relief Services. 2003. "Social Accountability Mechanisms: Citizen Engagement for Pro-Poor Policies and Reduced Corruption." Department of Policy and Strategic Issues, Catholic Relief Services, Baltimore. http://www.crs.org/about_us/newsroom/publications/social_accountability.pdf.

Chirwa, Ephraim. 2004. "Poverty Monitoring Systems in Malawi: An Analysis of Institutional Arrangements." Unpublished working paper, World Bank, Washington, DC.

Compton, D. W., M. Baizerman, and S. H. Stockdill, eds. 2002. *The Art, Craft, and Science of Evaluation Capacity Building*. American Evaluation Association New Directions for Evaluation 93. San Francisco: Jossey-Bass.

Coudouel, Aline, and Ferdinando Regalia. 2004. "Poverty Monitoring Systems: An Analysis of the Institutional Arrangements in Bolivia, Guyana, Honduras, and Nicaragua." Unpublished working paper, September, World Bank, Washington, DC.

Coyle, Erin, Zaza Curran, and Alison Evans. 2003. "PRS Monitoring in Africa." PRSP Synthesis Note 7 (June), Overseas Development Institute, London.

Development Bank of Southern Africa, African Development Bank, and World Bank. 2000. "Monitoring and Evaluation Capacity Development in Africa." Selected Proceedings from a seminar and workshop organized by the Development Bank of Southern Africa, the African Development Bank and the World Bank, Johannesburg, September 25–29.

Diamond, Jack. 2003. "Performance Budgeting: Managing the Reform Process." IMF Working Paper 03/33 (February), International Monetary Fund, Washington, DC.

Diaz, Margarita. 2004. "Institutional Arrangements of the Poverty Reduction Strategy Monitoring System: The Case of Honduras." Unpublished working paper, World Bank, Washington, DC.

Driscoll, Ruth. 2004. 'Progress Reviews and Performance Assessment in Poverty Reduction Strategies and Budget Support: A Survey of Current Thinking and Practice." With Karin Christiansen, Paolo de Renzio, Samantha Smith, Katarina Herneryd, and David Booth. Draft report submitted to Japan International Corporation Agency, October, Overseas Development Institute, London.

———. 2005. "Second-Generation Poverty Reduction Strategies: New Opportunities and Emerging Issues." With Alison Evans. *Development Policy Review* 23 (1): 5–25.

Dyer, Kate, and Chris Pain. 2004. "Civil Society Budget Monitoring for National Accountability." Report on a workshop, Lilongwe, Malawi, February 17–19, Oxfam, London.

Eberlei, Walter. 2001. "Institutionalized Participation in Processes beyond PRSP." Commissioned study, German Agency for Technical Cooperation, Eschborn, Germany.

Eberlei, Walter, and Heike Henn. 2003. "Parliaments in Sub-Saharan Africa: Actors in Poverty Reduction?" Published study, German Agency for Technical Cooperation, Eschborn, Germany.

EEC (Etude Economique Conseil) Canada. 2002. "Diagnostic Study of the Poverty Reduction Strategy Monitoring and Evaluation Systems in Burkina Faso, Benin, Côte d'Ivoire, Mali and Niger." Diagnostic study, October. Canadian International Development Agency, Quebec.

Elson, Diane, and Andy Norton. 2002. "What's Behind the Budget?: Politics, Rights and Accountability in the Budget Process." Commissioned study, June, Department for International Development, London.

Entwistle, Janet, Natasha Bajuk, Filippo Cavassini, and Federico Steinberg. 2005. *Country Case Studies: Bolivia, Ghana, Kyrgyz Republic, Senegal.* Vol. 2 of *An Operational Approach to Assessing Country Ownership of Poverty Reduction Strategies.* Washington, DC: Operations Policy and Country Services, World Bank. http://siteresources.worldbank.org/INTPRS1/Resources/383606-1106667815039/completevolumeii.pdf.

Entwistle, Janet, and Filippo Cavassini. 2005. *Analysis and Implications.* Vol. 1 of *An Operational Approach to Assessing Country Ownership of Poverty Reduction Strategies.* Washington, DC: Operations Policy and Country Services, World Bank. http://siteresources.worldbank.org/INTPRS1/Resources/383606-1106667815039/completevolumei.pdf.

Estrella, Marisol, ed. 2000. *Learning from Change: Issues and Experiences in Participatory Monitoring and Evaluation.* London: Intermediate Technology Publications, International Development Research Centre.

Evans, Alison, and Arthur van Diesen. 2002. "Tanzania's Poverty Monitoring System: A Review of Early Experience and Current Challenges." Report, February, Department for International Development, London and Dar es Salaam, Tanzania.

Foster, Mick. 2001. "Use of Surveys to Improve Public Expenditure Management." Paper, June, Centre for Aid and Public Expenditure and Overseas Development Institute, London.

Foster, Mick, Adrian Fozzard, Felix Naschold, and Tim Conway. 2002. "How, When and Why Does Poverty Get Budget Priority?: Poverty Reduction Strategy and Public Expenditure in Five African Countries, Synthesis Paper." Overseas Development Institute Working Paper 168 (May), Overseas Development Institute, London.

Foster, Mick, and Peter Mujimbi. 2002. "How, When and Why Does Poverty Get Budget Priority: Poverty Reduction Strategy and Public Expenditure in Uganda." Overseas Development Institute Working Paper 163 (April), Overseas Development Institute, London.

Fozzard, Adrian. 2001. "The Basic Budgeting Problem: Approaches to Resource Allocation in the Public Sector and Their Implications for Pro-Poor Budgeting." Working Paper 147, Overseas Development Institute, London.

German Federal Ministry for Economic Co-operation and Development. 2003. "German Bilateral Participation in the PRS Process: Cross-Sectional Analysis." Unpublished paper, German Federal Ministry for Economic Co-operation and Development, Bonn.

Gomonda, Nelson. 2001. "Qualitative Impact Monitoring of the Poverty Alleviation Policies and Programs in Malawi." Paper presented at "The Second Forum of Poverty Reduction Strategies," Dakar, September 10–13.

Gould, Jeremy, and Julia Ojanen. 2003. "Merging in the Circle: The Politics of Tanzania's Poverty Reduction Strategy." Policy Papers 2/2003, Institute of Development Studies, University of Helsinki, Helsinki.

GTZ (German Agency for Technical Cooperation). 2002. "Report of a Meeting of Experts on Reporting and Monitoring." Summary report of a meeting organized by the German Agency for Technical Cooperation and the Development Assistance Committee, Organisation for Economic Co-operation and Development, Task Force on Donor Practices, Berlin, March 26–27.

———. 2004a. *Main Report*. Vol. 1 of *National Monitoring of Strategies for Sustainable Poverty Reduction/PRSPs*. Eschborn, Germany: German Agency for Technical Cooperation.

———. 2004b. *Country Study: Nicaragua*. Vol. 2 of *National Monitoring of Strategies for Sustainable Poverty Reduction/PRSPs*. Eschborn, Germany: Mainstreaming Poverty Reduction Project, Governance and Democracy Division, German Agency for Technical Cooperation. http://www.gtz.de/de/dokumente/en-prsp-monitoring-country-study-nicaragua.pdf.

———. 2004c. *Country Study: Albania*. Vol. 2 of *National Monitoring of Strategies for Sustainable Poverty Reduction/PRSPs*. Eschborn, Germany: Mainstreaming Poverty Reduction Project, Governance and Democracy Division, German Agency for Technical Cooperation. http://www.gtz.de/de/dokumente/en-prsp-monitoring-country-study-albania.pdf.

Hauge, Arild O. 2003. "The Development of Monitoring and Evaluation Capacities to Improve Government Performance in Uganda." Evaluation Capacity Development Working Paper 10 (October), Operations Evaluation Department, World Bank, Washington, DC.

Heimans, Jeremy. 2002. "Strengthening Participation in Public Expenditure Management: Policy Recommendations for Key Stakeholders." Development Centre Policy Brief 22, Development Centre, Organisation for Economic Co-operation and Development, Paris.

Hill, Michael, ed. 1997. *The Policy Process: A Reader*. London: Prentice Hall.

Holmes, Malcolm. 2003. "A Review of Experience in Implementing Medium-Term Expenditure Frameworks in a PRSP Context: A Synthesis of Eight Country Studies." With Alison Evans. Draft working paper, July, Centre for Aid and Public Expenditure, Overseas Development Institute, London.

Hughes, A. 2002. "Lessons Learnt on Civil Society Engagement in PRSP Processes in Bolivia, Kenya and Uganda: A Report Emerging from the Bolivian–East African Sharing and Learning Exchange." Report, July, Institute of Development Studies, University of Sussex, Brighton, United Kingdom.

Hulsman-Vejsova, M., B. van de Putte, and R. Rist. 2001. "Building Evaluation Capacity for Poverty Reduction Strategies: Workshop Report." Ministry of Foreign Affairs, The Hague; Operations Evaluation Department, World Bank, Washington, DC.

Ilibeozova, Elvira. 2004. "Analysis of the Monitoring System in the Kyrgyz Republic." Unpublished paper, Department for International Development, London.

International Budget Network. 2001. "A Guide to Budget Work for NGOs." Guide, December, Center on Budget and Policy Priorities, Washington, DC.

International Monetary Fund and World Bank. 2002a. *Civil Society Organizations and Individual Contributions.* Vol. 2 of *External Comments and Contributions on the Joint Bank/Fund Staff Review of the PRSP Approach.* Washington, DC: International Monetary Fund and World Bank.

———. 2002b. "Review of the Poverty Reduction Strategy Paper (PRSP) Approach: Main Findings." Report, March, International Monetary Fund and World Bank, Washington, DC.

———. 2002c. "Better Measuring, Monitoring, and Managing for Development Results." Paper, Development Committee, International Monetary Fund and World Bank, Washington, DC.

———. 2005. "2005 Review of the Poverty Reduction Approach: Balancing Accountabilities and Scaling Up Results." Report, September 9, International Monetary Fund and World Bank, Washington, DC.

Jimenez, Elizabeth. 2004. "An Assessment of the Bolivian Poverty Monitoring and Evaluation System." Unpublished working paper, World Bank, Washington, DC.

Kakande, Margaret. 2002. "The Role of Participatory Monitoring and Evaluation in the PRSP: Uganda's Experience." Briefing notes for the international conference "Beyond the Review: Sustainable Poverty Alleviation and PRSP, Challenges for Developing Countries and Development Cooperation," Berlin, May 13–16.

Lawson, Andrew, David Booth, Alan Harding, David Hoole, and Felix Naschold. 2003. "Synthesis Report: General Budget Support Evaluability Study, Phase 1, Volume 1." Evaluation Report EV643 (October), Department for International Development, London.

Lawson, Max. "Monitoring Policy Outputs: Budget Monitoring in Malawi." Oxfam UK. http://www.internationalbudget.org/resources/Malawi.pdf.

Loureiro, João Dias. 2002. "Poverty Monitoring System, Implications for the National Statistical System: Mozambique Case Study." Case Study for the Seminar for Managers of National Statistical Offices on "Statistical Development and Poverty Reduction," Dar es Salaam, Tanzania, September 24–27. http://siteresources.worldbank.org/INTPAME/Resources/Country-studies/Mozambique_case_study_final(cleared).doc.

Lucas, Henry, David Evans, and Kath Pasteur. 2004. "Research on the Current State of PRS Monitoring Systems." Report, July, Department for International Development, London.

Machinjili, Charles. 2002. "How Can the Statistical System in a Country Best Build Capacity through a Locally Organized and Managed Training Program: Malawi Case Study." Seminar for Managers of National Statistical Offices on "Statistical

Development and Poverty Reduction," Dar es Salaam, Tanzania, September 24–27.

Mackay, Keith. 1999. "A Diagnostic Guide and Action Framework." Evaluation Capacity Development Working Paper 6 (January), Operations Evaluation Department, World Bank, Washington, DC.

———. 2004. "Two Generations of Performance Evaluation and Management Systems in Australia." Evaluation Capacity Development Working Paper 11 (March), Operations Evaluation Department, World Bank, Washington, DC.

———. 2006. "Institutionalization of Monitoring and Evaluation Systems to Improve Public Sector Management." Evaluation Capacity Development Working Paper 15 (January), Independent Evaluation Group, World Bank, Washington, DC.

McGee, Rosemary. 2000. "Participation in Poverty Reduction Strategies: A Synthesis of Experience with Participatory Approaches to Policy Design, Implementation and Monitoring." With Andy Norton. IDS Working Papers 109, Institute of Development Studies, University of Sussex, Brighton, United Kingdom.

Niger, Office of the Prime Minister. 2002. *Poverty Reduction Strategy*. Niamey, Niger: Permanent Secretariat of the PRSP, Office of the Prime Minister. http://povlibrary.worldbank.org/files/9355_NigerPRSP.pdf.

Overseas Development Institute. 2002. "PRS Monitoring: Issues from Consultants' Experience." Africa Regional Workshop on PRS Monitoring, Nairobi, November 12–13. Background Paper 2, Department for International Development, London.

Oxfam International. 2004. "From Donorship to Ownership?: Moving towards PRSP Round Two." Oxfam Briefing Paper 51 (January), Oxfam International, Oxford.

Oxford Policy Management. 2004. "Monitoring the Millennium Development Goals: Current Weaknesses and Possible Improvements." Report, January, Department for International Development, London.

Pain, Chris. 2003, "Monitoring the PRSP: Overview and Experience to Date." Paper presented to the Asian Development Bank Workshop, September. http://www.wiram.de/downloads/GTZ_PRS_MonitoringOverviewEvaluation.ppt.

Papps, Ivy, and Shkelzen Marku. 2004. "Poverty Monitoring Systems, an Analysis of Institutional Arrangements: The Case of Albania." Unpublished paper, Department for International Development, London.

Paris21 (Partnership in Statistics for Development in the 21st Century). 2004a. "Improved Statistical Support for Monitoring Development Goals: Country Case Study, Bolivia." Case study, Task Team, Partnership in Statistics for Development in the 21st Century, Paris.

———. 2004b. "Improved Statistical Support for Monitoring Development Goals: Country Case Study, Malawi." Case study, Task Team, Partnership in Statistics for Development in the 21st Century, Paris.

———. 2006. "Improved Statistical Support for Monitoring Development Goals: Report on Six Case Studies." Report, World Bank, Washington, DC.

Picciotto, Robert. 2004. "Visibility and Disappointment: The New Role of Development Evaluation." In *Rethinking the Development Experience: Essays Provoked by the Work of Robert Hirschmann*, ed. Lloyd Rodwin and Donald Schön. Washington, DC: The Brookings Institution.

Prennushi, Giovanna, Gloria Rubio, and Kalanidhi Subbarao. 2001. "Monitoring and Evaluation." In *Core Techniques and Cross-Cutting Issues*, Chapter 3: 105–30. Vol. 1 of *PRS Source Book*. Washington, DC: World Bank.

Roberts, John. 2003. "Public Expenditure for Development Results and Poverty Reduction." Working Paper 203 (February), Overseas Development Institute, London.

Rowden, Rick, and Jane Ocaya Irama. 2004. "Rethinking Participation: Questions for Civil Society about the Limits of Participation in PRSPs." Discussion paper, April, ActionAid Uganda and United States.

Schacter, Mark. 2000. "Evaluation Capacity Development: Sub-Saharan Africa, Lessons from Experience in Supporting Sound Governance." Evaluation Capacity Development Working Paper 7 (February), Operations Evaluation Department, World Bank, Washington, DC.

Schick, Allen. 1998. "Why Most Countries Should Not Try New Zealand's Reforms." *World Bank Research Observer* 13 (1): 123–31.

Scott, Christopher. 2004. "Building a Poverty Monitoring System in Honduras." Submitted report, May, U.K. Department for International Development, Honduras.

SGTS and Associates. 2001. *Overview and Recommendations*. Vol. 1 of *Civil Society Participation in Poverty Reduction Strategy Papers (PRSPs)*. London: Department for International Development.

Strategic Partnership with Africa. 2003. "Survey of the Alignment of Budget Support and Balance of Payments Support with National PRS Processes." Draft report by the Budget Support Working Group, December, U.K. Department for International Development, London; European Commission, Brussels.

Tanzania, Government of. 2001. "Poverty Monitoring Master Plan." December. Government of the United Republic of Tanzania, Dar es Salaam.

UNDP (United Nations Development Program). 2002. "UNDP's Engagement in Poverty Reduction Strategy Papers." Policy Note, August, United Nations Development Program, New York.

———. 2003a. *Main Report*. Vol. 1 of *Evaluation of UNDP's Role in the PRSP Process*. New York: Evaluation Office, UNDP.

———. 2003b. *Country Reports*. Vol. 2 of *Evaluation of UNDP's Role in the PRSP Process*. New York: Evaluation Office, UNDP.

United Nations Statistics Division. 2004. "Handbook on Poverty Statistics: Concepts, Methods and Policy Use." United Nations Statistics Division. http://unstats.un.org/ unsd/methods/poverty.

WHO (World Health Organization). 2004. "Poverty Reduction Strategy Papers: Their Significance for Health, Second Synthesis Report." Report, World Health Organization, Geneva.

Williamson, Tim. 2003. "Targets and Results in Public Sector Management: Uganda Case Study." Working Paper 205 (March), Overseas Development Institute, London.

World Bank. 2002. "Monitoring and Evaluation: Some Tools, Methods, and Approaches." Report, Operations Evaluation Department, World Bank, Washington, DC.

————. 2003. "Targets and Indicators for Millennium Development Goals and PRSPs: What Countries Have Chosen to Monitor." Report, Development Data Group, World Bank, Washington, DC.

————. 2004a. "Global Monitoring Report 2004: Policies and Actions for Achieving the Millennium Development Goals and Related Outcomes." Implementation Report, World Bank, Washington, DC.

————. 2004b. "The Poverty Reduction Strategy Initiative: An Independent Evaluation of the World Bank's Support through 2003." Report, May, Operations Evaluation Department, World Bank, Washington, DC.

————. 2004c. "Evaluation Capacity Development: OED Self-Evaluation." Report, June, Operations Evaluation Department, World Bank, Washington, DC.